When Ernest Hemingway committed suicide in 1961 he left four unfinished works – *A Moveable Feast, Islands in the Stream, The Garden of Eden*, and an untitled work on his travels in Africa. The edited versions of the three novels that were published between 1964 and 1986 have been presented to readers and scholars as discrete texts even though they are disjointed and fit uncomfortably into the body of Hemingway's work. Through extensive literary detective work Rose Marie Burwell has uncovered substantial evidence which reveals that Hemingway in fact designed the three published works as a trilogy, what she terms "his own portrait of the artist as painter and writer, and as son, husband, and father." She combines textual analysis with much new biographical information to create a compelling document of a period of Hemingway's life which other biographers have only begun to probe. Professor Burwell demonstrates that Hemingway inscribed in the four works he could neither complete nor abandon the life-long gender anxieties he had come to recognize as the legacy of "dangerous families." This book will ensure the critical reappraisal of the posthumous novels, and it will catalyze intense discussion among Hemingway's readers.

For Meffie with love and with thanks. Rose Marie

HEMINGWAY

CAMBRIDGE STUDIES IN AMERICAN LITERATURE
AND CULTURE

Editor:
Eric Sundquist, *University of California, Los Angeles*

Founding Editor:
Albert Gelpi, *Stanford University*

Advisory Board:
Nina Baym, *University of Illinois, Champaign-Urbana*
Sacvan Bercovitch, *Harvard University*
Albert Gelpi, *Stanford University*
Myra Jehlen, *University of Pennsylvania*
Carolyn Porter, *University of California, Berkeley*
Robert Stepto, *Yale University*
Tony Tanner, *King's College, Cambridge University*

Books in the series

HEMINGWAY

The Postwar Years and the Posthumous Novels

ROSE MARIE BURWELL
Northern Illinois University

CAMBRIDGE
UNIVERSITY PRESS

Published by the Press Syndicate of the University of Cambridge
The Pitt Building, Trumpington Street, Cambridge CB2 1RP
40 West 20th Street, New York, NY 10011-4211, USA
10 Stamford Road, Oakleigh, Melbourne 3166, Australia

© Cambridge University Press 1996

First published 1996

Printed in the United States of America

Library of Congress Cataloging-in-Publication Data
Burwell, Rose Marie, 1934–
Hemingway : the postwar years and the posthumous novels / Rose
Marie Burwell.
p.   cm. – (Cambridge studies in American literature and culture ; 96)
Includes index.
ISBN 0-521-48199-6 (hardcover)
1. Hemingway, Ernest, 1899–1961.   2. Hemingway, Ernest, 1899–1961.
Moveable feast.   3. Hemingway, Ernest, 1899–1961. Garden of
Eden.   4. Hemingway, Ernest, 1899–1961. Islands in the
stream.   5. Hemingway, Ernest, 1899–1961. Green hills of
Africa.   6. Autobiographical fiction, American – History and
criticism.   7. Novelists, American – 20th century –
Biography.   8. Journalists – United States – Biography.   9. Self in
literature.   10. Cycles – Literature.   I. Title.   II. Series.
812'.52 – dc20

95–14539
CIP

A catalog record for this book is available from the British Library

ISBN   0-521-48199-6   Hardback

THIS BOOK IS FOR GERSON

Contents

Illustrations

Preface

This book is a critical biography of Ernest Hemingway's postwar years, which in the language of literary studies should mean that it tells the story of his life from 1945 to 1961 while evaluating his works from that period. But I have had to define the task rather differently, for I am dealing with only four of the six novels Hemingway wrote during the postwar years – those that he could not complete, but continued writing, and that he said would be best left unpublished during his life. Added to this departure from standard critical biography is the fact that the thematic links among the four novels I examine resonate with episodes from Hemingway's early years, requiring a reassessment of the biographical information about his entire life.

Like many women who entered college in the 1950s and graduate school in the 1960s, I have had a long and ambivalent relationship with Ernest Hemingway. There was awe bordering on love for the man who wrote prose so lapidary that it conveyed in the finest Imagist sense that Francis Macomber had *become* the lion by presenting the two deaths in language that scans almost identically. And there was the resentment born of my sense of exclusion from so much of his work, for his lapidary prose seldom created a female character with an inner life that was not merely a male wish-fulfillment. Also, to one steeped in the puritan ethic – as I was, and as Hemingway had been – there was a sense that he had been wasteful with one of the greatest talents in modern literature.

As an undergraduate I was a science major who took literature courses for high-minded reasons such as spiritual nourishment. But my English professors, two male, one female, taught Hemingway according to the Code Hero theory: my objections that Nick Adams was damaged by his sudden experiences of life and death in "Indian Camp," and that his expression of immortality at the end was whistling in the early morning light, were not well-received.

In the years that followed, I thought often about Nick Adams. In "The Doctor and the Doctor's Wife" Nick's father sat on his bed, emptying and reloading his shotgun, as his wife uttered platitudes. In "Fathers and Sons" Nick remembered watching his father from the woodshed, his shotgun loaded, and thinking "I can blow him to hell." And in the same story, Nick, at thirty-eight, remembers his father's death in "a trap that he had helped only a little to set." When I began graduate study in English I wanted to know how Ernest Hemingway became so well acquainted with Nick Adams. That was 1962, and Hemingway had ended his life the year before. But in 1962, graduate programs in English were still dominated by the New Criticism, and although studies by Philip Young and Charles Fenton ventured into Hemingway's early life, I quickly realized that there was no surer way to make myself persona non grata (and perhaps to dry up the fellowship money on which I was dependent) than by pursuing biographical criticism in the seminars of New Critics. So I concentrated on the English Novel.

By the time I returned to serious reading of Hemingway, my six children were grown and I had nine grandchildren. In my classes and seminars I had long since found that the representations of childhood in fiction were under-read; and that critics were generally not interested in writing about children as fully created characters. Yet, I wondered, who could teach *Jane Eyre, Wuthering Heights,* the novels of Dickens and George Eliot and remain incurious about the lives of those children? Thus, when the invitation to review Mark Spilka's *Hemingway's Quarrel with Androgyny* arrived, and I reread *The Garden of Eden,* the elephant story framed there shone forth in a perfection that nearly obscured the rest of that strange novel.

I knew that *The Garden of Eden* had been heavily edited, and parallel with writing the review, I drafted what I thought would be an essay on the dilemma of the child in the elephant story. There, David Bourne is a younger version of the writer in the longer work I discuss in this volume; and like Nick Adams in "Indian Camp," he is coerced into a bloody ritual by a father whose approval he wants.

To write about *The Garden of Eden* I needed access to the manuscripts at the Kennedy Library. As I prepared for the trip to Boston, the indelible imprint of my graduate training and the disgrace of being guilty of biographical fallacy (my legacy from the New Critical oligarchy) combined in a dream made to order for an analyst (which, alas, I did not have). I had also reread *Islands in the Stream* (where there is much green-water imagery), for at the Kennedy Library I intended to examine the *Islands* manuscripts too. Although I had never worked there, a colleague had described how the Hemingway Room looks over the green water of Boston Bay. In this dream I was interviewing Ernest Hemingway. We were in a windowless, doorless room with walls of sea-water green. On my dream screen Hemingway was the figure of the Karsh portrait – turtleneck sweater, full head of salt-and-pepper hair, forthright and charming. Suddenly we were in bed together, and I found it most pleasant. But each time things began to get really interesting, a crack opened in the wall and an archival attendant handed me another file of manuscript!

Like the obedient graduate student I had once been, I turned in the dream from the man to the manuscripts. But in waking moments, Hemingway's letters, medical files, cancelled checks, book orders, and so forth began to fill my life as I traced through the posthumous novels the male children who knew from being too young how it would be to be too old.

The endnotes to this study constitute what one editor referred to as "another book": they are an integral and revealing part of the narrative of Ernest Hemingway's life, and both scholarly and general reader will, I think, find them compelling.

Acknowledgments

During the five years of research from which this book grew I have had the benefit of scholarly exchanges with many other laborers in the Hemingway vineyard. In thanking them for their generosity, and many of them for their hospitality, I am pleased to list Mark Spilka first, for it was in reviewing his *Hemingway's Quarrel with Androgyny* (1990) that I began to sense the serial nature of Hemingway's posthumous novels. As my research continued, often at the John F. Kennedy Library in Boston, Mark was always on call in nearby Providence, and his door was always open. Michael and Anne Reynolds have been a small, accessible, interactive reference library. Others who discussed, read, advised, and answered questions are Susan Beegel, Nadine Devost, Robin Gajdusek, Marion Mandel, Frank Scafella, Robert Scholes, Charlene Smith, Paul Smith, Bill Walton, Carol Weser, and Max and Frankie Westbrook. The use I have made of their advice, however, is solely my responsibility. Faculty colleagues who supported this project include Jim and Wanda Giles, Bill Johnson, Jim Miller, Mary Susan Schriber, Robert Self, and Valerie Yow. Closer to home, Hope Burwell and Gerson Ecker have listened and read, demanding a style accessible to those fortunate readers of Hemingway who remain innocent of critical terminology – those who do not, in the words of novelist Joe Halderman, "hemingway for a living."

For permission to quote from unpublished Hemingway manuscripts and letters, I owe thanks to the Hemingway Foundation and the Hemingway estate – John, Patrick, and Gregory Hemingway. For permission to quote from published Hemingway material, I thank Charles Scribner's Sons, an imprint of Macmillan Publishing. John and James Sanford and Carol Sanford Coolidge kindly gave permission to reproduce passages from the papers and manuscripts of their mother, Marcelline Hemingway Sanford. Lauri Anderson gave me permission to quote "A Short Unhappy Life." Portions of this book appeared in slightly different forms in *Texas Studies in Literature and Language* (35: 2 [Summer 1993]), and *Princeton University Library Chronicle* (LVI: 1 [Autumn 1994]). Thanks are due for the permissions of these journals.

Grants from The Hemingway Foundation enabled me to spend months in the Hemingway Archives at the John F. Kennedy Library, grateful for the tutelage there of Megan Desnoyers, Lisa Middents, and Stephen Plotkin. During my numerous trips to the Firestone Library at Princeton, Don Skemer's advice and assistance were invaluable. An Andrew Mellon grant made possible a summer of research at the Harry Ransom Humanities Research Center, where Cathy Henderson and Tom Staley were my guides.

Jim Giles owns the portrait of Hemingway by Melinda B. Weihmeir Wilcox which appears on the dust jacket. It appears there through Giles's generosity and that of Ms. Wilcox, for whom I searched many months. Her permission letter says: "I am amazed at the journey that 'Hemingway' has traveled. It is a testament to the thought that one should always do their best, for one never knows what may come of a seed that is sown." I thank her and invoke her words as a mantra for the entire book.

This study began during a sabbatical leave from Northern Illinois University in the fall of 1990; and it has been supported by travel grants from the Department of English, the College of Liberal Arts and Sciences, and the Graduate College. Through the efforts of Graduate Dean Jerold Zarr, permissions costs were defrayed by the Deans' Fund for Humanities Research.

Finally, I wish to express my gratitude to two people who made this project safe, comfortable, and affordable in ways that I have never taken for granted: Wilma Grayson, my friend and landlady in Princeton; and Chuck Criswell, my friend and the Volkswagen specialist who kept an aging Jetta running coolly for the 57,000 miles of my search for pieces to the posthumous Hemingway puzzle.

Chronology of events significant to this study*

1871	Clarence Edmonds Hemingway born, 4 September.
1872	Grace Hall Hemingway born, 15 June.
1896	Marriage of Grace Hall and Clarence Hemingway.
1898	Marcelline Hemingway born, 15 January.
1899	Ernest Hemingway born, 21 July.
1902	Ursula Hemingway born, 29 April.
1904	Madelaine (Sunny) Hemingway born, 28 November.
1911	Carol Hemingway born, 19 July.
1915	Leicester Hemingway born, 1 April.
1917	EH and Marcelline graduate from Oak Park High School.
1917	EH takes job with *Kansas City Star* in October.
1918	EH goes to Italy with Red Cross.
1918	EH is wounded at Fossalta, Italy.
1919	EH returns to Oak Park in January.
1919	Grace builds her own cottage at Longfield Farm.
1919	Clarence evicts Ruth Arnold from the Kenilworth Avenue home in August.
1920	EH takes job with Connable family in Toronto and begins to freelance for *Toronto Star*.
–	EH returns to Oak Park in May and to Michigan in summer.
–	Grace evicts EH from the family summer home shortly with twenty-first birthday letter.
–	EH takes job in Chicago in fall, meets Hadley Richardson.
1921	EH and Hadley marry at Horton Bay, 3 September.

*This chronology is based on Michael Reynolds, *Hemingway: An Annotated Chronology*, with the addition of events most relevant to this study and some changes in dates which reflect new documentation.

- Hemingways sail for France, 8 December. EH works as correspondent for *Toronto Star,* and writes fiction.
1922 Suitcase containing EH's manuscripts stolen from Hadley's train compartment, on 2 December.
1923 Hemingways go to Toronto in September to await birth of a baby. EH now regular with *Toronto Star.*
- John Hadley Nicanor (Bumby) Hemingway born, 4 October.
- EH visits parents in Oak Park alone at Christmas.
1924 Hemingways back in Paris in February.
- Bumby baptized with Alice B. Toklas and Gertrude Stein as godparents.
1925 Hemingways meet Pauline Pfeiffer in Paris, late March.
- EH meets Scott Fitzgerald in April.
- Pauline arrives in Schruns to spend Christmas vacation with the Hemingways.
1926 EH leaves Hadley in Schruns in late January.(They have a joint passport: she cannot re-enter France without him.) He begins trip to New York to discuss publication of *The Torrents of Spring* and *The Sun Also Rises* with Scribner's.
- EH returns from New York: spends 2–3 March in Paris with Pauline.
- Hemingways have been back in Paris since at least 1 April. Late April or early May, Hadley makes driving trip with Pauline and her sister Jinny, learns that EH is involved with Pauline.
- Hemingways separate in mid-August, return from Antibes to Paris, set up separate households, EH living in Gerald Murphy's studio at 69 rue Froidevaux.
- Hadley makes the "100-day separation" condition for a divorce, 24 September: rescinded, 16 November.
1927 Hadley receives divorce and custody of Bumby, 27 January.
- Pauline and EH are married on 10 May in Catholic ceremony.
1928 The Hemingways, Pauline pregnant, and EH well into *A Farewell to Arms,* arrive in Key West in March.
- EH meets parents briefly in Key West.
- Patrick Hemingway born in Kansas City, 28 June.
- EH visits parents in Oak Park in October.
- Clarence Hemingway commits suicide, 6 December.

1929 Hemingways set up trust fund for Grace Hemingway.

1931 After three years of renting residences in Key West, Hemingways purchase house at 907 Whitehead Street (with help from Pauline's uncle, Gus Pfeiffer).

– Gregory Hemingway born in Kansas City, 12 November.

1932 EH becomes involved with Jane Mason, probably in April.

1936 Affair with Jane Mason seems over by end of June.

– EH meets Martha Gellhorn at Sloppy Joe's, Key West, in December.

1937 EH makes first trip to cover Spanish Civil War in February. Affair with Martha Gellhorn begins.

1939 Family pressures mount, and EH goes to Cuba to write *For Whom the Bell Tolls*, 14 February. Martha sets up household at Finca Vigia in April.

– EH returns to Key West from Idaho, ca. 19 December to find house closed, Pauline and his sons gone. Within a week he moves to Cuba.

1940 EH and Martha are married in Wyoming, 21 November. He buys the Finca Vigia.

1942 EH's submarine hunting adventures begin.

1943 Martha leaves Cuba to report WWII for *Collier's* after an extended period at the Finca.

1944 EH goes to London as *Collier's* correspondent in April.

– Martha sails on dynamite freighter in May.

– EH meets Mary Welsh in London, 17 May.

– Bumby is reported missing in action, 27 October.

– EH ignores Martha's request of 3 November for a divorce.

– Mary agrees to try living with EH at the Finca, 14 November.

– EH announces to Patrick the end of marriage to Martha, 19 November.

– EH with Col. Charles (Buck) Lanham in the Hurtgenwald offensive from 15 November through early January. Returns to Cuba in mid-March, bringing Patrick and Gregory.

1945 Mary comes to Cuba to visit, 2 May. *New York Times* runs story, "Hemingway's Son is Liberated." Mary and EH begin divorce proceedings.

– Bumby comes to the Finca to recuperate in June.

– Buck Lanham and his wife visit at the Finca, 22 September–8 October.

- Ur-text that becomes *Across the River and into the Trees, The Old Man and the Sea, Islands in the Stream,* and *The Garden of Eden* is started in early October.

1946   EH and Mary are married in Havana, 14 March.

- Mary has ectopic pregnancy with nearly fatal ending in August.

1947   Pauline comes to the Finca in April to help care for Patrick who is ill there. She and Mary become good friends.

- Max Perkins dies, 17 June.

- Pauline and Mary remain at the Finca (when EH goes to Michigan and then Idaho in late August). They plan and start construction of the tower.

- Mary arrives at Sun Valley in October. Spends Thanksgiving week in California with Pauline, Patrick, and Gregory, then returns to Sun Valley. Pauline makes several trips from Key West to the Finca to supervise construction of the tower prior to EH and Mary's return in mid-February.

1948   *The Garden of Eden* begins as a separate work in June.

- Hemingways go to Italy in September, where he meets Adriana Ivancich in December.

1949   Hemingways meet Adriana's brother, Gianfranco, in January. He is taking a position with Sidarma Shipping Lines in Cuba.

- EH starts a story about duck hunting near Venice which becomes the frame for *Across the River.*

- Hemingways return to Europe in late November. He visits Aigues Mortes and Le Grau-du-Roi (where *The Garden of Eden* opens).

1950   Hemingways are in Venice in January where he sees Adriana regularly.

- Before leaving Venice for Paris on 8 March, EH invites Adriana and her mother to visit at the Finca Vigia.

- Adriana arrives in Paris on 15 March to study art. Charles Scribner arrives same week and announces they will use Adriana's design for the dust jacket of *Across the River.*

- Hemingways return to Cuba in April where he begins writing "Provisional Ending" for *Eden,* followed by the "Cuba" section of *Islands.*

- EH's first grandchild, Joan (Muffett), born to Bumby and Puck, 5 May.
- *Across the River* published to negative reviews, 7 September.
- Mary asks Charles Scribner Sr. to find her a job in New York, but does not follow through.
- Adriana Ivancich and her mother arrive 28 October; visit lasts until late January.

1951 EH works on *The Old Man and the Sea,* January through end of February. Calls it finished at 26,531 words.
- EH finishes "The Sea Chase" ["At Sea"] section of *Islands,* mid-May; will return to work on it in December, and call *Islands* finished 24 December.
- Grace Hemingway dies, 28 June.
- EH begins revising that part of "The Land, Sea, and Air Book" which was written in 1945–47, 29 June.
- EH has now decided to offer *Old Man* for separate publication, and by 8 July has refused *Cosmopolitan's* offer of $10,000 for a version that is just under 20,000 words.
- Pauline Hemingway dies, 2 October.
- Throughout 1951 EH turns down requests for his cooperation in the writing of books about him and his work (from Charles Fenton, Carlos Baker, and Philip Young). Encourages Baker to write book that becomes *Hemingway: the Writer as Artist* (1952).

1952 Charles Scribner Sr. dies, 11 February.
- *Life* agrees to pay $40,000 for *Old Man.* Publishes it in single issue, 1 September. Scribner's publication the following week has dust jacket designed by Adriana.

1953 Gianfranco, who has been living in Cuba since 1949 (first at the Finca and then on a farm he purchased with help from EH), returns to Italy.
- Hemingways leave for Europe in late June, begin African safari, 1 September.

1954 Plane crashes, at Murchison Falls, 23 January; and at Butiaba, 24 January.
- EH sees Adriana for last time, ca. 5 June.
- EH begins unpublished African book in July.
- EH receives the Nobel Prize in October.

1955 EH suffering from side-effects of plane crashes, continues work on African book.

1956 Last work on African book done in late July.

– Hemingways leave Cuba in late August for safari to be led by Patrick Hemingway.

– EH is ill in Spain; Egypt has closed Suez Canal. He returns to Paris and stays at the Ritz Hotel through 21 January. Finds papers left in Paris thirty years earlier.

1957 By May the Paris book has begun with a chapter on Fitzgerald.

– By December EH is working alternately on Paris book and *Eden*. This continues through early March 1959.

1959 Castro Revolution in Cuba, 1–2 January.

– EH makes contract with *Life* in February for a 10,000-word bullfighting piece that becomes the posthumous *The Dangerous Summer*.

– Hemingways buy house in Ketchum, Idaho, before returning to Cuba.

– Hemingways go to Spain where he will cover bullfights for the *Life* piece, late April.

– Mary Hemingway leaves Paris for Cuba, 16 October. EH has become involved with Valerie Danby-Smith during the summer. Mary insists on arrangements for an apartment in New York.

– EH deposits manuscript of Paris book with Scribner's and returns to Cuba in late October. Mary has established conditions on which she will continue to run the household. They go to Ketchum, ca. 20 November.

– Mary breaks elbow, 27 November. EH is quarrelsome and objects to helping her dress, etc.

1960 Mary agrees to hire Valerie Danby-Smith as EH's secretary. She arrives in Cuba by 8 February.

– EH is in serious depression, obsessively expanding *The Dangerous Summer*.

– EH goes to Spain, 4 August. Mary and Valerie remain in New York. His letters begin to express fear that he is having a breakdown.

– First installment of bullfighting piece appears in *Life*, 1 September.

- Mary sends Valerie to Spain to help EH, ca. 23 September.
- EH becomes increasingly paranoid, his temper more uncontrollable; returns to New York, 8 October.

1960 Hemingways have been in Ketchum since mid-November. He is suffering from hypertension, insomnia, and depression.

- EH enters Mayo Clinic (under name of George Saviers, his Ketchum physician) for treatment of hypertension, enlarged liver, paranoia, and depression. Has electroconvulsive therapy through December and January.

1961 Hemingways invited to Kennedy inauguration, but he is too ill to accept. Writes note to John F. Kennedy.

- EH discharged from Mayo Clinic, 22 January; flies to Idaho where he continues work on the Paris book.
- Depression and anxiety increase. On 18 April, writes Charles Scribner Jr. that Paris book cannot be published. Mary does not mail the letter.
- News of the failed Bay of Pigs invasion of Cuba appears in American newspapers. EH attempts suicide, Mary intervenes. He is sedated and hospitalized locally, 21 April.
- EH makes second suicide attempt, Dr. George Saviers intervenes, 23 April.
- EH is flown back to Mayo Clinic, probable third suicide attempt on the way, 25 April. More electroconvulsive therapy follows.
- EH is discharged from Mayo and returns to Ketchum by car, very anxious and paranoid, 26 June. Arrives 30 June.
- Suicide, 2 July.

Links among the four narratives that compose Hemingway's portrait of the artist

Period of artist's life and narrative setting	Work and dates of composition and publication	Reiterated thematic links
1922–26 in Paris	*A Moveable Feast* w. 1957–61 p. 1964	1. Hemingway as first-person, involved narrator. 2. Hadley's loss of the manuscripts. 3. Dangerous families. 4. Writing as an act of sexual possession.
1927 in South of France and in Spain	*The Garden of Eden* w. 1948–59 p. 1986	1. David Bourne, third-person, involved narrator is the age Hemingway was when his father died in 1928. 2. Wife burns the manuscripts. 3. Dangerous families (brutal father, excised mother). 4. Writer suspects his own sterility and seeks cross-fertilization of creative imagination via androgyny.
1936 and 1943 in Bimini, in Cuba, and at sea in the Caribbean	*Islands in the Stream* w. 1945–52 p. 1970	1. Thomas Hudson, third-person, involved narrator, remembers his earlier life in Paris as he engages in adventures created from Hemingway's submarine intelligence work. The production of art has turned to the pursuit of violence. 2. Loss of manuscripts remembered as a castration in deleted "Miami" section. 3. Absent mothers who are careless with children's lives. Males as better parents, living in a nearly conjugal relationship in a world of men without women.

After September 1953 at Kenya game preserve	African book w. Jul. 1954–Aug. 1956 Unpublished	1. Hemingway as first-person, involved narrator. 2. Remembered loss of manuscripts by the wife he "loved first and best." Other memories of Paris. 3. Remembered childhood in Midwest (excised mother). Questioning of tabus: homosexuality, polygamy, miscegenation, and cannibalism. 4. Aging writer seeking another identity and trying to conceive a child with native woman who neither reads nor writes, and does not know of such a thing as a writer. 5. Sterile wife has gone to Nairobi, taking the only typewriter.

UNPUBLISHED MANUSCRIPT EVIDENCE OF LINKS

1. Hemingway's statement that *Garden* is sequel to *Feast*.
2. Two episodes deleted from published novel that twin Roger Davis, the writer, with Thomas Hudson, the painter – then identify Davis/Hudson as the young artist of *Feast* and *Garden*.
3. Paris incidents of *Feast* begin in memory in the African book.
4. Elephant and *askari* who signify the powerlessness of childhood in *Garden* are in the African book – where they signify the isolation and powerlessness of the unproductive artist in old age.

Abbreviations

HRC: Humanities Research Center, University of Texas, Austin.

JFK: John Fitzgerald Kennedy Library, Boston, MA.

PUL: Firestone Library, Princeton University, Princeton, NJ.

Ernest Hemingway's spelling and punctuation were often eccentric: they have been regularized only where necessary for the clarity of a statement.

CHAPTER 1

A frame for Hemingway's portrait of the artist

When Ernest Hemingway took his own life on 2 July 1961, he left manuscripts of four unfinished novels. Three were extensively edited and published by Scribner's between 1964 and 1986:[1] about half of the fourth work, the African book, was excerpted in magazines; but it remains unedited, and there seem to be no plans for book publication. Hemingway had begun two of these narratives, *Islands in the Stream* and *The Garden of Eden,* in an ur-text that he started seven months after returning from work as a war correspondent for *Collier's* in March 1945, and that he sometimes referred to as "The Land, Sea, and Air Book." The other two (the African book and *A Moveable Feast*), were not part of the ur-text; but they grew out of the same thematic concerns with the creative imagination that had driven the ur-text. Together these four narratives form a serial sequence that was at times consciously modeled on Proust's *Remembrance of Things Past.*[2] The works form a tetralogy that is Hemingway's portrait of the artist as writer and painter, and as son, husband and father; but their serial nature, and their place in the body of his fiction, has been unrecognized, misconstrued, and undervalued because of the manuscript deletions made for publication, the order in which the three published works appeared, and the restrictions of archival material that clarifies much about their composition and intentions.

In their totality, the four narratives record Hemingway's fifteen-year search for a form and a style that would express his reflexive vision of the artist. It is a search he had begun at least as early as the fall of 1936 as he wrote in "The Snows of Kilimanjaro" of a dying writer's imaginative triumph over the distractions that have limited his art. There is a discernible movement toward what we have come to call *postmodern narrative* in these works. The inextricable mingling of painter and writer in Roger Davis, Thomas Hudson, David Bourne, and Nick Sheldon, and the telescoping of father and son in Thomas Hudson–Roger Davis–David Hudson–David Bourne and Bourne's father create protean characters unknown in English-language literature until the protagonists of Salman Rushdie's *Midnight's Children* and Philip Roth's *The Counterlife*. All of the writing is, at one level, about the cost of the creative process – to the artist and to those whose lives are united with his.

Two of the four posthumous narratives explore new possibilities for the male artist: *Eden*, with a writer-protagonist in his late twenties, considers and rejects cross-fertilization of the creative imagination through androgyny. The African book, with a writer-protagonist (named Hemingway) in his mid-fifties, contemplates and rejects escape from the artist's obligation to produce – and from the legend that has grown around him – through his integration into a culture where there are no writers. The remaining two works explore the beginning of the artist's vocation (*Feast*) and the artist as painter who, his vocation lost, has turned to self-destruction (*Islands*).

THE DANGEROUS MELTING OF AN ICEBERG

Although Hemingway had often referred to his typewriter as his only analyst, he could hardly have anticipated in 1945 when he began the novel he called "The Islands and the Stream" that sixteen years later, trying to bring closure to his book about the early years of a young American writer in Paris, he would have written his way to knowledge he could neither bear nor deny. But that, we now know, is what happened. In April 1961, ill, his memory impaired by electroconvulsive therapy, and trying to complete the Paris sketches that became *Feast*, he saw with blinding sight his own culpability in the destruction of the two personal relationships that had been most sustaining of him as a writer and most indicative of his integrity as a man. He recognized, perhaps for the first time, his role in the failure of his early marriages (to Hadley Richardson, 1921–27; and to Pauline Pfeiffer, 1927–40), and saw that he had blamed others for the end of his first marriage and denied responsibility for leaving Pauline – whom he had called his best critic – and entering into the cycle of self-destructive behavior inaugurated by his involvement with Martha Gellhorn in 1937 and his marriage to her in 1940. However, long before the final effort of bringing closure to the Paris book brought with it this self-knowledge, Hemingway had already inscribed the consequences of his actions in the four narratives that he looked upon as money in the bank, but would not publish during his life.

My own findings after more than three years of working with the manuscripts of the three posthumously published novels had established the pattern, intent, and unity of *Islands, Eden,* and *Feast* by the fall of 1992. That December the opening of the restricted portions of the Scribner's Archives at Princeton made available Hemingway's correspondence with his editors and publisher, extending my perception of the serial nature of the posthumous works to the African book, a typescript of which is among the Scribner's material. The letters between Hemingway and Charles Scribner Sr. revealed a kind of creative flash point at which his progenitor-like investment in the posthumous texts began. Communications between Hemingway and his editors provided mentions of work-in-progress that could be cross-checked against other information (manuscripts and oblique references in letters to other correspondents), making it possible to date the composition of most of his writing after WW II.[3] The summer of 1993, spent in the archives of the Humanities Research Center at the University of Texas, turned up new material about Hemingway's intentions in the African book and established the circumstances under which he had begun to write *Feast,* providing several significant pieces to the literary and biographical puzzle that I had come to think of as Hemingway's custody battle for masculine control of his texts. It was a battle that he carried on even as his private life – his personal relationships and his health – might have been a warning to a more introspective man; or to one less formed by the force of his own will and less immersed in the *machismo* of a Latin culture.

But Hemingway-the-man wrote the novels, and the novelist lived with the man's conflicts: art and life occupied the same space. Those conflicts permeated the vision that has been inscribed in the posthumous novels – but not necessarily inscribed in the same configurations they took in the writer's life. Although work on the narratives often overlapped, Hemingway returned to *Eden,* the most innovative, throughout his work on all the others, making it central to the tetralogy. He had begun the postwar writing with manic energy in October 1945, intent upon a war novel that would memorialize the experience he had shared with Colonel Charles (Buck) Lanham, commander of the 22nd Regiment, in the Hurtgen Forest. But Hemingway's inability to either live alone or to sustain a marriage was so blurred into his reasons for going to the war that the ur-text he began creating soon incorporated what he described as "relations between men and womenies."[4]

Working rapidly, Hemingway wrote first in the ur-text of a writer and of a painter – the latter of whom, in two sequences deleted from the final section of *Islands,* is also an incarnation of the writer and the painter in *Eden*; and he wrote too of the painter's three sons – who in the early manuscript version are the writer's sons. Second, in *Eden,* he wrote of two young painters (husband and wife) and of a writer and his wife, as well as the writer's childhood relationship with his father. Third, in the African book, he wrote of an aging writer named Hemingway who is serving as a game warden in Kenya as he remembers his childhood in the Midwest and his youth in Paris, and who tries to imagine a life in which he can be (and others can see him as) something other than a writer. In pursuit of that vision, he conceives a child with a young Wakumba woman who not only cannot read or write, but does not know that there are people who are only writers. Finally, in *Feast,* which begins in memories in the African book, he wrote of the same writer's life more than thirty years earlier in Paris.

Unremittingly, perhaps unconsciouly, Hemingway had inscribed in the four narratives those events that created anxiety and conflict in his own life as he used and abused his talent: (1) the determinative power of childhood and dangerous families; (2) the male artist's distrust of women and the feminine aspect of his own creative imagination; and (3) writing as an isolating and onanistic act which replaces intimate human relationships and produces a text that is the writer's parthenogenetic offspring.

Working throughout the postwar years at the four novels he could not bring to closure, Hemingway examined the life of the creative male from childhood through late middle age. He unified the narratives by invoking memory in a consciously Proustian manner, by twinning painters and writers as characters; by writing recurrently of the loss or destruction of the writer's manuscripts by his wife, and by focusing intensely on the growth and decline of the artist. Always Hemingway was aware that the narratives were very personal; and sometimes he would speculate that they could not be published while he was alive.[5]

Hemingway had often compared his fictional technique to the structure of an iceberg, giving to small details the burden of signifying what remained submerged. That he was a writer whose ethos, as well as his style, seemed forged as a protection against introspection, and that his simple prose actually demanded a great deal of his readers, has never been lost upon his best critics. But in the self-reflexivity of his portrait of the artist Hemingway had to use a narrative voice that could not evade introspection. *Eden,* as the central work in the tetralogy, contains the most obvious of these narrative innovations as the writer David Bourne explores his divided state in interior monologue and traces its origin in the elephant story. This is very close to the technique Hemingway had used in revealing Robert Jordan's past in *For Whom the Bell Tolls* (1940), making Jordan his most interiorly developed character to that point.[6] The narrative innovation of *Eden* was significantly obscured in its editing for publication, but the novel is replete with mirror narratives and character doubling – some consciously recognized by the writer-protagonist, others formally acknowledged by the arrangement of the text.

In the final months of his life Hemingway discovered that in venturing from the old narrative forms which had protected him from introspection, he had descended into the iceberg. The view from inside was Lear-like.[7] Memory and mortality ambushed him there; and filled with remorse, he tried to withdraw his book about the life of a young writer in Paris during the 1920s. The writer's name is Ernest Hemingway, and his experiences are recounted with such documentary detail that *A Moveable Feast* is still widely read as a memoir, although several weeks before he wrote Charles Scribner Jr. in his abortive attempt to withdraw the manuscript, Hemingway had written unequivocally that the Paris book was fiction – as all remembrance of things past is fiction (File 122; JFK).

Hemingway's heroes had always been fictional visions of himself, but they were also demonstrably other than himself, so that fictional distance protected the author. However, as he began his portrait of the artist, Hemingway knew that when these works reached print, he

could no longer expect to be shielded from assumptions that his
protagonists' obsessions and failures were also his own. Taking creative liberty with Nick Adams's statement that "the only writing that
was any good was what you made up, what you imagined . . . ," he
wove what had been with what might have been; and in creating
from his own experience, he informed the narratives with his own
anxiety.[8] The result is four schizophrenic fictional structures that he
could neither complete, nor expose, nor destroy; but that he did
intend for publication after his death, for he refers repeatedly in
letters to Charles Scribner, Sr. and Jr., of what he has written and
placed in a bank vault in Cuba as security for the cash advances he
received. He had the manuscripts microfilmed and put in the vaults
of two Havana banks, and as late as March 1961 he was anxious that
the rental be paid in a manner that would assure the preservation of
the contents (Mary Hemingway to Lee Samuels, 3 March 1961;
HRC). Although these four narratives are fragmented, incomplete,
repetitive, and partially repudiated, they are both a portrait of the
artist as an American and an unparalleled example of fiction as self-
analysis that is the only answer (albeit a partial one) to the question
so often asked: "What happened to Hemingway after WW II?"

TWO MEN WHO BECAME THEIR WORK

The question has remained as vexed as that of John F. Kennedy's
assassination. Although there is no mystery about who fired the gun
that ended Hemingway's life, the revisionings of the two deaths have
proceeded similarly in filmic and fictional accounts, where they
converge in a powerful short story that displaces Hemingway's death
into the death of one of his characters – much as the deaths of
Hemingway and Kennedy became part of the lived experience of so
many of us – and suggests the way in which the two violent deaths
have become benchmarks in American life.

The thematic center of the collection in which it appears, Lauri
Anderson's *Hunting Hemingway's Trout,* is the effect of the Hemingway image on American males. In "A Short Unhappy Life," the
protagonist, who is now a professor at the small Michigan college
he once attended, was assigned "The Short Happy Life of Francis
Macomber" in an undergraduate class on Wednesday, 20 November,
1963. But the Friday class was cancelled because of Kennedy's assas-

sination, and the Macomber story was never discussed. Now the deaths of Macomber and Kennedy have merged in his imagination:

> Lee Harvey Oswald, that son of a bitch, is probably the ultimate cause of my dilemma. If it weren't for him I might have discovered in 1963 whether or not Margot meant to shoot her husband. In 1963 I was only nineteen – still young and naive enough to accept whatever a professor wished to palm off as the truth. Unfortunately, I never got the truth. Instead I got a terrific headache and spent the day wandering about the campus in a migraine daze, trying to avoid TV sets and radios with their repetitive message of sudden death. The first full-fledged hero of my short life was dead, and all I could think about was Francis Macomber. In my grief I even got the deaths mixed up. I pictured Francis Macomber, a boyish grin frozen on his youthful face, pushing his whole body into the plush leather of the back seat of an open limousine. Bullets were splattering Francis's face into oblivion as Jackie and Margot sat beside him, smiling prettily for the cameras and wiping bits of gore from their faces.
>
> There's nothing I can do about the past now – about the way I am trapped forever with two entwined deaths on November twenty-second of 1963. The perplexity is there and will remain there, deep in my soul, in spite of my current efforts to discover a definite answer to at least one of the deaths, Francis's. (Anderson 49–50)

The association of Hemingway and Kennedy (who never met) began over two years before the president's assassination when William Walton, a friend of the Hemingways and of the Kennedys, helped Mary Hemingway obtain the visa she needed in order to retrieve her husband's manuscripts and papers from Cuba. Later, the permanent connection was established when Mary, firmly guided by Walton's sense of historical continuity, and her obligation to the president who made the recovery of her husband's papers possible, decided upon the Kennedy Library as their repository.[9] Jacqueline Kennedy and Mary Hemingway agreed in 1964 that the papers would come to rest at the Kennedy Library when it was completed. The conditions – that there be a Hemingway Room where the materials would be available to scholars, and that some of the Hemingways' personal items would be displayed there – were agreed upon in 1968, and in 1972 the materials began arriving at the library's temporary facility in "Bonwit Teller shopping bags, cardboard boxes, and dented trunks with French and Cuban labels.

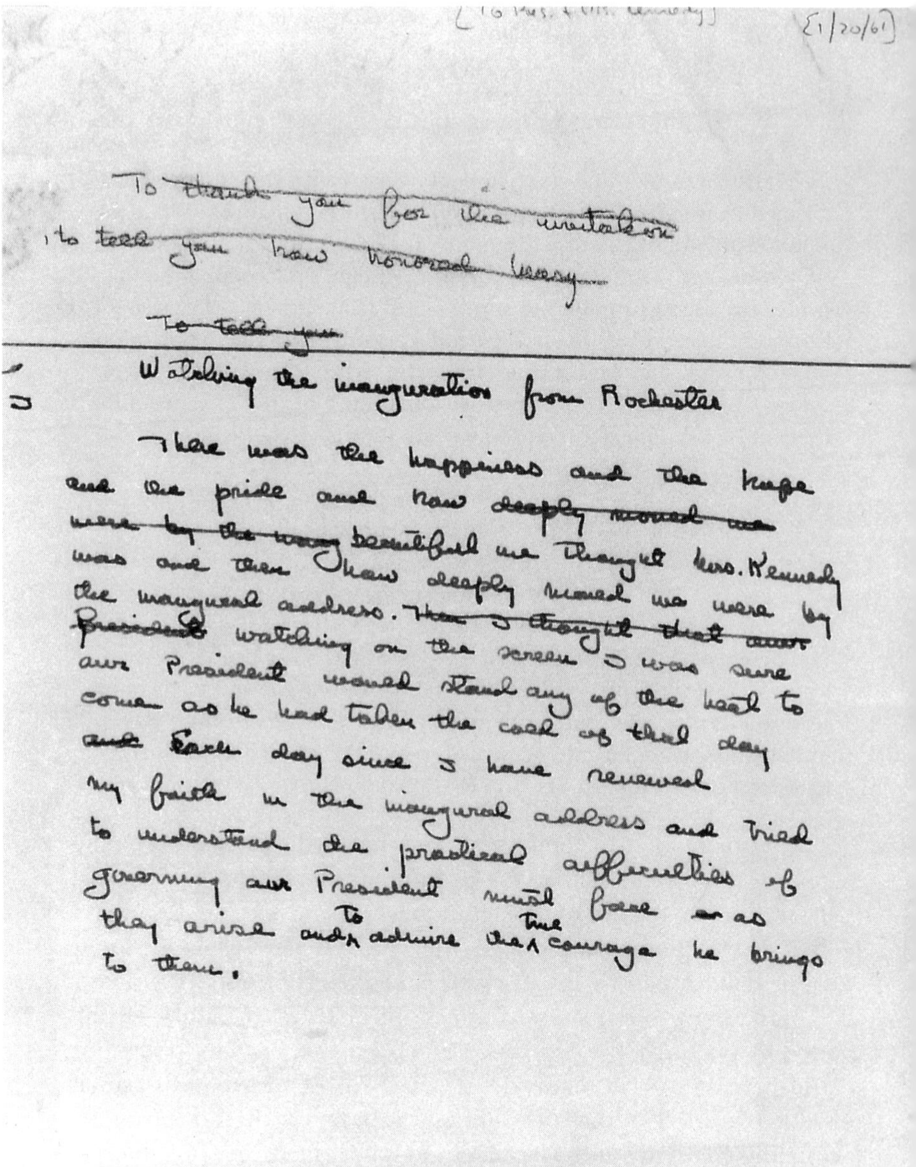

[To Mrs. & Mr. Kennedy] [1/20/61]

To ~~thank you for the invitation~~
, to ~~tell you how honored we were~~

~~To tell you~~

Watching the inauguration from Rochester

There was the happiness and the hope and the pride and how ~~deeply moved we were by the way~~ beautiful we thought Mrs. Kennedy was and then how deeply moved we were by the inaugural address. ~~Then I thought that our President~~ watching on the screen I was sure our President would stand any of the heat to come as he had taken the cold of that day ~~and~~ Each day since I have renewed my faith in the inaugural address and tried to understand the practical difficulties of governing our President must face ~~as~~ as they arise and to admire the true courage he brings to them.

Figure 1. In January 1961, John F. Kennedy invited the Hemingways to attend his inauguration. At the Mayo Clinic and unable to make the trip, Hemingway spent nearly four days composing the congratulatory note.

Figure 2. In 1962 Mary Hemingway attended the White House dinner honoring Nobel laureates. On Mary's right is Fredric March who read from "The Sea Chase." On Mrs. Kennedy's left is the widow of General George Marshall (John F. Kennedy Library, by permission of the Hemingway Society).

Hemingway papers were first opened for research in 1976 . . . [and] in 1980 Patrick Hemingway and Jacqueline Kennedy Onassis dedicated the Hemingway Room in the newly opened Kennedy Library at Columbia Point, Boston" (Megan Floyd Desnoyers, "Ernest Hemingway: A Storyteller's Legacy").

On 22 July 1961, three weeks after Hemingway's death, Mary had arrived at the Finca Vigía outside Havana to begin sorting the papers and manuscripts. On 1 August she wrote Walton – the uncharacteristically detailed heading, under the red-embossed letterhead of the

Finca Vigia, suggests that Mary Hemingway knew she was writing for
history:

> On Papa's typewriter – Tues., Aug. 1st, 1961
> Dear Willy –
> I have proposed informally to the Cuban Gov't that I give them the
> whole property in exchange for which they will give me assistance in
> taking back north Papa's papers and mine and a few personal things
> such as pictures. . . . I doubt that Papa would be totally in favor of this
> arrangement for disposal of the Finca; but since we cannot haul this
> place out to sea and sink it, as I hope to do with *Pilar* [Hemingway's
> boat], I think he would prefer this to any other arrangements we
> might make.[10]

But Mary could not arrange to have the *Pilar* scuttled because Gre-
gorio Fuentes, who had been first mate (and cook) on the boat
for eighteen years, feared the Cuban government's reaction. Today
researchers using the papers that Mary retrieved, and many other
documents that have accumulated since her first gift, sit in the
Hemingway Room at the Kennedy Library, where, looking out over
Boston Harbor, one can see John F. Kennedy's sailboat, the *Victura*,
anchored in a cement cradle on the seawall below – as the *Pilar*
is anchored on the grounds of the Finca Vigia, which is now a
museum.

In carrying out her trust as her husband's heir and literary executor, Mary Hemingway made it possible for the significance of the
posthumous works to become visible to scholars, even though she
may not herself have understood their relationship. Only when the
four works are seen serially can they be recognized as a thematically
coherent, though unfinished, unit. And only then are they visible as
the creative work that grew out of Hemingway's struggle to understand what had happened to his artistry in the face of premature
aging; of physical and mental conditions that we can now establish
were part of his genetic heritage (hemochromatosis and depression); of four ruined marriages that became the refractive indices of
male-female conflicts in his work; and of a narcissistic personality
that had always made writing the only intimate relationship Ernest
Hemingway could sustain.

In pursuing this study I have been fortunate in having had first
access to many new primary documents, and I sometimes thought

that if they were not in the archives or private collections where I used them, I would surely be suspected of inventing in order to support my perceptions of Hemingway's writing in the postwar years. But the new information would have made exaggeration or invention redundant; and much of the satisfaction in seeing this into print lies in the fact that the ordering and analysis of the many documents I have used now make possible greater understanding of both Hemingway the man and his portrait of the artist.

REASONABLE EXPECTATIONS

My second chapter will be a biographical consideration of the experiences that can be seen to have shaped Hemingway's anxiety about his art into the forms it took. Much of this material has either not appeared in biographies, or if it did, its significance to the posthumous works went unrecognized. I do not mean that I will read the fiction as biography, as has too often been done (once is too often!), but that when people, events, and image configurations from Hemingway's life are demonstrably reflected in the posthumously published novels or the African book, I have presented the biographical information as interpretive background.

In the four chapters that follow I will consider each book of the tetralogy in the order of its composition. Using both the published texts and the manuscript deletions for the three published works, as well as summary and paraphrase for the unpublished African book, I will trace the process by which pseudoautobiography became self-analysis, and self-excusing remembrance of things past became Hemingway's recognition of complicity in his creative decline as he strove – near the end of the life he would end – to complete the work that became *A Moveable Feast.*

Ernest Hemingway was not fond of literary scholars – he called them academic detectives who were always trying "to hang something" on him in order to get a Ph.D. and speculated that if he shot the one who was irritating him at the moment (Philip Young, whose book had begun in his Ph.D. thesis), he would bleed footnotes. Although I am one of those literary detectives, my Ph.D. is a quarter of a century old, and it is largely through the teaching, lectures, manuscript reviewing, conferences, and travel which make up academic life that I have become aware of how Hemingway's work, more than that of any other classic American writer, inhabits the hearts and memories of people the world over – those who read it for pleasure and wisdom, as well as those who teach and write about it. For that reason I have tried to make this a study that is as accessible in style and organization as it is sound in scholarship. And I have tried not to bleed footnotes.

CHAPTER 2

Recollections without tranquility: the biographical background

There is no shortage of Hemingway biographies: one appeared before Carlos Baker's 1969 *Hemingway: A Life Story,* the foundation on which all other serious biographers have built (Martha Gellhorn calls it the St. James version); and there have been eighteen primarily biographical books since 1969 – even counting the two serial biographies (by Peter Griffin, 2 volumes; and Michael Reynolds, 3 volumes) as single titles.

In addition there are the memoirs of Mary Hemingway, two books about Hadley Richardson Hemingway Mower, one about Martha Gellhorn that ventures into Hemingway's life, and an omnibus biography of the women who had extensive relationships with Hemingway.[1] However, a great deal of that part of Hemingway's life which is most relevant to the posthumous fiction is missing from or obscured in the biographies; or it has been presented in the distorting context of a single-trauma interpretation. The notable exception in the coverage of Hemingway's early years is the work of Michael Reynolds, which has reached April 1929 in the third volume and promises to be definitive. The incompleteness of Hemingway biographies results also from the writers' emphasizing one period or aspect of Hemingway's life to the exclusion of others – necessarily so with the two serial biographies and the thematically focused (but meticulously researched) works of Matthew Bruccoli, John Raeburn, and Mark Spilka.

The books about Hemingway's wives tend, as one would expect, to be *their* stories. Only one biographical study, Spilka's *Hemingway's Quarrel with Androgyny,* is fundamentally concerned with Hemingway's relationships with women as they have shaped the texts of his fiction.

Because the posthumous novels return repeatedly to the threat
that families and women pose to the creative artist, and to the artist's
inability to live and create in a world of men without women, it is
the early relationships of Ernest Hemingway with his family, and
those with his second, third, and final, wives that provide the essential contextual background for the posthumous novels.

This chapter does not strive for full coverage of any period of
Ernest Hemingway's life: the principle of selectivity is simply that of
providing the background for his portrait of the artist. On the other
hand, I will try to minimize the distortion inherent in selectivity by
dealing with patterns, not isolated incidents. The focus here will be
on the family dynamic in which Hemingway was raised, on his
relationships with his wives, and on his perceptions – which were
often projections – of the difficulties that other creative artists had
with the women in their lives, for these are the recurrent patterns in
the posthumous novels. In using the wealth of newly available material, my intent is to create a chronological narrative of those events
in Hemingway's life that I view as significant because they are important in his serial portrait of the artist. I have concluded that an
event is in this category if I can recognize the biographical resonances of a fictional configuration.

PASTORAL PIETY – THE HEMINGWAY HOME

Born in 1899, the second child and first son of Grace Hall and
Clarence Hemingway, Ernest had a childhood that seems typical of
the time, except that few Oak Park families carried on their entire
summer life as though they were living on the frontier half a century
earlier.[2] However, the fact that ultimately Clarence Hemingway and
three of his six children took their own lives suggests that something
quite untypical was present in the Hemingway home. Today we
know what Ernest Hemingway did not – that his father suffered from
recurrent bouts of depression that began to leave a record in his
correspondence in 1903 (when Ernest was four years old) and
deepened as he reached middle age. Clarence probably also suffered from hemochromatosis, a hereditary condition that becomes
symptomatic mostly in males in which the body does not break down
iron, and in middle age the excess of iron begins to cause mental
and physical illness.[3] (See Susan Beegel, "Hemingway and Hemochromatosis.")

Figure 3. The Hemingway family in 1905: Marcelline, Clarence holding Made-laine (Sunny), Grace holding Ursula, and Ernest (John F. Kennedy Library).

Both of Hemingway's parents were of English background and identified culturally and religiously with the optimistic tradition of nineteenth century British muscular Christianity which saw the business and professional middle class as the rank upon which moral and social leadership had devolved after the Industrial Revolution.[4] They accepted this charge with all the sense of being among the elect that their Puritan ancestors had assumed.[5] For example, in 1895 Grace wrote Clarence (who was on board ship to Scotland for a medical externship) of her success in convincing "all the better class of people" to support the Social Settlement Board of which she is a member. It is a letter that documents Grace's sense of her own superiority and unquestioning ability in several ways, for in it she indulges in her lifelong habit of repeating in letters the compliments she has received; and she gives Clarence, who is not yet her fiancé, much directive advice (21 May 1895; HRC).

On the righteousness of their views, Clarence and Grace Hemingway were initially in accord, for nine years later, while she was

visiting her brother Leicester, Clarence sent Grace a local newspaper
report of scandal among members of Oak Park's most prestigious
social club with the comment that "the Colonial Club and all other
clubs here are home destroyers. Time will tell a lot of tales. Thank
God we are not Club people – But *Home* & Nature folks" (18 Jan.
1904; HRC). However, it becomes clear from the correspondence
of the following decades that Clarence's obsessive concern with
conventionality and his recurring bouts of mental agitation, including several episodes that appear to be suicide plans, wore on Grace,
and that their thinking gradually diverged (see Michael Reynolds,
"Hemingway's Home").

When word of Ernest and Hadley's divorce appeared in the *Detroit
Free Press,* giving Hemingway's home as Toronto (where his last
American employment had been), Clarence tried to pretend that it
was a rumor and hoped that the Chicago and Oak Park newspapers
would not pick it up (Clarence–EH, 6 Mar. 1927; JFK). Five months
later, not knowing that Hemingway had already married Pauline,
Clarence wrote:

> I pray you may reform yourself and start aright to regain your wife.
> We are grieved and feel disgraced in a way you know not. I wish all
> the "Love Pirates" were in hell. Our family has never had such an
> incident before and trust you may still make your get-away from that
> individual who split your home. (8 Aug. 1927; JFK)

But Clarence's use of "we" was wishful thinking, for he and Grace
wrote to their son separately, and six months earlier, while Clarence
was still trying to deny the divorce rumors, she had written:

> I'm sorry to hear that your marriage has gone on the rocks, but
> most marriages ought to. I hold very modern and heretical views on
> marriage – but keep them under my hat. (20 Feb. 1927; JFK)

After their marriage in 1896, Grace and Clarence had adopted a
strenuous style of living that blended the spirit of muscular Christianity with that of the American frontier. The year before Ernest's
birth, they chose the upper peninsula of Michigan as the place
where they would begin the creation of a myth that became part of
the larger myth which has surrounded Ernest Hemingway ever since.
In the summer of 1898, Grace and Clarence decided to build a

summer place on Bear Lake (later named Lake Walloon), and during the winter drew plans for the cottage, named Windemere (a misspelling of Windermere) after that lake in the northwest country of England where the romantic myth of English country life began. Ernest was born on 21 July of the following summer, and on his one-month birthday, his father was in Michigan arranging for the construction of the cottage that would be his home for nineteen of the twenty summers that followed: the missing season (1918) he spent in a hospital in Italy. Grace apparently joined Clarence in Michigan when baby Ernest was seven weeks old, beginning the story that he was dedicated to nature in Michigan in September, and to God in Oak Park in October of his first year, a fact (or a myth) that is first told in Grace Hemingway's hand in volume 1 of the five-volume scrapbook at the Kennedy Library which she kept for her oldest son.[6]

SINGLE-PARENT SUMMERS

The result of Grace and Clarence's commitment to this life in which vigorous outdoor activity was a concomitant of Christian grace, was Ernest's early and constant exposure to hunting, fishing, and nature lore in a family environment where gender roles were quite fluid. (In the early years of the marriage, income from Grace's voice and music lessons sometimes exceeded that from Clarence's medical practice; and Grace learned to shoot and fish, while Clarence canned food and was the better cook.) But it was also a life in which the considerable burden of maintaining discipline among the Hemingway children fell largely upon Grace during more than three months of the summer, and under living conditions that drove her to the brink of exhaustion each year. Although their correspondence (*daily* letters) shows that Clarence supported Grace in her disciplinary actions, in Ernest's memory she became the "bitch" he consistently labeled her in later years, while his father became a weakling and, as Ernest fancied himself, a victim of his mother's tyranny.[7]

For example, when his mother evicted him from Windemere just after his twenty-first birthday, she was doing what his father had wished done four years earlier during the summer that Grace had remained in Oak Park for medical reasons, and Clarence had to assume the disciplinarian role at Windemere.[8] During that summer after Ernest and Marcelline's graduation from high school (1917), Clarence was the single parent, and his complaints are those that Grace had made nearly every summer since the older children had reached their teens: "Ernest is just as *headstrong* and abusive and threatening as ever," and Marcelline is uncontrollable, he wrote.[9] He wants Ernest, who he believes is leading Ursula astray, out of the house; and hopes that the job his brother Tyler is trying to arrange for him at the *Kansas City Star* will materialize.

Ernest took the job in Kansas City that October, and the following May he left to serve as a Red Cross ambulance driver, but he returned to Windemere during the summers of 1919 and 1920, and his increasing divergence from the way of living that his parents could contenance again created rebellious behavior among the Hemingway children. When Ernest was finally told to pack it in, it was Grace who delivered the message as, shortly after his twenty-first birthday, she handed him an eviction notice in the form of the famous birthday letter that at least one biographer has seen as part of an archetypal wound behind the darkness in "Big Two-Hearted River" (Lynn, *Hemingway*, 103–04).

There must have been at least three (handwritten!) copies of the birthday letter, since two survive at the Humanities Research Center, and presumably Grace handed one to her son. Clarence praised it as "a masterpiece [and] the right conception of the Mother's part of the game of Family life." In later years Hemingway created from the incident various versions of having spent most of his early years on the road because of the "all-American bitch." Although the letter is a solipsistic masterpiece of Victorian rhetoric with its strained monetary metaphors, there is no evidence that it inflicted a deep wound. In fact, Ernest, who had already accused his mother of having the *Atlantic* around the cottage as an intellectual prop, probably had a good laugh over the style – even at twenty-one. Two months later Grace and Ernest were making peace, and in September 1921, he and Hadley were married in Horton Bay, Michigan, and honeymooned at his mother's cottage across the lake from Windemere. Michael Reynolds documents the events of this summer (in *The Young Hemingway*, chapter 5) and reproduces the letter in full. The excerpt here suggests the degree to which Grace saw herself as the subject of the letter.

My Dear Son Ernest,

For three years, since you decided, at the age of eighteen years, that you did not need any further advice or guidance from your parents, I have tried to keep silence and let you work out your own salvation; by that I mean, your own philosophy of life – your code of ethics dealing with men, women, and children. Now, at the age of twenty-one . . . I shall brave your anger, and speak this once more to you.

A mother's love seems to me like a bank. Each child that is born to her, enters the world with a large and prosperous bank account, seemingly inexhaustible. For the first five years he draws, and draws – physical labor and pain – loss of sleep – watching and soothing, waiting upon, bathing, dressing, amusing. The Mother is practically a body slave to his every whim.

There are no deposits in the bank account during all the early years. "Cheery-o," thinks the mother, "some day he will be a comfort to me and return all I am doing for him," and she is content.

Then, for the next ten years, or so, up to adolescence, while the bank is heavily drawn on, for love and sympathy, championship in time of trouble or injustice, nursing thru illnesses, teaching and guiding, developing the young body and mind and soul, at all and any expense to the often exhausted parents during this time – there are a few deposits of pennies, in the way of services willingly done, some thoughtfulness and "thank yous."

Truly, the bank account is perilously low, for there is nothing coming in, no deposits, unless occasional spells of regret for past conduct make him come to her with an "I'm sorry and will truly try to do better."

But now, adolescence is past – full manhood is here. The bank is still paying out love, sympathy with wrongs, and enthusiasm for all ventures; courtesies and entertainment of friends who have nothing in common with mother, who, unless they are well bred, scarcely notice her existence.

The bank goes on handing out understanding and interest in budding love affairs, joy in plans of every sort. The account needs some deposits, by this time, some good sized ones in the way of gratitude and appreciation, interest in Mother's ideas and affairs. Little comforts provided for the home; a desire to favor any of Mother's peculiar prejudices, on no account to outrage her ideals – Flowers, fruit, candy, or something pretty to wear, brought home to mother, with a kiss or a squeeze – the unfailing desire to make much of her feeble efforts, to praise her cooking, back up her little schemes;

a real interest in hearing her sing, or play the piano, or tell stories that she loves to tell. . . . These are merely a few of the deposits which keep the account in good standing.

Many mothers I know are receiving these, and much more substantial gifts and returns from sons of less abilities than my son. Unless you, my son, Ernest, come to yourself, cease your lazy loafing, and pleasure seeking – borrowing with no thought of returning – stop trying to graft a living off anybody and everybody – spending all your earnings lavishly and wastefully on luxuries for yourself – stop trading on your handsome face, to fool little gullible girls, and neglecting your duties to God and your Savior Jesus Christ – unless, in other words you come into your manhood – there is nothing before you but bankruptcy: *You have overdrawn.* (Dated 24 July, but apparently handed to Ernest on 27 July 1920; HRC)

ERNEST AND MARCELLINE AS GRACE'S TWINS

The rhetoric of the birthday letter suggests not only that a lapse in behavior was a personal affront to Grace Hemingway, but that where self-involvement was at issue, the apple hadn't fallen far from the tree. Further evidence of Grace's difficulty in seeing her children, particularly the two oldest, as other than extensions of herself lies in the twinning of Ernest and Marcelline that has received much attention in the Lynn, Meyers, and Spilka biographies. Grace was open about her fantasy of being the mother of same-sex twins, and I am inclined to think that, with the tendency of the narcissistic personality to see others only in relationship to itself which she displayed in the birthday letter, she felt licensed in earlier years to act out her fantasy by treating Marcelline and Ernest as toys. In short, the motive for the twinning was probably simpler than the assumptions of some critics – that she wanted to make Marcelline a boy, or Ernest a girl, or to control the visible manifestations of both their sexes.

The twinning took the form of similar or identical clothing and hair styles for the two oldest children, and of Marcelline's twice being held back in school (in kindergarten, where she remained until she was seven and a half, and in eighth grade, when she was taken out of school for a full year) so that she and Ernest would be in the same high school class. Marcelline has left a record of the pain that this trifling caused her, for the complications of the cross-dressing were ended only by the intrusion of a second-grade teacher into the family matter when Marcelline was eight years and eight months old. Further, in her memoir, *At the Hemingways,* Marcelline relates the events that brought an end to the twinning in terms quite different than she had rendered them in the early manuscript versions of the book.[10]

Hemingway kept his silence; and after his father's suicide in 1928, he assumed support of Grace and his two siblings (the bank deposits that the birthday letter suggested?). But his threat to cut off support if she gave an interview to *McCalls* in 1949 may reflect a fear that the "twin" photos would surface (*Letters,* 675). His adult preoccupation with the erotic qualities of hair, and his attempts to change his own hair color suggest that the impact of at least that part of the twinning was far from negative. Although he was in the same schoolroom with Marcelline, and must have been a witness to the ridicule she endured because of his mother's whim, there is no evidence he recognized that Marcelline, as well as he, had suffered from his mother's manipulations. The question that this evidence raises is not, it seems to me, the one biographers have asked rhetorically as they prepare to answer it affirmatively: "Did his mother's actions create for Hemingway a larger drama of sexual confusion?" (Lynn, *Hemingway,* 58). Rather, in view of Hemingway's difficulty with human relationships, the critical question is, How did witnessing Marcelline's humiliation affect his ability and willingness to truly see others? And to experience empathy? For after he was five, the twinning switched to Marcelline's being dressed and coifed as a boy, and no longer involved female garb for him.[11]

Hemingway's relationships with the women he married, and the posthumous novels, particularly *The Garden of Eden,* suggest that it was his empathetic faculty which was damaged in childhood, at least in part by his mother's failure to see her children as other than an extension of herself. Marcelline seems to have buried the matter, but at considerable psychic cost (for she suffered from depression) and, as she matured, to have become very much like her mother,[12] while Ernest, who could hold a grudge forever, recounted many permutations of his mother's domineering character, but never spoke or wrote of the twinning.

LEARNING TO KILL

The scrapbooks which Grace Hemingway kept for Ernest (as she did for the other children) document further the degree to which it was the parents' inclinations rather than the children's needs that structured family relations in the Hemingway home, and how that may have affected Hemingway as a man and a writer. They suggest too Clarence's mental state, for he smiles in only three of the many photos in all the five volumes, and often appears depressed or distracted. Grace has captioned the photos (in a fine Palmer method hand), and if the treacly language she uses represents that of everyday discourse in the Hemingway home, Frederic Henry's mistrust of abstract words must have begun there. Pictures of Ernest's first Christmas are underwritten with "The darling little man seemed to enjoy his first Christmas[,] may God spare him to see many more."

Other incidents in the scrapbooks illustrate just how much the home was the construct of Grace and Clarence's values, and suggest how detrimental this may have been to Ernest. Examples of parental obtuseness that must have required the child Ernest to dichotomize or deny his emotions are reflected in both *Islands* and *Garden*. In volume 1, Grace records Ernest's fondness for owl stories, noting that at sixteen months, in response to a regime of Clarence's devising, Ernest had his supper at 5:30 p.m., and was not fed again until 6:30 a.m., and that for a month he has awakened "beg[ging] for an owl story at all time [*sic*] of night, waking the family." But by the end of November, he began going to sleep "without a word, *putting the pillow over his face*" (my emphasis). In volume 2, a photo of Ernest at four is labeled "The Hunter and His Game." He holds aloft a giant owl! The final entry in volume 1 says:

> Ernest Miller went to Ringling Brothers Circus at about 21 months and enjoyed it hugely. He saw performing elephants and is never tired of having you tell him about them. Early, oh *so* early in the morning you hear "Tell Ernie about dat big Elempant, Da-bear" [Daddy Bear]. He loves to walk like an elephant and imitates all sorts of animals.

In September 1949, Hemingway wrote his mother that he had looked at the scrapbooks again. He thanked her for assembling them and remarked particularly on the pleasure that the photos of his father had given him, closing with fond wishes to her and her companion Ruth Arnold (*Letters*, 675).

Both Marcelline Hemingway Sanford and Edward Wagenknecht, a high school classmate who became a literature professor, remember Hemingway's sustained interest in elephants. In a 1990 newsletter of the Oak Park-River Forest Historical Society, a contemporary of Hemingway recalled that the annual unloading of elephants and other animals for a circus performance in Oak Park took place at the intersection of Madison and Cuyler Streets in the village (about a mile from the Hemingway home) and was a great attraction for children. During Hemingway's childhood the rotunda of the Field Museum of Natural History in Chicago displayed two elephants that remain there today. Marcelline remembers that on trips to the museum with their father they saw "stuffed animals looking lifelike . . . with their glass eyes shining out at us, just as though they could see us the way we could see them" (Sanford, *At the Hemingways*, 38). In 1935, giving instructions for the photos to be used in the serialization of *The Green Hills of Africa*, Hemingway told Max Perkins that the layout man "should be able to get [them] to look as they look alive in the african hall of the museum of natural history [*sic*]" (22 Feb.; PUL).

Hemingway never hunted elephants. His direct statement in "On the Blue Water" – that killing an elephant would destroy his taste for hunting all lesser animals just as surely as drinking lye would destroy his taste for fine wine – suggests that elephant hunting was taboo for him. In *Eden* he gave to the death of the elephant a signifying burden that links this taboo to the killer instincts of a father who was indifferent to his eight-year-old son's empathy with the old animal.

Another resonant episode from Hemingway's early years is preserved in the scrapbooks. In volumes 1 and 2 Grace notes the game of "Mamma Kitty/Baby Kitty" that she and Ernest played. (Twenty years later she would cloyingly remind him of the days when she was his Mamma Kitty.) Hemingway had cat names for both his first and last wives: Hadley's cherishing of the appellations is evident in the "Kitten to Waxin" letters published by James Nagel; and his adult attachment to cats is legendary: the famous Boise of *Islands* was only one of the many cats resident at the Finca Vigia. In volume 2, a letter of 8 July 1907 from Clarence (who was in Oak Park) to Ernest (who was at Windemere with his mother), describes enthusiastically his shooting a cat. Prefacing the account with "Don't tell," he writes:

> Mr. Tom cat turned a sommer-sault in the air; and will never steal eggs or baby chickens again – so you can see your Daddy is still a good "Eagle Eye" with the trigger when there is game or tom cats.

In *Hemingway in Cuba,* Norberto Fuentes recounts an incident at the Finca Vigia in which one of Mary's favorite cats had been injured by an auto and Hemingway sent a servant, Rene, for his gun. Rene asked, "Do I shoot him, Papa?" Hemingway "grabbed the gun from him and through clenched teeth said '*Dame aca, con que a los mios los mato yo* [Give it to me, damn it, I kill my own]' " (80).

RUMORS OF LESBIANISM

Perhaps the final matter of Hemingway's years in the family home that may be reflected in the posthumous novels is the rumor that Grace had a lesbian relationship with her student and household helper Ruth Arnold. The letters between Grace and Clarence Hemingway, and between Grace and Ruth Arnold which are at the Humanities Research Center, establish that Clarence's eviction of Ruth Arnold from the Hemingway home (where she had lived for eight years) in August 1919 was the culmination of one of his recurrent periods of paranoia. Further, there is evidence that the state into which he had worked himself may have begun with a rumor arising from an internecine quarrel in the church choir that Grace directed.[13] The Grace-Ruth Arnold letters establish that Ruth Arnold as a young woman was both effusive and starved for the attention Grace gave her. Some of her letters to Grace are about the boys who are paying attention to her, and eventually she married and had a daughter. Further, the year following the harsh events of the summer of 1919, Clarence seems to have put the relationship back into a nonthreatening perspective and been happy that Grace had Ruth's help and companionship in Michigan. For her part, Ruth Arnold was sensitive to whatever had caused his outburst, and she writes Grace that she will not think of joining her and the children until "the Doctor" has stayed in Michigan as long as he can. The two shared an interest in music and a mystical religious sensibility, and in the late years of Grace's life Ruth once again became, so to speak, her household helper, for they lived together, and she cared for the aging Grace as if she were her own mother. Ernest greeted and thanked Ruth Arnold in his infrequent letters to his mother, but when he was in the blaming mode, which was often, he seems to have subscribed to the belief that their relationship was suspect, for his son told a biographer that his father would not let him visit his grandmother because she was androgynous.[14]

CHILDHOOD'S LEGACY: LONELINESS, DEPENDENCY, MISTRUST

Drafting his Nobel Prize acceptance speech in 1954, Hemingway wrote, but did not incorporate, this passage:

> There is no lonelier man than the writer when he is writing except the suicide. Nor is there any happier, nor more exhausted man when he has written well. If he has written well everything that is him has gone into the writing and he faces another morning when he must do it again. There is always another morning and another morning. (File 609a; JFK)

He was describing emotional isolation that he knew well, and in this statement Hemingway locates his very self at the center of his ability to write well, a dangerous concentration of ego identity in a single and mutable site that child psychiatry generally agrees is related to narcissistic parenting – which is itself likely to produce narcissism in the child who is raised in such an emotional climate.

Child analyst Alice Miller gives a particularly clear consideration of the ways in which the child's early necessity to develop an independent sense of self can be thwarted by responding instead to the needs of parents. She is in basic agreement with the other major scholars of the separation phase of childhood in which the construction of the self normally occurs (Heinz Kohut, Margaret Mahler, and D. W. Winnicott). Theories of this group have much in common with the Lacanian "mirroring phase" theory which stresses the crucial need of a parent who truly sees the very young child and is able to reflect back to him a self that is grand enough, secure enough, to continue forming apart from the mirroring parent. This mirroring, without the introjection of their own needs, is, I suggest, a stance of which neither Grace or Clarence Hemingway was capable.

This study is concerned only tangentially with Ernest Hemingway's parents – the task of writing that family history awaits another scholar, and a great deal of material for it is contained in the Hemingway family papers at the Humanities Research Center and in the archives of the Ernest Hemingway Museum in Oak Park. However, a sketch of Grace and Clarence's backgrounds suggests the chain of parenting that I believe shaped Hemingway into an often dark and lonely man, habitually seeking the public eye, yet unable to carry on in that glare the writing that was his only measure of self-worth.

Grace always identified herself as "Grace Hall Hemingway," at a time when most married women dropped their maiden names. In continuing to perform and to teach voice and music, Grace, who had had a debut in Madison Square Garden in 1895 (the year after her mother's death) was also living her mother's unfulfilled desire for a musical career. After marrying Clarence in 1896, she incorporated into her life the mandate her mother had given as she supported her voice studies – she insisted upon keeping a portion of her time and income free from the needs of her family to use for her own development. While her independence has drawn criticism from some biographers, it is a matter of record that she contributed a considerable portion of the income to the Hemingway household during the early part of the marriage. However, when Ernest was an infant, she seems to have been far too self-involved to have provided the atmosphere in which he could develop a self not contingent upon being the child she wanted him to be.

The record of Grace's relationship with her youngest daughter, Carol Hemingway Gardner (b. 1911), which is contained in their correspondence at the Humanities Research Center, shows a very different kind of parenting, a relationship that she apparently became capable of only when she no longer had to defend against the needs of her family in order to keep a part of her life for herself. Their letters reveal that Carol was a well-adjusted woman, and that Grace was consistently generous to her when both their incomes were limited. She clearly remembered and empathized with the dilemma of a young mother with intellectual and artistic leanings who was trying to raise a family on a small income.

Clarence did not live to reach that angle of repose. He had brought to the marriage and parenting his father's desire to do Christian social work, which Anson Hemingway had put aside for a real estate business in order to support his large family. Clarence's brother, Willoughby, had become a physician and a medical missionary in China, while Clarence found expression for his thwarted desires in his commitment to a medical practice where patients' needs took priority over their ability to pay, and in the more disruptive need to serve that over the years became an obsession with assuming responsibility for every detail of the family's lives. How well Philip Larkin understood families when he wrote:

> They fuck you up, your mum and dad.
> They may not mean to, but they do.
> They fill you with the faults they had
> And add some extra, just for you.
> ("This Be The Verse," 1971)

This residue of loneliness would bring Hemingway into conflict with women all of his life, for he was extraordinarily dependent and could not write unless he had a primary relationship – no matter that he fled each for the company of men almost as soon as it had become established and returned at his convenience. Despite the fact that almost from the beginning of his life as a writer, Hemingway mistrusted the impact of women on his work, his marriages were serial: he never broke with a wife until her successor had committed herself to him and set in motion her arrangements for the life they would share. In 1926, when Hadley made a hundred-day separation between him and Pauline the condition of her granting him a divorce, he lived alone in Gerald Murphy's studio and became so depressed that he could not work, and contemplated suicide (Baker, *A Life*, 174–76).

During his long, frequent (and voluntary) separations from Pauline, when he went to Bimini or Cuba for weeks at a time, Hemingway had a stream of affectionate letters and frequent visits from her; and after April 1932, he often had the company of Jane Mason. By December 1939, when Pauline was alienated enough by his very public relationship with Martha Gellhorn to take the children and leave Key West, Hemingway had been involved with Martha for nearly three years; and she had established a home for them at the Finca Vigia outside Havana.

But Martha's absences for her work assignments with *Collier's* soon became the source of conflict. Hemingway blamed his irascibility and inability to create on her not being at home. In a letter of 12 March 1944 he tells Maxwell Perkins that he is "punchy from Martha haveing been away so long" (JFK).

When Martha had reached the point of no return, and Hemingway met Mary Welsh in London in May 1944, he transferred his affections to her almost immediately – as a letter of 31 July and 1 August shows (*Letters*, 558–559). Yet only when he and Mary have agreed upon a life together in which she will take over the domestic and business/literary advisory aspects of his life and become his "partner" does Hemingway announce to his children the end of his marriage to Martha. To Bumby, the oldest, he wrote a locker room scenario of trading off his "equity" in Martha for a good third baseman, concluding, "when want to write need to have wife around as is tough racket and impossible be alone after doing it" (12 Oct. 1944; JFK). To Patrick he wrote, "Going to get me somebody who wants to stick around with me and let me be the writer of the family" (19 Nov. 1944; *Letters*, 576).

During forced separations from Mary in 1945 Hemingway frequently wrote her more than once a day, as Clarence had written Grace during her absences. In a letter of 9 April he says:

> I ought to get so I can be alone. But I can't. . . . I miss you as though they had cut my heart out with one of those things you take cores out of apples. (JFK)

Fourteen months earlier, he had used the identical phrase in a letter to Martha.

Ultimately Hemingway's behavior so alienated Mary during the summer of 1959 that she set down conditions on which she would return to Cuba. In letters to A. E. Hotchner, who had been with him during the summer, Hemingway describes his life with Mary as being without warmth (8 Nov. 1959; JFK). The following February Mary agreed that Valerie Danby-Smith, with whom Hemingway had become involved the previous summer in Spain, could come to Cuba as his secretary. When Hemingway returned to Spain in the summer of 1960 and began to disintegrate, Mary sent Valerie to help him; and on her return from Spain, Valerie remained in New York, receiving financial support from Hemingway in Idaho. His letter of 25 October 1960 to Valerie makes clear that he had now become very dependent upon her, but that his mental and physical deterioration kept him with Mary in Ketchum, Idaho. He explains to her the arrangements he has made for correspondence so that her letters will not "annoy" Mary, and adds:

> I love you very much and miss your help all the time. This is a rough fall and the whole purpose of being here to work is destroyed unless I know you are well and doing well. So far it has been like being in Limbo or you being in Limbo or both. (JFK)

But Hemingway's dependency was always mixed with a fear and mistrust of women that was probably more complex in its origin than we will ever know. Certainly there was the belief that his mother had called the shots in his childhood, a belief that his parents' correspondence shows as erroneous, for his father was often a very agitated and troubled man, and it is clear that in any conflict Grace chose the way that impinged least upon her own time – which meant that Clarence's rigidity was enforced by Grace. But the belief in his mother's dominance, like his suspicion of her androgyny, was truth to Hemingway. There was also the easy assumption that his mother had driven his father to suicide, which is also dispelled by their letters – but Hemingway never lived with his family after his Christmas visit in 1919; and after leaving the United States in 1921, he saw his father only three times (Christmas 1924; Apr. 1928, a brief meeting in Florida; and Oct. 1928). He did not know what his parents' correspondence at the Humanities Research Center shows – that after three tumultuous decades their marriage had reached a state of relative serenity, and his father was looking forward to a retirement in which they could travel and Grace could continue the painting that had recently begun to bring her recognition, and in which Clarence took pride. Nor did he ever know that the depression (and probably hemochromatosis) from which his father suffered led him to exaggerate the seriousness of his diabetes. His long-visible pessimism and paranoia ultimately combined with financial losses – which, like every other problem, he fretted over endlessly – to trigger Clarence's suicide. But blaming his mother satisfied a lot of needs for Ernest Hemingway.[15]

In all of the posthumous novels Hemingway reiterated his distrust of women's entry into the creative process by rendering it in terms of Hadley's loss of his manuscripts in 1922; she had attempted to bring them to him in Switzerland, and they were stolen from the

train when she left the suitcase unattended (see Michael Reynolds, *The Paris Years*, 86, 88–90). Although Hemingway would very nearly canonize Hadley in later years – calling her in the African book "The wife that I loved first and best" – the depth with which the artist in him experienced this loss is rendered as a sexual wound in an episode deleted from *Islands*. The double bind of dependency and distrust are a combination guaranteed to undermine better constituted psyches than Ernest Hemingway's had ever been.

WRITING ANXIETY AND FATHER FIGURES

Long before Hemingway began to inscribe the destructive power of the feminine in his posthumous texts, he assumed that the wives of his artist friends, Scott Fitzgerald, Waldo Pierce, Evan Shipman, and Mike Strater, were destructive to their work. Later he would praise Charles Sweeny, a mysterious and hard to trace soldier of fortune that I believe was one of the three most influential males in Hemingway's life, as the only man he ever knew who was able to handle women.

A second important figure was Charles (Buck) Lanham, the WWII friend whom Hemingway advised on the relative merits of fighting through a contested divorce (and having his military pension attached) or trying to have his wife committed to a mental institution.

The third important man in his life who fuelled Hemingway's already well-developed distrust of women was Max Perkins. His long-time Scribner's editor, Perkins was at the center of an information network through which Hemingway kept track of Fitzgerald and Sweeny (both Scribner's authors), as well as Pierce, Shipman, and Strater.

Hemingway and Perkins were complementary personalities, each genially coveting what the other had. Perkins, with five daughters, admitted that he was uncomfortable with women, and sometimes envied Hemingway his family of boys, while Hemingway confessed to Perkins that he wanted a daughter. In 1933, planning a daughter's wedding, Perkins says:

> You live in a family that is six-sevenths feminine, and you are kept
> mighty busy with a lot of psychology and strange things that you don't
> have to deal with in a family that is four-fifths male. (14 Aug.; PUL)

Hemingway had frequently invited Perkins to visit him in Key West; (eventually he did) one of Perkins's explanations of why he hadn't yet visited is interesting:

> Maybe I might come down to Key West. I would like to do it mighty well. I'd like to spend an afternoon on the dock looking at those lazy turtles swimming around. The trouble is there is another author in Florida, Marjorie Rawlings. She is a fine author too, and a fine woman. But I never did feel comfortable alone with women (I suppose there is some complex involved in it) and the idea of visiting one with nobody else around (she is divorced) scares me to death. (28 Dec. 1934; PUL)

Perkins's uneasiness with women, and his grumbling about the necessity of giving teas for "lady authors," are only mildly misogynistic for his time; and it is interesting to note that he felt Zelda Fitzgerald had talent which might be put to the hieratic service of supporting Scott so that he could write.[16]

But in keeping Hemingway updated on the activities of the writers and painters they both knew who were having marital and creative problems, Perkins fed the mother-haunted Hemingway's obsession with the destructive effect of women on male creativity.

Perkins's nurturing of his authors was legendary, and Hemingway became as jealous of his attentions to Thomas Wolfe as he later became of Charles Scribner's support of James Jones.[17] Thus, when Perkins reported to Hemingway that critics were deprecating his detachment from the Depression as self-indulgence, and urged him to expand the Harry Morgan stories into a novel that would compete with "the proletarian boys, the Marxists," Hemingway wrote *To Have and Have Not*. Ten years earlier he had begun and put aside a picaresque novel. Now he used a Fielding-like technique with parallel narrative lines, seeking to juxtapose high and low life in Key West to suggest working-class solidarity as a refuge from individual tragedy.[18] But the double plot just didn't go that way, and the novel ended instead by dramatizing the double delusion of believing that fate is escapable. Harry Morgan dies when a robber he had shot three times revives long enough to shoot him in the stomach: his death is as much the legacy of chance as Catherine Barkley's narrow hips or Jake Barnes's war wound.

Reviews of *To Have and Have Not* (1937) ranged from unenthusiastic to dismissive, but Hemingway's letters show that he was not particularly troubled.

NEW MATERIAL, NEW WIFE, AND THE LANGUAGE
OF RESISTANCE

Hemingway's equanimity with the reviews of *To Have* in 1937 was in
no small way a reflection of the fact that before the finished manuscript had been sent to Scribner's, he had already embarked on an
exciting series of events that would produce *For Whom the Bell Tolls*
(1940) and result in a marriage that would forever make his creative
and personal lives inseparable – if they ever had been. The experience of the Spanish Civil War, and the mismatching of Hemingway
with Martha Gellhorn that developed there worked to crystallize his
sense of the destructive power of women that had begun in childhood. In 1953 he would link his mother and Martha by describing
them as the two most ambitious women he ever knew – and confess-
ing that he was afraid of ambitious women.

Whatever Grace and Clarence Hemingway had done, or failed to
do, it was inevitable that Hemingway would eventually find himself
protecting his art from a vision of female power, because the very
forging of his lapidary style had been done in resistance to the
platitudinous language of his upbringing that he regarded as feminine. The language of his childhood was to him, quite literally,
mother tongue, despite the fact that his father's sensibility informed
the pious utterances he rejected as a falsification of human emotions
as thoroughly, and for a longer time, than his mother's.[19]

If he were to function as a creative artist, and as a heterosexual
male – and I see no evidence that Hemingway was not heterosexual – he would find himself in conflict with women, for the deepest
roots of his self-identity united his maleness and his vocation as a
writer. That Hemingway sensed he needed a feminine component
to his creative imagination, as well as a companion against loneliness, is clear both biographically and artistically as he chose (with
the significant and psychologically costly exception of Martha Gellhorn) boyish wives, and taught them to hunt and fish as part of his
courtship.[20] For example, Pauline writes him during their forced
separation in 1926, "We're the same guy." Even in his early fiction
Hemingway created couples who think of themselves as the same
person (Catherine Barkley-Frederic Henry; Robert Jordan-Maria).
Zelda Fitzgerald sensed, but misunderstood, just how inseparable
Hemingway's maleness and his art were when, in 1926, she called

the ambivalent and sometimes tumultuous attraction between Scott and Hemingway a homoerotic one.

As he aged, this hypermasculine identity that Hemingway had eagerly helped to create in his youth, became a mask behind which he was trapped; and the masculine-feminine tension was a truly debilitating conflict for a man as dependent upon women as Hemingway remained throughout his life.

During the more than ten years of Hemingway's second marriage, Pauline Pfeiffer devoted her inherited wealth, as well as her considerable intelligence and energy, to the service of Hemingway as a man and writer. But no lasting trust of the female or the feminine came from her devotion, despite the fact that in 1940 – after he had forced her to make the choice that ended the marriage (just as he had done with Hadley in 1926) – Hemingway still thought Pauline his best critic. She had also accepted, perhaps encouraged, his initial explorations with hair coloring that are the first visible evidence of his extra-textual experiments with androgyny.[21]

Hemingway's third marriage, to Martha Gellhorn, quickly obviated any trust of women in the demesne of his art that might eventually have emerged from his years with Pauline. After Martha, protecting the masculine texts would become a consistent subtext in the four posthumous works, where the writer's ability to create becomes a progenitive act, while protection of the text becomes a symbolic custody battle that the writer fights with the women in his life, and his fictional artists wage in their work.

ROMANCING THE NOBEL AND PLAYING DANGEROUS GAMES

Martha Gellhorn was twenty-eight, ten years younger than Hemingway, and fourteen years younger than Pauline when they met in Key West during late December 1936. Although she was on vacation with her mother and brother at the time, it is clear that Ernest Hemingway was part of her itinerary, for in Key West she had headed for Sloppy Joe's, the bar that was well-known as his haunt; and when her family returned to St. Louis, Martha stayed on. Far closer in personality to Hemingway than to either of his two previous wives, who had devoted themselves to creating an atmosphere where he could thrive as a writer, Martha was restless, intellectually curious, self-disciplined, and ambitious. Almost nomadic, she seems to have remained intelligently self-protective in any romantic relationship. These were traits that did not change.[22]

Martha was aware that there was a growing perception of her work as the most reliable chronicle of the toll the Depression was taking on the lives of those displaced by farm foreclosures, and she was becoming nationally known as a protégée of Eleanor Roosevelt. When Hemingway met her, Martha's picture had recently appeared on the cover of the *Saturday Review of Literature* (26 September 1936), where her first volume of stories was reviewed.[23]

In inviting Martha to the house on Whitehead Street, he was setting in motion a chain of events like those that had led (in 1926) to the end of his first marriage. Then Pauline had been the single, younger, glamorous, aggressive woman from St. Louis who opened her campaign for him by becoming a friend of the family. She spent a vacation skiing with Hemingway, Hadley, and Bumby in Schruns in 1925–26, beginning an affair that would end in Hadley and Hemingway's divorce, and his marriage to her in May 1927. Hemingway would use these events as benchmarks of the writer's decline in *Feast* and *Eden*.

Martha was a frequent visitor to the Hemingways, in December and early January (1936–37); and on returning to St. Louis, she reported to Pauline how fond she was of both of them (and the children). She and Hemingway had been together on the train from Miami to Jacksonville – it is not clear whether this was by prearrangement – as he traveled to New York to sign on with the North American Newspaper Alliance to cover the war in Spain. In the letter, Martha describes their journey, the pleasure of eating a good steak, as well as quietly and sleepily digesting it with "Ernestino" (Martha Gellhorn-Pauline Hemingway, 14 Jan. 1937; PUL).

Eleven years earlier Pauline, in Paris, had written an equally revealing and gustatory letter of appreciation to Hadley, who had remained in Schruns with two-year-old Bumby while Ernest returned to Paris on his way to New York to discuss the publication arrangements for *The Torrents of Spring* (and by extension those for *The Sun Also Rises*):

> I've seen your husband E. Hemingway several times – sandwiched in like good red meat between thick slices of soggy bread. (29 Jan. 1926; JFK)

There is no record of how Pauline reacted to Martha's letter – or whether the man who inspired red meat fantasies saw either letter on returning to his current wife; but until his suppressed letter of 18 April 1961 regarding the Paris book that became *Feast,* Hemingway never acknowledged that the end of his second marriage was a repeat performance. Nor did he ever show for Pauline, who had been an extraordinary helpmate, the reverence and gratitude that he displayed for Hadley when he made her the heroine of *Feast.* Hadley (who had some independent income) had revoked her hundred-day separation edict in mid-November 1926 and had accepted the royalties from *The Sun Also Rises* as a settlement of the marriage; and Hemingway said that he had never loved her more than when she freed him. Pauline (who had considerable independent income) had finally called him to account for his neglect of her and the children and his public liaison with Martha Gellhorn; and part of that accounting was support for the two boys and herself.[24] In the years that followed, Hemingway remarked that Pauline had stolen him from Hadley, and that in her calculated campaign for him she had underestimated the power of his remorse. Martha was simply doing to Pauline as Pauline had done to Hadley – and he, by implication, bore no more responsibility for the theft than did the suitcase Hadley had left unattended in the Gare de Lyon.

Hadley and Pauline had been indulgent, tolerant wives and had bent their own lives to the curve of Hemingway's self-absorbed oscillation between isolating bouts of writing and vigorous pursuits of sports. The third time around he did not fare so well. When biographers, feminist critics, and Hemingway's sons assign blame for the failure of his third marriage, which cut Hemingway loose from the domestic security he needed but never failed to abuse, Martha has generally been shriven. But Hemingway's brother and his male friends, especially Buck Lanham, take the opposite view, their information coming from Hemingway, who was hardly a disinterested party.[25]

Martha Gellhorn (b. 1908) lives in Wales and London, and remains a regular contributor to British and American periodicals such as the *Times Literary Supplement, Granta,* and the *New Republic.* She has said little, and that reluctantly, about her years with Hemingway, nothing at all about the expectations she had when she entered the marriage.[26] Many of her personal papers, including her letters to

Hemingway, have been deposited at Boston University, where they are closed to scholars. Fortunately, other documents provide information about her years with Hemingway that Martha alone could never provide – even if she were to be uncharacteristically forthcoming. They furnish a splendid unifying framework for assessing the impact of Hemingway's third marriage on his complex vision of the incompatibility of feminine influence and masculine text.

The Scribner's III Archives contain Max Perkins's and Charles Scribner Sr.'s correspondence with Hemingway; and the Scribner's IV Archives contain Martha's correspondence with Charles Scribner Sr. before, during, and after her marriage to Hemingway. The Perkins-Hemingway letters supplement Hemingway's exchange with Scribner, filling in blanks and providing a more disinterested view of the Gellhorn-Hemingway relationship than either Hemingway or Scribner, who were both once captivated by Martha, could possibly render.[27]

Max Perkins and Charles Scribner knew the direction of Hemingway's relationship with Martha from its beginning, for the pair was not subtle, and both Perkins and Scribner had pipelines to people who saw them together in New York and Europe, and reported back to the Scribner's network what has been interpreted as Martha's pursuit and Hemingway's lack of resistance.[28] From 1937 to 1939, Pauline was sometimes forced to locate her husband through inquiries or messages transmitted by Scribner's – lending a certain poetic justice to the fact that in 1943–44, Hemingway had to resort to the same manner of reaching Martha. For his part, Charles Scribner became Martha's confidant and admirer.[29]

Personal considerations aside, the Scribner's firm had no small interest at stake when they assumed an accessory role in the Hemingway-Gellhorn affair. He was an important author on their list and Scribner's policy, as Perkins once articulated it to Hemingway (who at the time was trying to persuade the firm to take on Ford Madox Ford), was to sign writers early in their careers and build with them (Perkins-EH, 14 Nov. 1930; PUL). They had done this with Hemingway, publishing *The Torrents of Spring* (1926) when Horace Liveright refused it, and thereby obtaining *The Sun Also Rises* (1926) and *Farewell to Arms* (1929), both of which had become modern classics. But the books that Hemingway had produced for them in the 1930s, *Death in the Afternoon* (1932), *The Green Hills of*

Africa (1935) and *To Have and Have Not* (1937), had not kept the promise of *Sun* and *Farewell*. Although Perkins was anxious about the danger to Hemingway in becoming a war correspondent, his letters establish that he never overlooked the potential of literary material in any activity that Hemingway undertook. From that vantage, Scribner's saw that the Spanish Civil War experience and Martha Gellhorn, who was a part of Hemingway's involvement there from the beginning, might well increase the value of their investment. They were right, of course – in the short run.

When Hemingway urged Martha to change publishers and Scribner's to acquire her third book, *A Stricken Field* (1940), the firm had multiple reasons for agreeing. Not only was she the "intended" of an important member of their stable; she was also a comer in her own right who had a connection of long standing in the White House, for her mother and Eleanor Roosevelt were personal friends, and she was a frequent visitor there who had the ear of Mrs. Roosevelt and the president.

Thirty-six letters from Martha to Charles Scribner Sr. survive. From them, and from the correspondence between Scribner, Perkins, and Hemingway, emerge some informative glimpses of Ernest Hemingway and Martha Gellhorn in the years prior to, during, and just after their marriage. The correspondence contains references to events which form the creative basis of significant episodes in the posthumous fiction. The letters of Hemingway and of Martha to Charles Scribner Sr. are particularly valuable in establishing that Martha Gellhorn and Ernest Hemingway were two ambitious, self-involved individuals who happened also to be romantically involved with one another. They show each intent upon his or her own part of the drama, with neither calculating in advance the cost of this mutual usage to himself or herself. When the final reckoning was done, Hemingway won the Nobel, but Martha was more resilient.

Between February 1937 and November 1938 Hemingway made four extended trips to the front in Spain. From March 1937 onward, Martha, a correspondent for *Collier's*, was either with him or finding a way to complete her other work and get back to where he was. His writing during these twenty-one months was largely journalistic, and his marriage to Pauline was increasingly strained by his absences and by press attention to his relationship with Martha. Although Hemingway may not have realized it at the time, his Valentine's Day,

Figure 4. Hemingway and Christopher Columbus at the Finca in the 1950s
(John F. Kennedy Library, courtesy of *Look* and Earl Thiesen).

1939, flight from family interference was a significant event, the opening date for the final phase of his inextricable linking of women to the destruction of his art.

After being with his family in Key West for Christmas, Hemingway returned to New York (and Martha) on 2 January 1939. But in three weeks he was back in Key West, where Pauline's uncle, Gus Pfeiffer, who had been their patron since before the marriage, had arrived with his wife for a visit. Their visit was followed immediately by one from Grace Hemingway. Hemingway had little tolerance for such concentrated family presence, especially when he could not help suspecting that it was prompted by media rumors that his second marriage was in trouble. On the day after his mother's departure, he took the *Pilar* to Havana, where within two weeks he was steadily at work on *Bell*, the novel that Scribner's had hoped would be the outcome of his experience in Spain. In late March or early April, Martha arrived, rented the Finca Vigia, and set up a household for herself and Hemingway. The novel was finished in mid-July 1940: "The bridge is blown!" Martha announced in a letter to Charles Scribner Sr. That December, a month after their marriage, Hemingway bought the Finca for $12,500.

Neither Martha's nor Hemingway's letters hint at Nobel Prize expectations prior to the publication of *Bell* on 21 October 1940. But in December 1941 their separate letters to Scribner, castigating him for failing to record Sinclair Lewis's address to the Limited Edition Club when it bestowed on Hemingway the Triennial Golden Medal for *Bell*, reveal that the first progeny of the Finca Vigia was to have been the Nobel Prize for literature. Hemingway had declined to attend the Limited Edition Club ceremony in New York, but from Sun Valley he had wired Charles Scribner Sr. to have Lewis's tribute taken down by a stenographer, which Scribner failed to do – perhaps because he had an advance copy of the speech and knew that it would not please Hemingway. In it Lewis named Hemingway as one of the six greatest living novelists – putting him in the curious company of Theodore Dreiser, Willa Cather, Somerset Maugham, H.G. Wells, and Jules Romains. Hemingway would get a bit of his own back when he portrayed Lewis so recognizably and cruelly in *Across the River and into the Trees* (1950). Whatever the explanation for Scribner's lapse, Hemingway's letter of 12 December reveals what his and Martha's hopes had been:

I wrote Max exactly how I felt about not getting Sinclair Lewis's speech so won't go into that. It is over and I'm fucked on that. Had driven all the way from Idaho to Arizona looking forward, like a dope, to reading it and then from Arizona here. Now know I never will and that something that I could have had will never have. It was the only thing connected with writing I ever wanted to keep and the fact that by taking it down and re-printing it as a pamphlet you could have probably gotten me the Nobel prize is *not* what I mean. Chances are there aren't going to be any Nobel prizes any more [a conclusion that Hemingway had mysteriously arrived at, perhaps related to the war] and anyhow this was what I wanted instead. (*Letters*, 532)

The following day Martha wrote Scribner that she was "too mad yesterday" to write about her own book, *The Heart of Another,* which Scribner's had published three weeks earlier (PUL).

Other of Martha's letters to Scribner make clear that she saw her parturient role as that of managing publicity and promotion through managing Charles Scribner Sr. Scribner's letters to Hemingway after the marriage ended establish his awareness that Martha had once found him useful. She went about her task with enthusiasm, having many new photos of Hemingway taken for the jacket of *Bell,* pleading with Scribner to let her choose the photo for Book-of-the-Month Club publicity, cajoling him to discard the old scruffy shots, and scolding him for the seedy photo the *New York Times* had used in their review. In a letter of late July 1940, while Hemingway was in New York delivering the finished manuscript of *Bell,* Martha had written Scribner how pleased she was that *Bell* had been selected by the Book-of-the-Month Club, for that would give it the stamp of respectability (PUL).

Six weeks later (two weeks before Hemingway returned the last of the corrected galley proofs), Martha wrote Scribner that she has had thirty-six photos of Hemingway made for publicity, and eleven were "lousy." She intends to get better shots for Scribner's to send to book review departments and asks that no photo be used on the book jacket unless she can get a good one (ca. 1 Sept. 1940; PUL). Two days later, while Martha is in St. Louis, bored and waiting for Hemingway to pick her up on his way to Sun Valley, she rather disingenuously warns Charles Scribner that he must not joke too much about being fond of her or "Ernest will get cross" (PUL).

Even before the marriage, Martha was uneasy about the loss of identity and mobility that being Ernest Hemingway's wife would entail. When Charles Scribner referred to her as "your wife" in a letter to Ernest, she suspected them of conspiring to interest her in writing a book about Cuba that would keep her in residence at the Finca Vigia, and she told Scribner that she was not yet married and found the prospect of matrimony frightening enough without being addressed as a wife before the fact (23 Aug. 1940; PUL). Two months later, with *Bell* published to the best reviews since *Farewell,* and awaiting news that Pauline's divorce was final, she wrote Scribner from Sun Valley that *Collier's* had given the Burma Road assignment she wanted to someone else and conceded that if she were not on the spot, the best jobs would go to others. She then resolves to take anything she is assigned and be grateful she has work (29 Oct. 1940; PUL).

Two months after the marriage (on 21 Nov. 1940) Martha was preparing for the China assignment – which was what *Collier's* did give her; and she was clearly hungry for the attention and intellectual stimulation that Charles Scribner provided. In a letter of January 1941 she tells him she will be in New York and asks if she may come out to his house on a Saturday night and stay over to talk, for she seldom sees those people she loves best, sees a great deal of those to whom she is indifferent, and spends her time largely in running errands for others (PUL).

Hemingway went to China with Martha and seems to have thrived on the living conditions that Martha found trying. It was his first witnessing of WWII. Back at the Finca Vigia the following summer, Martha reports to Scribner that all her mental energy is given to domestic problems such as resurfacing the tennis court and hanging pictures (16 July 1941; PUL). She had been at the Finca since the second week of June and would remain at Hemingway's side – in Cuba, Mexico and Idaho – until mid-July 1942 (with time out only for a two-week visit to her mother in May). It was the longest unbroken period they were ever together, and her letters to Scribner continue to reveal that she is bored and feels ill-used. In October 1941 she is at Sun Valley with Hemingway and his sons where their stay has been extended because of good shooting weather. She complains that she has had no time to work on her own writing, having spent hours sorting and filing Ernest's letters and doing household errands, and anticipates that the packing – which will fall to her – will be like getting a battalion on the march.

In spite of Martha's feeling of being ill-used, and despite the fact that *Collier's* had assignments she could take at any time, their longest interval together was ended not by Martha's departure on an assignment, but by Hemingway's embarking on his scheme to hunt German submarines in the Caribbean.

"THE SEA-BORNE COMIC STRIP WE OPERATED IN THE CARIBBEAN ZONE"[30]

In April or May of 1942, with the support of the American ambassador and the Cuban prime minister – and to the great displeasure of the FBI – Hemingway began gathering intelligence about pro-German activities in Cuba. In a short time, the land-based intelligence activities metamorphosed into his using the *Pilar* to patrol for submarines in the Caribbean, a scheme that seems to have been concocted and approved during the last two weeks of May while Martha was visiting her mother in St. Louis. In mid-July Martha began a *Collier's* assignment on German submarine activity in the Caribbean that would take her to Haiti, Puerto Rico, St. Kitts, St. Thomas, St. Martins, and Dutch Guiana before she returned to Cuba in late September to write her articles for *Collier's*. Some insights into her experience during the trips, and into the way that what she saw ultimately clarified her own marital situation, can be glimpsed in *Travels With Myself and Another,* published thirty-six years later.[31]

In mid-October Martha delivered the *Collier's* assignment in New York, then spent several days at the White House and returned to Cuba longing to have some stability in her life with Hemingway.[32] Although he turned the submarine patrol over to others for a time after Martha's return, there was no privacy at the Finca, for Hemingway had asked the State Department to assign Gustavo Duran, a friend from his Spanish Civil War days, as his second in command; and with his characteristic, and often grandiose hospitality, had invited Duran and his wife to live at the Finca.[33] Martha, trying to write *Liana,* and craving time alone with Ernest, was resentful of both the lack of privacy and the disruptive effect on her writing of the constant traffic of men involved in the intelligence operation.

Hemingway was not writing: he had completed the preface to *Men at War* the previous August and would publish no fiction until *Across the River* appeared in September 1950 – a creative hiatus of ten years! Throughout November and December Hemingway drank heavily and quarreled with Martha. On 30 December she left for another visit with her mother.

It seems safe to speculate that Martha's visit in St. Louis produced in her the resolution to make one more concentrated effort at salvaging the marriage which had become so different from what she remembered of her early years with Hemingway. (At a distance of more than three decades, she would conclude that the best times were over before the marriage occurred.) Martha's mother may well have counseled her to remain in Cuba as long as she could, for Edna Gellhorn and Ernest were mutually admiring, and more than ten years after his marriage ended Hemingway wrote of her, "The only true nice and lovely mother I ever knew was Martha's. But in the cross her reasonableness and goodness did not come through" (EH-Wallace Meyer, 5 July 1956; PUL). Bill Walton, a close friend of Martha after 1945, said nearly fifty years later that "Edna had Ernest on a leash, and he loved it" (author's interview). Certainly, Charles Scribner assumed that Martha had discussed her marital problems with her mother when, early in 1945, he asked Edna about the future of the marriage.[34]

Martha returned from St. Louis to settle in once again at the Finca (the Durans had moved to a hotel), working on *Liana,* and beginning to oversee major repairs to the house and grounds. But Hemingway resumed the submarine patrols, leaving on 21 May for two months at sea. Martha had no illusions about their value: she considered them a childish waste of Hemingway's time by which he avoided writing, and dubbed the operation "the Crook Factory," a name that Hemingway soon adopted.

Gustavo Duran also made no secret of his contempt for the subchasing, and Hemingway must have felt that both his wife and the man he had chosen to be his second in command were traitors. Years later, Martha would describe this period to Carlos Baker as one in which she believed Hemingway was "literally insane" (Baker to Prudencio Perdera, 26 Jan. 1965; HRC). As the facts of those months have become known, the intelligence operation does seem more like Tom Sawyer playing cowboys and submarines than the risk-taking heroics Hemingway wrote of in *Islands*. His two younger sons sometimes shared the sea adventures that Gregory later described in *Papa* as "Don Quixote vs. the Wolf Pack" and Patrick wrote of with gentle humor in *"Islands in the Stream:* A Son Remembers."

The FBI file which tells at least part of the story of the "sea-borne comic strip" is nothing if not entertaining.[35] J. Edgar Hoover did not want to cross American Ambassador Spruille Braden, a Hemingway admirer who was supporting the intelligence operation to the tune of twice the dollar amount that had been reported to the State Department, and providing gas for the *Pilar*. Hoover feared both Martha's influence in the White House and Hemingway's pen – the latter especially after receiving the following memo of 13 August 1943 from R. G. Leddy, legal attache at the embassy who had already been burned by Hemingway's introducing him as "a member of the Gestapo" at a jai alai match they attended together:

> [Hemingway is] currently engaged in writing a book based on his experiences in [intelligence] work. Hemingway states that 11 of the people whom he has known during the last year in Cuba in connection with intelligence work will appear in his book, including Ambassador Braden. We are not yet informed as to what role the representative of the FBI will play, but in view of Hemingway's known sentiments, will probably be portrayed as the dull, heavy-footed, unimaginative professional policeman type.

Although Hemingway and his crew never closed with a submarine, other episodes noted in the FBI file must at least have added levity to their adventures, for the memo of a briefing on Hemingway's exploits given by C. H. Carlson to D. M. Ladd of the FBI on 13 June 1943 indicates: (1) Hemingway has expanded from using four to six full-time operatives and has twenty undercover workers at Mantazanas, Camaguey, and Santiago de Cuba, "all down the Island," – costing not the $500 per month that Braden had reported, but $1,000 per month (plus embassy gasoline). (2) An informant told the FBI that a box left in a Basque bar by a "suspect" contained espionage information. After many memos the FBI examines the box: it contains a cheap edition of *The Life of St. Teresa.* Further developments include:

> After reading in the *New York Times* about a new type of oxygen-powered submarine used by the Germans, Hemingway instituted an investigation of the supply and distribution of oxygen and oxygen tanks in Cuba and immediately advised that "at last with this development we have come to the point after months of work where we are about to crack the submarine refuelling problem."

His investigation was referred to the legal attaché (the already cautious Leddy) by the embassy and a check was made on the supply and distribution of oxygen and oxygen tanks throughout Cuba – with the result that the available supplies were well-accounted for: "Nothing further was heard from Hemingway about the subject," Carlson says. He recommends in closing that in view of Hemingway's prestige, and because Hemingway claims to have political influence (Martha's connection with the Roosevelts), "great discretion be exercised in avoiding an incident with Ernest Hemingway" (Hemingway's FBI file; JFK).

The effect that this period had on Martha's hopes for the marriage can be seen developing in her confiding letters to Charles Scribner, whom she had told in late February 1943 that she would like to be covering the German campaign in North Africa, but saw no way of reconciling that with being a wife and a writer and so would stay at the Finca at least until her book (*Liana*) was finished. Her enumeration of excluded choices is revealing, for Martha recognizes once again, as she had in November 1941 while preparing for the family's return from Idaho, that to be Ernest Hemingway's wife is to be absorbed into the domestic arrangements that consume her writing time. But here she also realizes that to be reporting from a war zone would deprive her of both her marriage and her writing.

However, as the summer progressed, with Hemingway either absent at sea or surrounded by a rowdy, drunken entourage of aspiring spies at the Finca, and with her novel finished two months earlier, Martha was approaching the moment of choice. To Scribner, she wrote on 27 September 1943 that her supervision of renovations at the Finca made her feel more like an adding machine than a human being and she was off for a visit to her mother – to be the cared for rather than the caretaker; and she closes the letter by telling him she is depressed.

Disgusted with life at the Finca, Martha made arrangements to become *Collier's* European war correspondent and urged Hemingway to accompany her, reminding him how well they had worked together in Spain. But he resisted. Charles Scribner sent her orchids at the Gladstone Hotel in New York, and on 25 October 1943, Martha sailed alone, leaving the American Embassy in London as a forwarding address. Her letters to Hemingway during the next several months reveal her sense of failure and loss as she comes to accept that the marriage is over. But even as she ran, "a fugitive from a finca," Martha wrote Hemingway: "I am yours first of all and you are my main concern. . . . You tell me what you want and that is what I will do" (Oct. 1943, quoted in Bernice Kert, *The Hemingway Women*, 383).

When Martha fled Cuba to return to her *Collier's* position, she knew at some level the danger to herself in not recognizing her untenable position in the marriage, for she had just spent nearly two years writing *Liana*. More than a year earlier Martha had told Hemingway that *Liana* was about people she really didn't understand. But in 1943 Martha's typewriter helped her to see the implications of her own actions in much the same way that Hemingway's would aid him in 1961 as he labored to complete *Feast*. In the novel she had just finished, Liana, a young mulatto woman living on the Caribbean island of St. Boniface during the war, is married to Marc Royer, a wealthy, powerful, sensual man twenty years her senior. First sought by Royer for her physical beauty, Liana learns that she is of little significance either to him or to Pierre Vauclain, a young Frenchman whom he hired to tutor her, and who has become her lover. The two male characters are allegorically drawn, Vauclain representing the uneasily feminine side of the male, Royer the brutally masculine side. Both men see their destinies in romantically self-aggrandizing plans for civilian leadership in the war effort, which creates between them a male bond that obviates Royer's cold-blooded pride at possessing Liana, as well as Pierre's enchantment at Liana's eagerness to learn from him. Socially displaced by her marriage, and left out of account by both men, Liana commits suicide. Although it is less carefully crafted than Jean Rhys's *The Wide Sargasso Sea*, *Liana* is an eerie forerunner of the Rhys classic and a novel that Rhys looked to for a model as she strove to write a book she had planned for forty years (*The Letters of Jean Rhys*, 45, 46).

NEW WIFE, OLD ANXIETIES – BLAMING MARY FOR MARTHA

Hemingway's agenda for his third marriage, even though he probably had not reduced it to a list, had been rather more complex than Martha's. He wanted the Nobel Prize, of course, and eventually would receive it; he wanted a writing partnership in which Martha would be his protégée; and he wanted a daughter. But to the latter there was an obstacle that became the lasting focus of Hemingway's bitterness toward Martha and the source of his identifying his texts as his offspring.

When Martha married Hemingway, she believed that she could not bear a child because of complications from an abortion several years earlier. He married Mary Welsh in March 1946. Not until 1950, when he was set in a pattern of abuse toward Mary – which was motivated in part by her inability to conceive after an ectopic pregnancy in 1946 – did Hemingway learn that at least four months before their marriage, Martha had confided to Charles Scribner Sr. that she could not have a child.[36] By the time that Scribner accidentally brought this to Hemingway's attention, he had destablized his marriage to Mary, and transmuted twenty-year-old Adriana Ivancich into the complex daughter, sister, double, and muse who would energize him in writing the two postwar novels published during his life (*Across the River* and *The Old Man and the Sea*). When Scribner mentioned to Hemingway what he thought Hemingway had long known – that he had married Martha knowing that she was unable to conceive – he was probably motivated by a desire to protect Mary and thus to preserve the Hemingway marriage, for Mary had asked Scribner to help find her a job in New York in order that she might leave Hemingway.[37] In his accidental disclosure, Scribner had probably been counseling Hemingway (both as a friend and a valuable property) to recognize and appreciate that Mary was a better caretaker than Martha had been. But in doing so he reminded Hemingway of what he thought Hemingway was willingly forgetting – that he had married Martha knowing she could not produce the daughter he wanted.

The revelation came at a time when Hemingway was filled with anxiety: he was making changes in the galleys of *Across the River* (at Scribner's request) because Martha had threatened to leave the firm if it were published with the scurrilous passages about her intact. He was tormented by his love for Adriana Ivancich, which he had inscribed in the novel; and Scribner's revelation about Martha's barrenness had arrived almost concurrently with the birth of Hemingway's first grandchild on 5 May 1950 – a girl! He was furious with his friend and publisher. The man whom he had once considered his rival in influence over Martha was now compelling him to make these deletions; and he railed that Scribner should have told him about Martha *before* he married her, or never have told him at all. Scribner responded:

> As I remember, at the time she told me that you would not believe that it was possible for her not to have a baby when married to you, no matter how much she explained it. (16 May 1950; PUL)

Scribner's recollection of the confidence Martha had made is probably true, for Hemingway was singularly unpaternal when his three sons were young;[38] and although he had over the years remarked that he would like to have a daughter, he linked his affair with Martha Gellhorn to wanting children only after Pauline had taken their children and left Key West.[39]

However, Hemingway's decision to wed Mary Welsh in 1945, although it had been reached very quickly and in a frame of mind close to panic, was quite calculated. The determination to marry her consciously incorporated his desire to have a wife who would remain with him, would take over the domestic and business arrangements of his life, would not be a competitor (as he now fancied Martha had been), and would produce another family for him.

There are a number of letters between Mary and Ernest during 1944 and 1945 that discuss their expectations. Most are at the Kennedy Library; and, ironically, Mary summarizes what she intended to contribute to and expected to get from the marriage in a letter of 6 May 1950 telling Hemingway why she is planning to leave him:

> Maybe it is ambiguous for me to explain my reasons for leaving. But I write them down because I think this time you should have the opportunity of knowing precisely how I feel about this marriage.

It began in 1944 in bed in the Ritz Hotel in Paris and my own reasons for it were two: I thought you were a straight and honorable and brave man and magnetically endearing to me. And because, although I was suspicious of your over-drinking, you said so often that your chief desire was to be GOOD and adult and to live your one and only life intelligently, I believed you and in you.

About your work, you scoffed at others who couldn't go the distance on a good book. . . And you said you loved to write and were never happier than when doing so. It was therefore not unnatural for me to assume that, working, you could if you want to, be a companionable and considerate husband – as well [as] gay and charming and sturdy in spirit, which you are when you are not drunk.

What I expected to contribute to the marriage were: absolute loyalty to you and devotion to your projects; cheerful and intelligent (if possible) and enterprizing service to you and your family and house and possessions in any capacities I knew or could learn; conscientious care of whatever things or jobs you intrusted to me, and in daily living, a certain good balance, alertness and tenderness towards you.

With these mutual contributions, it looked in 1944 as though we could actually achieve the fine life of mutual trust and kindness . . . we both wanted. But now in May 1950, my view of this marriage is that we have both been failures.

As far as I can analyse it, my principal failure is that somehow I have lost your interest in me, your devotion, and also your respect.

Your principal failure is that, primarily because of your accumulating ego and your increasing lapses into over-drinking, you have not been the good man you said you intended to be. Instead you have been careless and increasingly unthinking of my feelings, at times to the extent of brutality. . . .

If there were any sign of remorse after such bouts . . . I could believe that we might . . . make things better. But for a long time now your only reaction to the possibility that you have been mistaken is a petulant irritability, protecting your steel-bound ego, that your rectitude or infallibility should be questioned . . . . (JFK)

There are sixteen lesser known letters written by Hemingway to Mary between 8 November and 27 December 1944 in Norberto Fuentes, *Hemingway in Cuba*. They provide first-person testimony to the basis of Mary's assumptions about the union she was entering with Hemingway. But in the Fuentes book there is also a fragment of a letter to an unknown recipient which contains internal references to a mink coat that establish the subject as his quarrels with Mary, and suggest how much he was retaliating for her inability to bear him a daughter. Mary's ectopic pregnancy in 1946, and what she describes as the occlusion of her remaining fallopian tube, diagnosed in 1949, were almost certainly the result of a pelvic inflammatory condition (of which venereal disease could be one cause). The gynecological problems that hint at it are mentioned in Hemingway's letters to her in 1945 and 1946 (just prior to, and just after the marriage) when she is in Chicago. His remarks here date from after 1950, when he purchased a mink coat for Mary:

> I think most sterile women were clapped early and just didn't notice it. Most of them don't even know when they have the clap or the old rale and they give it to you with true love and affection. They always have to be jealous of something and if you give them no cause for jealousy except your work they will be jealous of that. (Fuentes, *Hemingway in Cuba,* 416)

I have found no evidence that Mary ever knew she was being punished for what Hemingway remembered, perhaps inaccurately, as a fraud that Martha had perpetrated against him. But the fact remains that once again – or more accurately, twice again, since he linked Mary's and Martha's inability to bear children – Hemingway saw his writing, which was becoming ever more difficult to produce, as his only "get," a term that signifies both the nonexistent child and the treasured texts in *Eden.* In *Islands* he would envision a life where women are safely confined by memory and dreams, and troubled male artists raise their children in the storybook adventure life of Frederick Marryat novels. But it is not a world where either the author or his characters can thrive, for when the children are gone – victims of their mother's carelessness or of war – the artist turns from creation to violence, as the author, his get unborn in a Havana bank vault, turned to self-violence in his life.

CHAPTER 3

Islands in the Stream: A World of Men Without Women

The novel that we know as *Islands in the Stream* (1970) had its genesis in a sprawling ur-text which Hemingway began in the fall of 1945 to memorialize the experience he had shared with Buck Lanham during his ten months of covering the European war.[1] But from its inception the narrative of the ur-text was also about the creative problems of a protean artist who is sometimes a writer named Roger Davis or David Bourne, and sometimes a painter named Thomas Hudson or Nick Sheldon. From this ur-text came not only the posthumous *Islands* and *The Garden of Eden* (1986), but also the two novels published during Hemingway's life, *Across the River and into the Trees* (1950) and *The Old Man and the Sea* (1952).

"ALL MY WORK IS A PART OF ALL MY WORK . . ."[2]

Hemingway's letters from 1946 to 1952 make confusing mentions of (1) "the Land, Sea, and Air Book," (2) "the Sea Book," and (3) "the Big Book." Further, he was often less than candid about what he was writing, and where it fit into the three books. Given the concern with creativity that is common to the posthumous novels, perhaps he did not himself know. However, since the opening in September 1992 of Hemingway's correspondence with his editors and with the two Charles Scribners, it is possible to clarify the three-book scheme.

(1) "The Land, Sea, and Air Book" was a dream that never became a reality. "The Land" section, which dealt with the war in Europe, was reduced and incorporated into *Across the River*.[3] "The Sea" section was "The Sea Book" that became *Islands*. "The Air

51

Book" never got beyond a fragment about flying with the RAF which is at Princeton.

(2) "The Big Book" turns out almost always to refer to the ever expanding work that became *Eden*.[4]

(3) "The Sea Book" initially had four parts: (i) the material that became *Old Man* which Hemingway referred to as "The Sea in Being"; (ii) "Bimini" and "Miami," which he referred to as "The Sea When Young"; (iii) "Cuba," which he referred to as "The Sea When Absent"; and (iv) "At Sea," which he called "The Sea Chase."

"Bimini," "Miami," and *Old Man* were set in 1936; "Cuba," and "At Sea" in 1943. When *Old Man* was removed, the three remaining sections became *Islands,* but the "Miami" portion of "The Sea When Young," which follows Roger Davis across the country toward Montana, was dropped. However, much of "Miami," which was thematically absorbed into *Eden,* was published as a story, "The Strange Country," in *The Complete Short Stories* (1987). There the concern of the creative artist with families and with intimate relationships that threaten to impinge upon his writing remains visible.

Lee Samuels had microfilmed 1,600 pages of what was still called "The Sea Book" by early in July 1951, with Hemingway retaining the original for revisions. The microfilm, which was deposited in the Banco Nacional of Havana, where it remained in mid-February 1961, has never been located.[5] Although Hemingway continued to mention "The Sea Book" to Scribner's as a three-part work that could be published in separate volumes, I can find no evidence that he worked on it after December 1951.

WARTIME FRIENDSHIPS AND THE POSTWAR WRITING

Hemingway had gone reluctantly and late to report on WW II, filled with anger, quite literally in a mood to kill, and half-hoping to die a heroic death witnessed by the kind of men he most admired.[6] He was still rankled by the failure of *For Whom the Bell Tolls* to receive a major literary award or make him a serious contender for the Nobel Prize, and was humiliated by the ineffectiveness of his submarine hunting operation. Further, he knew that Martha's growing contempt for his conduct in the Crook Factory operation he later described "a sea-borne comic strip" was no small factor in the deterioration of their marriage.

There is no doubt that Hemingway's status as a writer had drawn Martha Gellhorn to him in 1936; but in the fall of 1943 he was not writing.[7] He drank heavily, quarreled with Martha when she was at the Finca, and was himself often at sea for weeks. But, whatever Hemingway later claimed in private life and inscribed in his fiction, Martha did not see him as a mentor to advance her own writing career; nor was she competing with him.[8] In fact, the record shows that during 1942–43 Hemingway told Max Perkins what a pleasure it was to return from sea and read Martha's work on the novel that became *Liana,* and that he joked with his sons about retiring and letting Martha be the writer in the family.[9] Martha had chosen early to support herself by journalism; but she also took her other writing seriously and considered the "bilgers" she wrote in later years a kind of whoring that paid for such pleasures as time to be idle in the sun at a house she loved in Cuernavaca (Gellhorn-Charles Scribner, 12 Aug. 1949; PUL). Between assignments she needed serenity and privacy to work on her own writing; instead, from the middle of 1942 until she left Cuba for good in April 1944, Martha struggled to avoid being consumed by the needs of the Finca, where now more than ever, there was open house for Hemingway's mates.[10]

Hemingway had told Max Perkins shortly after Pearl Harbor that if he went to *this* war, it would only be in order to get material for a novel; and in August 1943, he asked Archibald MacLeish (in Washington) if he could have him sent to the war, not to write propaganda, but so that he could have something good written after the war (MacLeish-Carlos Baker, 10 Aug. 1943; PUL). When Martha's prodding finally moved him to sign on with *Collier's* in late April 1944, he was able to take her job because a magazine was permitted only one correspondent in a war zone. Without press credentials, she could not get a transportation assignment to Europe, and while he flew to London (and declined to help her get a seat), she crossed the North Sea with a convoy – the only passenger on a ship loaded with explosives.[11]

Although Hemingway's departure for the European front had been an act of angry despair, his return was filled with hope for a new life that (whether he recognized it or not) would be essentially like the one Pauline had arranged for him in Key West – and from which he had begun fleeing to the islands in the gulf stream and to Havana even before the house on Whitehead Street was settled. Hemingway had made it clear to Mary Welsh that he wanted a stable domestic establishment with her in residence, a family life that would include another child (which he always imagined as a daughter), and a household centered on his writing – with Mary as a ready typist.[12]

He also wanted to write a great war novel that would be a tribute to Colonel Buck Lanham. Hemingway was fond of saying that war was life reduced to its most elemental, and in the ten months that he was a *Collier's* correspondent (May 1944–March 1945) circumstances allowed him to once again reduce his life to elemental needs. The wisdom of his rapid attachment to Mary Welsh soon became problematic for both of them; but the friendship that he formed with Buck Lanham in Normandy and the Hurtgen Forest was to last for the rest of his life. As Hemingway had yearned to wear a military uniform, Lanham was a frustrated poet: and their experience gave each a vicarious life he could not otherwise have had. Bill Walton, who was often with Lanham and Hemingway, remembered that "for Buck, having Ernest there was as if Shakespeare had come down from heaven to tell him how to fight the war" (author's interview). The day before he left Europe on 3 March 1945, Hemingway told Lanham that he hoped to write about their experiences properly, "if only as a means of expressing my bumbling, pathetic devotion."

On 2 April 1945 Hemingway wrote Lanham that he was homesick for him and the 22nd Regiment, concluding with, "I don't give a damn about writing and would rather be back with you." But on 14 April he told Max Perkins that he was getting in shape to write about what he had learned at war: "You see it is all done with people, not just weapons, nor logistics, but always people – and I'm finally getting so I know about people a little." Here is Hemingway's earliest revelation that he intends to treat character differently than in earlier fiction. Although he probably could not have articulated it at the time, his iceberg theory had begun to dissolve with the interiority of Robert Jordan in *Bell*. Now, in his first postwar novel, Hemingway began to work by what he would eventually call *remate*, a technique that certainly facilitated – and may have suggested – the significant twinning, cloning and splitting of painters and writers in *Islands* and *Eden*.[13]

Figure 5. In a few months of 1944, Hemingway and Lanham formed a friendship that endured for the rest of their lives. Shown here at Lanham's Command
Post Bleialf (on German soil), 18 September 1944 (John F. Kennedy Library).

Buck Lanham and his wife Pete visited Hemingway at the Finca
in late September 1945. Seven weeks after their departure he announced to Perkins that he had finished 250 pages of a new book.
It was rare for Hemingway to share with anyone the details of what
he was writing, and Perkins received no other information; but
during the next seven months Hemingway confided many other
details to Lanham. On 7 December he wrote that he had done 275
pages and was not yet within six years of the war; and on 20 January
1946 that he was "still at 1936 . . . but take it fairly well thru 1935 –
that only leaves 9 years to D-Day but maybe we can just say 'nine
years passed our hero was pissed off as ever.' " On 21 February he
has 460 pages done, is deeply depressed, thinks the book will be
"awfully long," and probably the last he will write. It is significant
that he is also quarrelling with Mary, for a complication in his
writing and difficulty with the woman on whom he was currently

Figure 6. Buck Lanham and his wife Pete visited Hemingway at the Finca Vigía in late September 1945 (John F. Kennedy Library).

dependent was a combination guaranteed to bring on a depression that made Hemingway contemplate death (they were married on 14 March).

By 30 June 1946 the book had reached 1,000 pages, and he tells Lanham that he is in the fornication part (which he enjoys writing), discloses that the book now begins in 1936 and will expose their "Lost Leader," and that "relations between men and womenies probably big part of this book."[14] But he also warns Lanham subtly that he will not be as forthcoming about his writing as he has been heretofore: "If anyone knew what book was about would be attacked, pooped on, destroyed and copied long before out. All I can say is a long book . . . and want to get non-fighting and fighting into it eventually."[15]

That part of the ur-text which Hemingway refers to as beginning in 1936 became "Bimini" and most of *Old Man*.[16] The part that was to expose General Barton's role in the debacle of the Hurtgen Forest eventually formed a portion of *Across the River*. And the part where relations between men and women were foregrounded was the inception of *Eden*, which I believe Hemingway began to contemplate as a separate work in 1947 and to write as a separate work in 1948.[17] *Eden* grew concurrently with *Islands*, and continued growing for eight years after *Islands* had been put in a Havana bank vault; but mentions of work on *Eden* are rare and cryptic – not surprising considering its subject.

FROM "THE SEA BOOK" TO *ISLANDS IN THE STREAM*

When Hemingway finished what is now the final section of the book he thought of as "The Islands and the Stream" on 18 May 1951, he first decided that a recently completed shorter version of *Old Man* would be a part of it.[18] However, by 8 July he had decided to publish *Old Man* separately and had rejected *Cosmopolitan*'s offer of $10,000 for the 20,000-word novella. Fourteen months later *Life* paid him $40,000 for the 26,531-word version.[19] He had also approached *Collier's* and the *Saturday Evening Post* about publishing "The Sea Book" in *three* serial segments.

Once Hemingway had made the decision to offer *Old Man* for publication separate from "The Sea Book" – where it has never seemed to belong – he began rewriting "Bimini" and "Miami," which like the published version of *Old Man,* were set in 1936. The aesthetic necessity in these revisions, never quite achieved, was to provide motivation for Thomas Hudson's actions in "Cuba" and "At Sea," the two sections set in February 1943 during the last weeks of Hudson's life.

Hudson is a painter who has abandoned his art for the pursuit of German submarines; and as the "Cuba" section opens, he has recently learned of the death of his oldest son in combat. He is estranged from and filled with bitterness toward his third wife, whom he married sometime after the death of his two younger sons in 1936. Hudson is a man for whom the pleasure of work, which for many of Hemingway's earlier protagonists was creative work, has been replaced by duty. Among the few lines from this very uneven novel that will be remembered for their terse, understated beauty (in the way that we remember lines like "After a while I went out and left the hospital and walked back to the hotel in the rain") is Hudson's injunction to himself as he leaves his finca for his last assignment: "Your boy you lose. Love you lose. Honor has been gone for a long time. Duty you do " (*Islands in the Stream* [hereafter IS in citations], 326). A few days later, as Hudson acknowledges that the duty he chose over his painting is murder, he becomes a man waiting for an opportunity to give his life away (IS, 356).

"MIAMI" DISAPPEARS AND "BIMINI" DEVELOPS

Although it is not absolutely clear whether Hemingway intended finally to use "Miami" in "The Sea Book," the preponderance of evidence is that he did not. First, by the time he began discussing serial publication of "The Sea Book" with Wallace Meyer in early 1952, he was referring to *three* works. Since the decision to separate *Old Man* had been made nearly a year earlier, and because "Miami" does not have the presence of Hudson's sons that is necessary to qualify it as one of the three, he would have meant "Bimini," "Cuba," and "At Sea." Second, the typescript of "Miami," which follows Roger north and west toward Hudson's Montana ranch, bears no holograph corrections in Hemingway's hand as that of "Bimini" does (File 102; JFK). Third, the most important elements of "Miami" had already been transmuted into the major themes of *Eden,* where they develop as (1) the conflict between a writer's fear of women in the

Figure 7. Hemingway aboard the *Pilar* off Bimini, 1935 or 1936 (John F. Kennedy Library).

vicinity of his writing and a young woman's desire to create literature rather than children, (2) dangerous families and their legacy, and (3) the loss of the writer's early work in the suitcase stolen in 1922.[20]

A fourth explanation for the disappearance of "Miami" just after Hemingway's decision to publish *Old Man* separately – an explanation consistent with the creative anxiety that provides the thematic unity of all the works which emerged from the ur-text except *Across the River* – is that Hemingway may have originally intended to bring Roger back from Montana and into the novel with the old fisherman's story as evidence of his recovery. The old fisherman whose lines are "as thick around as big pencils" (*The Old Man and the Sea* [hereafter OM in citations], 28), but who has not had a catch for so long that he is becoming an outcast is, I believe, another avatar of the writer. To have put his story in the frame of Roger Davis's triumph would have unified the otherwise tenuously related tale of the old fisherman who went out too far – and who, like Roger, has a beloved son-figure, but no wife or child of his own – with the creative struggle that underlies the entire book. It would also explain why

Figure 8. Hemingway and Bumby aboard the *Pilar* (John F. Kennedy Library).

Hemingway placed Roger rather than Hudson at David's side during the shark scare of which David says he just went out too far, and throughout his struggle with the fish where the writing subtext is visible. Finally, such a framing device adumbrates the metafictional way that Hemingway used the elephant story in *Eden,* for that story was written more than four years before it was incorporated into the novel.

Hemingway told Charles Scribner on 8 July 1951 that he would begin rewriting 977 pages he had not seen since 1947 (PUL). This is "Bimini" and "Miami," but the holograph of "Miami" ends at page 907 with Roger and Helena driving toward Montana, and I believe that the missing 70 pages were the old fisherman's story that became *Old Man.* There is no holograph of *Old Man* at the Kennedy Library, and the virtually clean typescript, with word counts that go as high as 1,805 per day, makes it clear that Hemingway was working with something he had done thoroughly before (Files 190–1 and 190–2).[21]

At one point Hemingway had intended that "Miami" follow "Bimini" and occupy the position where he placed "Cuba" in 1950, for the Kennedy Library contains a manuscript where the opening

Figure 9. Hemingway with Patrick, Bumby, and Gregory on the dock in Bimini, 1936. Here Hemingway saw a marlin that had been stripped of its flesh by sharks, an image central to *The Old Man and the Sea* (John F. Kennedy Library).

chapter of "Miami" is designated "Book Two" in Hemingway's hand (File 98–14, p. 680). Further, Hemingway's references in letters to the section "The Sea When Absent" predate the writing of "Cuba," and the locution is far more indicative of Roger's cross-country journey in "Miami" than of Thomas Hudson's single day ashore in "Cuba."

While "Miami" disappeared, "Bimini" underwent major revisions, and the observation made by several critics – that in the novel Roger Davis and Thomas Hudson are one character – is a recognition that Hemingway was dealing with the unitary origin of creativity and was using the *remate* technique to explore problems common to a writer and a painter. In fact, there are several points in the manuscripts at which Hemingway seems to have forgotten the distinction between the two artists and their differing mediums: in one instance the narrator refers to himself in the same paragraph as working on a story and as painting every morning. In a draft of David's struggle with the giant fish, Hudson is a writer, not a painter; and Davis has painted in the past, finding it easier than writing.[22] Further, in the novel Hudson tells Davis:

> Maybe in painting the tradition and the line are clearer and there are more people helping you. Even when you break from the straight line of a great painting it is always there to help you. (IS, 78)

Although the three most significant changes during the revision of "Bimini" were all necessary to the characterization of Hudson that Hemingway had recently completed in "Cuba" and "At Sea," they are also complex documentation of Hemingway's growing awareness that this novel was really about the tension between deeply reciprocal human relationships and creativity, which had long beset him: (1) Names were changed – George Davis became Thomas Hudson; Roger Hancock became Roger Davis; and the names of the oldest and youngest boys (Andy and Tom) were transposed. (2) The children, who had belonged to Davis, became Hudson's; and he acquired two ex-wives and a current wife from whom he is estranged. (3) The ending was changed completely to add the deaths of David and Andy, and a chapter (much reduced in the novel) was added that reveals Hudson's refusal to mourn or to feel as he travels to France for their funeral.[23] A change in the narrational scheme is less significant, for in moving from a first-person narration by George Davis/Thomas Hudson to a third-person omniscient narration focalized through Hudson, Hemingway did not reduce Hudson's centrality.

It was common for Hemingway to change the names of characters between drafts of a story. He had called David Bourne first "John," and then "Phil" in some of the early pages of *Eden* (the latter a given name that he liked for writers).[24] Therefore, his changing of Roger Hancock to Roger Davis, and George Davis to Thomas Hudson, is not in itself noteworthy. In discarding "Hancock" and "George," he was also erasing family names, the maiden name of his maternal grandmother (Caroline Hancock) and the given name of a paternal uncle whom he believed culpable in his father's suicide (George Hemingway). However, it is significant that as each character loses a tie to the author's family, Roger acquires the surname that had belonged to George, for this transaction is a marriage-like merging of the two personalities that determines the metaphors of domesticity pervading "Bimini." The disappearance from Thomas Hudson's life (in "Cuba" and "At Sea") of this striving for a familial/domestic order is a vision of what Hemingway had learned at great cost about the incompatibility of creativity and consuming *machismo* in his third marriage, but seemed unable to apply in his fourth – even at the very time he was inscribing it in "Cuba." [25]

Hudson and Davis are artists with long histories of dissipating their creativity in drinking, brawling, and troubled relationships with women. On Bimini they have created a Mt. Athos in the Caribbean where even the servants are male. There Hudson claims they have reached a *modus vivendi* that eliminates the complications of women but retains the structure and companionship of a stable domestic life – if the painter can only wean the writer away from personalizing his sexual attractions. [26]

The life that Davis, Hudson, and the three sons lead during the boys' school holidays is very nearly conjugal, and in the early manuscript George Davis thinks of the children's impending departure:

> I had been lonely for a long part of my life but later I had learned how not to be lonely. But in avoiding loneliness my life had taken on certain forms and habits that were protections but were almost *old-maidish even though they were, on the surface, the opposite* [my emphasis] and haveing the children at the house had broken them up and made me much happier . . . I was lonesome for the boys before they had ever gone away. I knew how Roger felt about them and how he missed them and I wished we could both have them all the time. But that isn't the way things go. (File 98.5, pp. 291–92; JFK)

In these observations, Roger is treated as another parent – one with whom George must share custody; and Hemingway has made George keenly aware that a kind of behavioral cross-dressing is necessary – old maidish habits that support an ultra-masculine, exclusively male, lifestyle – if existence is not to degenerate into the barrenness of the cold house with an empty larder in "Cuba" or the brutishness of life in "At Sea."

The contrast between "Bimini" and "Cuba" reflects the danger inherent in Hemingway's own need for a world of men without women, a world that he could actuate only in his imagination.

But the revisions Hemingway made in "Bimini" – transferring parentage of the sons to Hudson, and then having David and Andy die – are inadequate to explaining Hudson's character in "Cuba" and "At Sea." The author seems to offer the deaths of David and Andy as the blow that loosed Hudson from his life of monastically disciplined creativity and inclined him toward another failed marriage and his present Hobbesian existence; but the lost younger sons have no part in Hudson's memories in "Cuba" except as refracted through a time when Boise, the cat, had been happy (IS, 204, 210). And in "At Sea," they appear only once – nameless, in Hudson's dream – and are not again remembered (IS, 343). Nor is it the death of his remaining son, Tom, that causes Hudson to give up painting, for his work as an artist ceased some time earlier.[27] The near obliteration of David and Andy from Hudson's memory after "Bimini," the silence of the text on his relationship with young Tom during the seven years that have passed, and the disappearance of Roger from the narrative cause a textual gap that leaves Hudson's creative decline unexplained, and his alternating self-hatred and grandiosity unconvincing.[28]

In transposing Tom's and Andrew's names during revisions, Hemingway ordered the plot so that the death in action of the son who bears his father's name destroys the last link between the past (as artist) and the present (as paramilitary man). Hudson has chosen a life at the level signified by the recurrent animal images in "Cuba" and "At Sea," but he is doomed to continue seeing the islands and the stream where he plays the most dangerous game through the eyes of the painter he once was.

Consistent with the strong autobiographical matrix of the posthumous novels, there are also elements of the "Bimini" revisions that were solely the inscription of Hemingway's obsessions. In the first writing of "Bimini," the youngest boy, still named Tom, has "a head that is hundreds of years old" and a dark side. He is a devil, but an attractive devil (File 98.4, pp. 186–88; JFK). In the revisions this is Andrew, and a case against him begins early by narrational assertions that

the smallest boy was . . . a copy of Thomas Hudson . . . and was born being very old. He was a devil too, . . . and he had a dark side to him that nobody except Thomas Hudson could ever understand. . . . He was a boy born to be quite wicked who was being very good and he carried his wickedness around with him . . . he was a bad boy and. . . . was just being good while his badness grew inside him. [Thomas Hudson] knew Andrew was Andrew and a little boy and that it was unfair to judge him. . . . [b]ut there was something about him that you could not trust. (IS, 53, 143–44)

When Andrew, David, and their mother are killed, Hudson and Eddy, the cook, speculate incongruously that this "little boy" may have been driving because "He's conceited enough" (IS, 195). Pauline Hemingway had died suddenly while the revision of "Bimini" was under way, and Hemingway had blamed their youngest son, Gregory, for her death.[29]

Additional evidence of the complex emotions stirred in Hemingway by Pauline's death were removed from "Bimini" in the editing process: while crossing to the boys' funeral on the *Ile de France*, Hudson meets his former brother-in-law, who tells him that despite Barbara's death, he will not recover any of "the alimony fund." In 1929, shortly after his father's suicide, Ernest and Pauline had set up a trust fund for his mother with $50,000 borrowed from Pauline's uncle and from Scribner's. When Grace Hemingway died in June 1951, Hemingway learned that he would not recover the principal remaining in the trust. With the former brother-in-law's taunt, Hemingway inscribed his bitterness at this discovery.

In altered or deleted portions of "Bimini," Hemingway paid off other grudges: against Wallace Stevens (with whom he had exchanged blows in Key West in 1936) and against Archibald MacLeish (who had once criticized him as lacking social consciousness). Mr. Edwards, the pedophile who approached young Tom was named Mr. Stevens, and the group with which Audrey arrives in Bimini includes a dull man who works on *Fortune* (as MacLeish did). (Baker-Hemingway manuscripts 0365, Box 25; PUL)

THE OBSCURING OF CONCERN WITH CREATIVITY IN *ISLANDS*

The visible concern of the creative artist with his work that gradually emerges from the tension between the honeymoon narrative and the African stories in *Eden* is absent in *Islands*. The writer is never seen in the act of writing, as he is in *Eden* and *A Moveable Feast;* nor is he consciously seeking a way of life that could give him another

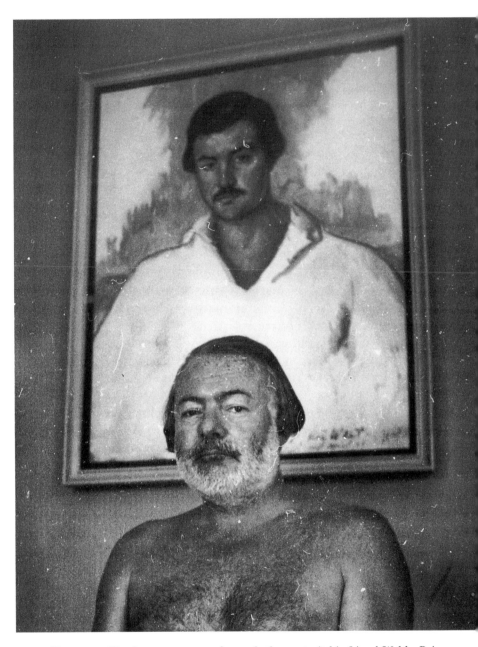

Figure 10. Hemingway ca. 1941 beneath the portrait his friend Waldo Peirce had painted of him in Paris during the 1920s (John F. Kennedy Library).

identity as he is in the African book. For Roger Davis, talking about the women, drinking, and brawling that were destructive to his creativity has become a substitute for it. His forte is parenting Thomas Hudson's sons, who are glad to have an extra parent – one who can see them as more important than his art during their school holiday.

Although Hudson clings to his routine of daily painting as if it were a salvational ritual, he is no better realized as a painter than Frederic Henry was as an architect, his discussion of painting no more insightful than that of an informed spectator. Even with Roger, who has also painted, Hudson never talks of his craft; instead, the act of painting locates him safely in a lofty and voyeuristic position that is a buffer between himself and the sons who will be with him for only six weeks. The motions of creation which structure Hudson's life suggest that he is superior to Roger – who is unable to write, or stay out of a fight, or resist an aggressively worshipful younger woman. But they also reveal him as less able to function as a parent than Roger.

Hudson remains aloof from David's battle with the fish, which is one of two passages in the novel where the linguistic nuances suggest writing as a sub-text. There Roger advises David, "Try and rest inside the action except when you are working on him" (IS, 130). This is a directive with strong verbal echoes in David Bourne's aesthetic perception as he continues his second African story "completely detached from everything except the story . . . he was living in it as he built it" (*The Garden of Eden* [hereafter GE in citations], 128). In the second such passage (also during David's struggle with the fish), Hudson descends from his position on the flying bridge to take the wheel in the cockpit, and his descent is like the writer moving from detached to involved narration: "It was strange to be on the same level as the action after having looked down on it for so many hours. . . . It was like moving down from a box seat onto the stage" (IS, 136).

The twinning of Davis and Hudson, and the assignment of true parental concern to Roger Davis, suggest that Hemingway recognized how little he was able to be genuinely attentive to personal relationships and how much his writing served as his only substitute for intimacy and as the tenuous, single, structuring principle of his life. For Thomas Hudson, when creation ceases, the chaos of "Cuba" ensues: when Ernest Hemingway could no longer write, he could not live.[30]

There are two spots of good comedy in "Bimini": the plan Hudson and Bobby make for the huge painting to hang behind the bar in the Ponce de Leon; and the "pretend rummy" scene, the drunken charade the boys perform there later – but both have dark undertones. The huge painting with devouring waterspouts seems to be a joke as Hudson and Bobby plan it; and although the discussion is of Bosch, Brueghel, and "that magneto man" (Mantegna), the escalating size and scope of Bobby's painting echo the manic plans of Gulley Jimson, the self-destructive painter in *The Horse's Mouth*. The joke ends when Hudson promptly follows through, for in a few weeks, the painting hangs behind the bar at the Ponce de Leon, and patrons want to buy it.[31] In the pretend-rummy scene Hudson does not drink the placebo Roger is drinking, but Bacardi, which is "warm and inspiring" (IS, 165).

So the creative activity that absorbs David Bourne and brings him into conflict with his bride in *Eden* is largely talk about creating in "Bimini." This textual void emanates from both the mediocrity of Hudson's painting and from circumstances of the special bond between Roger Davis and David Hudson and their genealogical connection with David Bourne, for the writer's conflicts which Hemingway had begun to develop in "Miami" were siphoned into *Eden*, where Roger is "rebourne" as a writer named David. This causes writing to recede from the text in *Islands* rather than emerge as it does in *Eden*, until, with the departure of Roger Davis, it disappears. Left behind are only a few rueful allusions, in "Cuba," to Hemingway's difficulty with "The Land, Sea, and Air Book." Finally the very drive to create, which was so often dissipated in talk in "Bimini," is annihilated when Thomas Hudson ceases to paint at some undesignated time between the closure of "Bimini" in 1936 and the opening of "Cuba" early in 1943.

"CUBA," A STORY WITH MARTHA OFFSTAGE

Hemingway's desire for a daughter had been a significant part of his agenda after he lost his sons in the divorce that allowed him to marry Martha Gellhorn,[32] and it remained strong in his fourth marriage, even after Mary's nearly fatal ectopic pregnancy in 1946.

Figure 11. Hemingway's desire for a daughter had been the cause of conflict in all of his marriages. On 5 May 1950, when the fourth marriage was strained by his infatuation with Adriana Ivancich, his first grandchild, Muffet (Joan), was born to Bumby and his wife. Shown here on the steps of the Finca Vigia with Muffet, 12 May 1953 (John F. Kennedy Library).

On 21 May 1950, just five days after receiving the letter from Scribner which contained the details of Martha's disclosure that she knew she could not have children before she married Hemingway, he told Scribner that he had written a story of over 30,000 words and was planning to add another 10,000 to 15,000 words. "It's a hell of a story. Think you will like it." On 1 June, he adds that Martha is in the story, "but only off stage" (PUL). Three days later Hemingway told Adriana Ivancich that he had just finished a long story, the happenings of just one day when a storm had driven him in from the antisubmarine work he was doing then (HRC). Part of this story – probably everything except the interlude that develops with the appearance of Hudson's first wife at the bar in Havana – had been first written in June or July of 1948 when Hemingway described to Peter Viertel a story about the commander and crew of a sub-chasing operation who spend the day in Havana just before they leave on the operation that forms the final chapter of *Islands*. The difficulty Hemingway was having moving the narrative forward, and the loneliness he felt in working on it, are suggested by his offering Peter Viertel a collaborative role and inviting him and his wife to Cuba so that they might work together.

He was writing the story during the period when he was also furious with Martha for forcing revisions in the galleys of *Across the River*. "Cuba" is set in the period of the events that Hemingway left offstage, and details of the narrative reflect how conscious he was of the erosion of his own creativity during the nearly two years when he became a hunter of men (and Martha believed he was sometimes insane). On 25 July 1943 Hemingway wrote Max Perkins that he was just in from fifty-eight days at sea and tired. The letter continues: "Haven't written anything in a year. If Martha is abroad I'm too damned lonely here unless kids are here or am at sea." He is blaming his failure to write on a domestic situation that he misrepresents, for although he had been at sea since 21 May, he had picked up his two younger sons in Havana on 13 June and taken them on the submarine hunt; and Martha wasn't abroad. She was at the Finca, trying to supervise restorations and working on *Liana*.[33] Clearly Scribner's disclosure of Martha's alleged deception, along with Hemingway's anger at having to make changes in *Across the River* because of her objections, dredged from the bottomless pit of his memory (where grudges could endure forever) recollections of what life had been like during the years that he was hunting submarines rather than writing. His letter to Perkins, along with the textual gap in *Islands* created by the lack of resonance of David and Andy's deaths, suggests that Thomas Hudson's movement from self-disciplined creativity in the midst of his all-male family to dissipation and the pursuit of violence in the company of men to whom he feels superior is not an extension of his grief. It is evidence of Hudson's (and Ernest Hemingway's) inability to either develop and sustain intimate human relationships or function creatively without them.

However, in drawing on his own experiences to create the narrative, Hemingway does not consistently use Thomas Hudson to shrive or mythologize himself. This is a distinction missed by many readers, including Carlos Baker in his editing of the novel.[34] On the contrary, Hudson's inadequacy is established in "Cuba" both from his own interior monologues and from his *remate* comparison with Ignacio Natera Revello. When Hudson leaves the embassy, he wishes that reality were as pleasant as appearance, that the sea harbored only natural dangers, that he was himself as solid as Lt. Commander Archer thinks he is, and that his public image – that of a powerful killer suggested by the fantasy of carrying Torpex under his arms – allowed him to be human, because "I think you have more fun as a human being even though it is much more painful" (IS, 257–58).[35]

Ignacio Natera Revello, the tiresome Cuban Hudson drinks with at the Floridita, is a rebounding surface for Hemingway's *remate* shots that undercut Hudson, who thinks of Revello as having "snob" and "bore" after his name "like people who put III after their names. Thomas Hudson the third. Thomas Hudson the turd" (IS, 260). Both men wear English brogues, know that the American ambassador is a fool, start drinking early in the day, and are seldom sober. After hours of drinking, rolling dice, and trading insults, Revello asks about young Tom, and Hudson responds that he is dead. Seeking some words of comfort for Hudson, Revello metamorphoses from a Cuban snob and bore into an affected user of British English pretending to technical knowledge of RAF flying that he does not have. So Revello and Hudson are, each in his own way, posturing.

But Revello expresses genuine sorrow at young Tom's death, albeit in Wilfred Owen and Rupert Brooke clichés, while a few hours later Hudson improbably beds his ex-wife after a day of marathon drinking, then informs her in a single syllable – "Sure" – that their son is dead and offers to comfort her with a Kipling recitation. Thomas Hudson the turd indeed! (IS, 319, 324).

"OUR DREAMS OF SAFETY MUST DISAPPEAR"[36]

For many of Hemingway's protagonists the response to irreparable loss was work, often creative work: Nick Adams heals the equivocal darkness of "Big Two-Hearted River" by becoming the writer who is writing the story in a Paris café. Jake Barnes is a journalist with ambitions. Frederic Henry dictates *A Farewell to Arms*. Robert Jordan plans to write a good novel if he makes it back to Missoula, Montana. But Thomas Hudson moves from creation to destruction.

Hudson's inability to heal himself through his work is not the result of inconsolable grief for the dead sons, but of his absolute inability to create without a mirroring relationship – and his equally

Figure 12. Martha Gellhorn, ca. 1940. Her attraction to Hemingway was inextricably mixed with her admiration for him as a productive writer (copyright Studio Paris).

absolute inability to sustain one. In the first draft of "Bimini" Roger suggests that George modify the lectern in front of the window (where he stands drinking martinis and reading the newspaper after a day of work) by putting a rail on it and a mirror behind, like a bar (Baker/Hemingway manuscripts 0365, Box 25, Folder 1, PUL). Here the standing desk that Hemingway often used becomes metonymically the writing, drinking, and self-regarding that are a necessary ritual in *Eden*.

Hudson's sons must die, and Roger must disappear from the narrative if Hudson is to proceed on the self-absorbed course that explains his dissipated, barren life in "Cuba." The relationships with his sons and Roger are circumscribed by the deference patterns of father-child and productive painter-nonproductive writer and could not indefinitely reflect back to Hudson the uncritical assurance of creative superiority he basks in throughout "Bimini." Without it he cannot create. Therefore, in the unpersuasive way that earlier novel-

Figure 13. Writing has become a form of self-examination for Hemingway in the posthumous novels. Shown at the Dorchester Hotel in 1940 (John F. Kennedy Library).

ists used a *deus ex machina* device, Hemingway excised Hudson's sons and Roger from the narrative. Whether Hemingway would have realized, if he had prepared the book for publication, that the death of Hudson's creativity must arise out of his internal conflicts is a question we cannot answer. Nor do the manuscripts give any help. The only love relationship that Hudson admits to (aside from Boise the cat) is his continuing attachment to his first wife, who is safely beyond needing him in any reciprocal way. There was a third marriage – after David's and Andy's deaths – but the wife is absent and has no more place in his memory than his sons or Roger, a void that is consistent with his refusal or inability to form reciprocal human relationships.

In "Bimini," Hemingway began for the first time to explore the most intense, enduring, dangerous love of which human beings are capable – the love of a parent for a child. And it is from the text of "Bimini" that the source of Hudson's inability to sustain human relationships in "Cuba" must be gleaned. That Hemingway took up

Figure 14. With his oldest son, Bumby, a German prisoner of war, Hemingway returned from work as a *Collier's* reporter in Europe with keen interest in gathering his family together once again. Shown here as he and Patrick changed planes in Miami, 14 March 1945 (John F. Kennedy Library, courtesy Pan American World Airways).

the positive aspect of parental love in the fall of 1945 was undoubtedly related to feelings aroused by the deaths of young men he had witnessed in the Hurtgen Forest, by his gratitude that his oldest son had recently returned safely from a prisoner-of-war camp, by again being able to see his two younger sons, and by his hope that his fourth marriage would produce a daughter.[37]

However, the subject of parental love held such an emotional charge for Hemingway that he initially protected the narrating "I" (George Davis) by making the children Roger's in the first writing and by ending "Bimini" with George's resignation expressed in an androgynous voice that changes to the familiar stoicism of the Hemingway male only as he returns to the company of Bobby, the bartender at the Ponce de Leon:

Figure 15. Bumby arrived in Cuba to recuperate in early June. Shown here: Patrick, Bumby, Ernest, and Gregory at the Cazadores del Cerro Shooting Club, fall 1945 (John F. Kennedy Library).

I knew the boys had to go. I had known that ever since they came. And that was normal and right and they were not my boys and I had no right to love them the way I did. But I was happy I did love them. And proud of it and proud of them and the day after they left all I could think about was how nurses must love the kids they raise when they are good kids and how awful and lonely they must feel when the children grow up and go away to school and yet how proud . . . . I knew all about that. But that was the way it was . . . So they were gone and I stopped at Bobby's on the way home.

"Going to be god-damn lonely," Bobby said.

"Yes," I said, "It's going to be god-damn lonely."

And it was. (Baker-Hemingway manuscripts 0365, Box 25, Folder 6; PUL)

But once the children are Thomas Hudson's, the prophetic, spiraling terror of three episodes during the last summer of David and Andrew's lives becomes evident. The near disaster with the shark, the battle with the fish, and the drunken charade all embed disclosures about Hudson that prepare for his derelict condition in "Cuba" and "At Sea."

David, the son that Hudson believes is most like himself, directs the reader to the source of Hudson's inability to risk intimate human relationships as Hemingway must have begun trying to understand the problem in himself after *Bell*. For after that novel, Hemingway's view of families becomes less intent upon simplistic blaming: the domineering mother and weak father are replaced by what in *Feast* he would call "dangerous families."

Just as Roger Davis and Thomas Hudson are two manifestations of a single creative individual, Davis and David Hudson are linked in a mysterious way that presages their joint metamorphosis into David Bourne when the "Miami" section is absorbed into *Eden*. We will see that in deleted portions of "At Sea," Thomas Hudson was also an avatar of David Bourne during his youth in France and Austria.

In "Bimini" Hudson is mute about his own childhood, and although he has known Roger for a long time, he was unaware that he had lost a younger brother. The trinitarian unity of Roger Davis-David Hudson-Thomas Hudson is transmitted from "Bimini" to "At Sea" by a kind of genetic-associative path that reveals in "Cuba" the childhood origins of Thomas Hudson's inability to form attachments.[38] But the revelation does not occur until long after Roger Davis has disappeared from the text and David Hudson is dead, a delay that causes yet another textual lacuna.

With the drowning of his younger brother in a canoeing accident when Roger was 12, he – like Nick Adams – learned too young about death and the crazing of parental love (IS, 75). And it is only Roger who recognizes that permitting David's long struggle with the fish was as wrong as leaving him exposed to the shark attack on the previous day. Hudson, aloof on the flying bridge throughout most of both ordeals, denies the physical damage to the boy's back, hands, and feet by rendering the bloody hands and "lacquered-looking oozing feet" in the images of the bleeding icons which infest Latin American churches (IS, 136). Hudson responds to young Tom's concern with the injuries David is sustaining: "[T]here is a time boys have to do things if they are ever going to be men. That's where Dave is now," establishing a significant opposition between Roger Davis (as anxious father) and Thomas Hudson (as detached

Figure 16. By the time of his second safari (1953–54), Hemingway had lost much of his taste for hunting and in the later years of his life often preferred observing animals. Shown here in Idaho, winter 1959 (John F. Kennedy Library, courtesy A. E. Hotchner).

artist) in their willingness to recognize the perils of making men through physical ordeals.

But in "Cuba," we can reckon the cost of Hudson's denials as he tells Lil of his boyhood brush with death when he was trapped beneath logs, in water "that was brown from the logs in it. The water that's like your drink was in a little stream that flowed into that river." Hudson makes a joke of the terror, telling Lil, "I drowned," and then that having pushed his way between two logs, he "had an arm over each log. I loved each log very much" (IS, 278). But this is gallows humor, a reprise of his conversation with Lieutenant Commander Archer, where Hudson wishes he were as solid as he appears to be, and having an arm over each log echoes his fantasy of carrying Torpex under his arms (IS, 257).[39] An essential part of Hudson did perish at some time back in his western boyhood (like Roger Davis and David Bourne, he is from Oklahoma) where there was a dark underside to the ritualized killing by which boys become

Figures 17 and 18. Hemingway and ten-year-old Gregory at antelope hunt, Idaho, 1941 (John F. Kennedy Library, probably by Robert Capa).

men.[40] He goes on to tell Lil that the water from a stream where he nearly drowned was as brown as her whisky drink – which is also as brown as the water in the channel where he runs aground when his physical death finally comes. Hudson's death, like Harry's death in "The Snows of Kilimanjaro," solves the two problems which beset creative artists through all of the posthumous novels, that of the paintings/stories that will never be created outside the imagination; and of never understanding those who love them (IS, 414, 455, 466).

David Hudson also learned too young that the world his father offers him is dangerous – even in the high, cold air of Montana. But the burden of his knowledge was lost in manuscript elisions, and therefore he sounds more precious than prescient when he tries to discuss with his father the weight of manhood created this way: "I know too much for a kid, papa. . . . [E]verything I know hurts me. I feel it and it does something to me. It's like a vicarious sin" (IS, 162).

Thomas Hudson responds to David's disturbing confession with anxiety about the rummy joke the boys are planning. This apparent *non sequituer* points to the events in the earlier manuscript where David's knowing too much began. There (while the boys were still Roger's sons) the father had jeopardized his vacation custody of David and Andrew by allowing David (at eight, the age of David Bourne in the elephant story in *Eden*) to drink wine until he is drunk. A visitor at the Montana ranch informed Andy and David's mother that David is drunk every night, and a manuscript insert tells of the bitter conflict that followed as the boys' mother tried to keep their father from having them with him (File 98.9, pp. 521, 525, and 541–42 insert; JFK). David's memory of the parental struggle, along with his awareness of how much of his father and Roger's attention is given to their drinking, constitutes his inchoate sorrow that is like "a vicarious sin."

All of the sons want to be with their father and Roger, but know that they are in the hands of two men with precarious control over their own lives. This is evident not only in their concern with the adults' drinking and in their attempt to express openly, through the charade at the Ponce de Leon, what they fear secretly, but also in the displacement of their concern with Roger and Hudson's drinking into the ongoing discussion of whether Eddy is a rummy.

Hudson's cryptic assertion that Andy "was just being good while his badness grew inside him" (IS, 53) has its basis in his youngest son's ability to recognize, and his refusal to be silent about, the patterns of evasion which his father, Roger, and Eddy indulge in their daily lives, while at the same time they engage the boys in the dangerous pursuits that are supposed to establish manhood. During the meal that follows the shark episode – which nearly becomes a reprise of the death of Roger's brother (also named David) – Andy counts Eddy's drinks and asks if he is a rummy. And during the ordeal of the fish, young Tom's way of being useful is making drinks for the adults and mentally inventing insulated coasters of cork blocks so that the ice in them will last longer.

In "Cuba," Thomas Hudson "fondly" uses "a sheet of moulded cork that came to within a half-inch of the rim of the glass" to hold a drink as his surly chauffeur drives him into Havana (IS, 240, 241–42, 244). The accoutrements of drinking survive the eager-to-please

Figure 19. At antelope hunt, Pahsimeroi Valley, Idaho, September 1941. Standing: left, Bumby; right, Patrick. Front row: Hemingway, Taylor Williams, and Gregory second from right (John F. Kennedy Library, courtesy Lloyd Arnold).

son who made them, just as Boise the cat survives the boys who found him at a bar in Cojimar – where they spent Christmas morning with their father.[41]

Andrew's questioning about what makes a person a rummy is persistent, and the night after David's ordeal with the fish, Hudson reflects that "he had not liked the way Andrew had behaved" (IS, 143). But in the manuscript David too wants to understand who is a rummy and who is not as he says to Roger Davis: "It seems to me a little like this. That if we like somebody and they drink too much they're not a rummy. But if we don't like somebody and they drink too much they are a rummy" (File 98–14, p. 659; JFK).[42]

When Hudson implicates Tom, David, and Andy in his drinking routines, he is entrapping them like his own father entrapped him

Figure 20. Martha Gellhorn and Gregory at antelope hunt, September 1941
(John F. Kennedy Library, probably by Robert Capa).

in the killing of ducks which he recalls in "At Sea" and like young
David Bourne's father entrapped him in the slaughter of the old
elephant in *Eden*. One of the forms that the powerlessness of childhood takes is wanting or being compelled to please a parent, and in
the process becoming implicated in parental actions that are cruel
and/or frightening – for example, Nick Adams's exposure to a
suicide and a caesarean section performed without anesthetic in
"Indian Camp."

   Hemingway had held the potential pain of permanent emotional
relationships at a distance in his early work by denial or stoicism;
but like Roger Davis, David Hudson, and David Bourne, he had
known many forms of entrapment as a child, and he was terminally
wary of permanent emotional relationships. His more than a quarter
of a century of refusing to deal with them – in his life as well as in
his work – is manifest in Thomas Hudson's inability to sustain the
human relationships he needs in order to create.

Figure 21. Gregory: the hunter and his game, September 1941 (John F. Kennedy Library, probably by Robert Capa).

LOOKING BACKWARD FROM DESTRUCTION TO CREATION

Hudson's home outside Havana, with its unused bedroom, empty
larder, and undisciplined servants, contrasts sharply with the well-
ordered life of companionable males in "Bimini": it is the reality –
as Hemingway's memory has shaped it – of life when he returned to
the Finca Vigia from submarine hunting in 1942–43 to find Martha
either absent on assignment or appalled by the narrowing of his
perspective and involved in her own writing. As Thomas Hudson
considers moving the best of his paintings from his bedroom because "I'm never in my bedroom anymore," he is a descendant of
Jake Barnes – with the disturbing difference that Hudson made this
suicidal, talent-wasting choice when, as he admits later, he could
have chosen his art over the murderous duty he is involved in.[43]

Boise the cat is the vehicle for an interior monologue that discloses the totality of Hudson's alienation from all but the life of
appetites and violence that he shares with his crew – and with the
suicidal pig in "At Sea." Further, the relationship with Boise is also a
debased and dehumanizing version of Hudson's relationship with
Roger in the "Bimini" section. Then he was content to participate
voyeuristically in Roger Davis's relationship with Audrey – whose
attention oscillates between the two men before settling on Roger.[44]
Now he jokes with Boise about sharing a woman who will accept a
diet of fruit rats. And his banter about the wantonness of another
cat, Princessa, becomes the masturbatory memory of an extended
period of sexual frustration with a princess which yielded a bond
with her husband and the recognition of a fellow passenger that for
Hudson art took priority over any woman (IS, 226, 229–30).[45]

But by February 1943, Hudson has not painted (and Hemingway
had not written) for a long time. As if to remind himself of a time
when life still held the promise of creation, Hudson makes a mental
list of the things he will not think about. It is a list that inscribes
Hemingway's own creative anxiety: "Let's just have *the sea in being*
. . ." (my emphasis), Hudson decides. This had long been Hemingway's working title for the story which became *Old Man*, the story of
an old fisherman who went out too far.

> Now you take a bath. . . . Then you dress for Havana. Then you ride
> into town. . . . What the hell is wrong with you? Plenty is wrong with

Figure 22. Hemingway descends the front steps of the Finca Vigía carrying Boise, the mango-eating cat of *Islands in the Stream* (John F. Kennedy Library, courtesy Hans and Malmberg, Stockholm).

me, he thought. Plenty. The *land* of plenty. The *sea* of plenty. The *air*
of plenty. (my emphasis; IS, 235, 237)

Here is Hemingway's anxiety about "The Land, Sea, and Air Book"
he has been unable to write.

" 'AT SEA' — HE HAD TRADED IN REMORSE . . ."[46]

When Hudson leaves his home at the end of "Cuba," he is like a
resolved suicide awaiting the action of an assassin with whom he has
made a contract to surprise him. He gives the letters and pictures of
Tom to the boy's mother, and plans to deposit at the embassy a will
making the finca hers. Many images of the section prepared for
this – the empty house, with the wind blowing under doors, the
bartender at the Floridita who looks like a death's head, Ignacio
Revello's toast ("I hope you die"), and Hudson's statement that he
has no use for money. His only consolation during the last days and
nights of his life is that he has something to do and is doing it in the
company of good men.

There is a change of tone between "Cuba" and "At Sea" that is
probably the reflection of Hemingway's view of the narrative events
in each section. In "Cuba," his recently revived bitterness toward
Martha and the memory of the talent-wasting chaos his private
life became during the submarine hunting years allowed for ironic
treatment of Thomas Hudson. However, in "At Sea," Hemingway's
bond with the men who were actually part of his *Pilar* crew is
reflected in Hudson as a kind of saint possessed of stoic endurance;
and the author never undercuts him. The characterization by *remate*
which was done using Roger Davis in "Bimini" and Ignacio Revello
in "Cuba" is here rebounded off Willie, who speaks the pidgin
English Hemingway sometimes affected after the war, has a very
precarious, hate-driven hold on reality and who tells the dying Hudson, "You never understand anybody who loves you." Hudson's verbal cruelty in "Cuba" is gone now, and the conciliatory way that he
exercises command over his crew of "half saints and desperate men,"
as well as the treatment he orders for the dying German prisoner,
show a man striving through duty to attain a virtue that escaped him
in the self-isolated world of his art.

Six days of chasing the German submarine crew provide the

structure of "At Sea," and although the details of the pursuit are excessive and repetitive, they are often the best of Hemingway's writing in this uneven novel. He must have believed this too, for the only part of *Islands* Hemingway exposed during his life was a reading from "At Sea" that he sent to A. E. Hotchner, which was not released until 1965 ("The Sea Chase," Caedmon Records, TC 1185). As Hudson moves willingly, at times recklessly, toward the physical death that comes like an embrace, there are a number of passages revealing that remorse, the horse he claims to have traded in for duty, is still very much in the running (IS, 383). Although most of "At Sea" is given to Hudson's command decisions and to thinking himself into the heads of his quarry as he pursues them, the natural world where he searches for clues directs him back to the painting he knows could have been a way to continue his life instead of becoming a murderer, "Because we are all murderers, he told himself. We are all on both sides, if we are any good, and no good will come of any of it" (IS, 356).

The resonances of life on Bimini that appear near the beginning of "At Sea," along with Hudson's memories of life there and in Paris that appear near the end of this final section, are Hemingway's effort to connect Hudson's present life of destruction to some earlier damage to his creativity; but the connection was obscured by the deletion of two long episodes from near the center of "At Sea." Those episodes suggest that the damage came from another form of entrapment, one inherent in the life of men without women that Hudson had arranged in "Bimini" – Hudson's attraction to, and fear of, a more fluid gender alignment than the conditioning of his Western childhood could accommodate. The deletions also reveal the younger Thomas Hudson as an avatar of Nick Sheldon and David Bourne.

The first resonance of "Bimini" occurs as Hudson lies on the beach at the unnamed cay where the massacre is discovered. There he sees with a painter's eye the gray, sanded driftwood he had once collected, cherished, and hated to burn; and his attention to the shape and texture evokes both the impossibility and the consequences of that dichotomous, exclusively male world in which creativity and lasting intimate relationships were incompatible. As he admires the driftwood, which he would like to paint, and thinks it should be in an exhibition at the Salon d'Automne, his pistol lies between his legs. A moment later he tells himself: "A beach tells many lies but somewhere the truth is always written." The truth written on this beach concerns not just the submarine crew he is pursuing: it is also a reflection of what Hudson has lost from his life, for he moves closer to the driftwood that he will never paint, and that will not warm his home, and addresses the pistol lying between his legs:

> "How long have you been my girl?"
> "Don't answer. Lie there good and I will see you kill something better than land crabs when the time comes." (IS, 338–339)

Later, we learn that the sheepskin machine gun covers, which are impregnated with oil to protect the guns from rusting at sea, are like cradles and the guns are called *niños* (male children). So Hudson has come to think of his penis as a gun and consummation as killing: guns, not paintings or books, are the well-cared-for progeny in this life where creativity has ceased. The impossibility now of living otherwise comes to Hudson in a dream on the sand by the driftwood: the dead sons are alive, Tom's mother lies on top of him as he used to love her to do, and he penetrates her – with the moistened .358 Magnum!

But then with the wonderful, treacherous possibilities of dreams, the girl says, "Let me take the pistol off and put it by your leg. The pistol's in the way of everything." And the dreaming Hudson replies, "Lay it by the bed, [a]nd make everything the way it should be" (IS, 344). This lovemaking is different from and more dangerous than the masturbatory fantasy of "Cuba." What follows is that mysterious erotic exchange of sex roles that David and Catherine Bourne seek – in which the penis does not have to be a weapon, for the penis as a pistol gets in the way of everything – and either lover can give or can take, and all distinction between taking and giving disappears. But for both Bourne and Hudson, who in this *Fantasia*-like merging of art and artists are the same man, the blurring of sexual differences is a danger against which the male creative imagination must be protected.

Of course, androgyny is frightening – venturing from any place where the authority of culture both defines what one should be and evaluates how well one meets its standard is likely to be frightening. But the artist is by definition a cultural critic, and to be rendered unable to create by the stasis of a gender role is an entrapment of the adult artist in the narrow vision of his childhood, a constraint that Thomas Hudson has experienced and that Ernest Hemingway was striving to overcome in the posthumous novels. The reader cannot know the origin of this anxiety about feminization that Hudson experienced in his younger years with his attraction to androgynous sexual positions and hair styles; but it is somehow connected with his later *déjà vu* recognition that all his life he had felt both in command and a prisoner of his need to be in command (IS, 414).

In Hudson's late frontier youth, an inclination toward androgyny would have elicited the epithet applied to Peters, the radio operator – "half-cunt." What the reader *can* deduce is the toll Hudson's need to be in command has taken on his relationships with women, for Thomas Hudson's sons die in the grip of the two most dangerous forces Ernest Hemingway could imagine: a talented, ambitious mother intent upon having her own way, and an indifferent war machine.

The two deleted episodes which connect Hudson and Bourne in their creative struggle were a part of the manuscript following the third paragraph of chapter 11 in the novel (Files 112, 113; JFK). It is not clear who made the decision to delete them; but their manuscript format and position in the narrative indicate to me that it was not Hemingway. Each of the deleted flashbacks is close to Hemingway's typical second draft: typed, with triple spacing between the words and bearing interlinear holograph corrections, the format that usually preceded typing of a finished manuscript. Across the cover sheet of File 113 is written in Mary Hemingway's hand "Discarded mss (Removed from The Sea Chase)."

While the initial revelation of Hudson's earlier years came in the dream of androgynous lovemaking with his first wife that remains in the novel – but which the resistant reader in 1970 could interpret as "normal," female-superior heterosexuality – the deleted episodes are waking memories in which Hudson carries on an argument with himself about his early ability to yield control and how well he painted under the conditions in which he did not have to pretend to be a human Torpex device:

> So now you spend your life hunting people to kill them which is surely as low as a man can be. So think about her and how she always

made you do things while now you make others do them. . . . [D]o
not think like that, you son of a bitch, because you still have work to
do. . . . It will be nice when you get back to that [painting], he
thought. Maybe you will have a better idea how to do it. At least you
have seen the sea. . . . By now you can almost say that you have seen
her and if you could do her and the mountains the way they should
be done that would make up, maybe, for the lost murder years and
the unsuccessful and successful homicides. (File 113, p. 87; JFK)

This memory comes just after Hudson has been cleansed by a
drought-breaking rain and is lying on the deck trying to avoid
thinking of the manhunt to come. And it has been evoked by a
resurgence of his creative drive, for a short time earlier he watched
his crew bathing on the stern and told himself that he should be
painting the scene rather than seeing it as Cézanne's bathers or
wishing Eakins had painted it (IS, 382). From the deleted memories,
Hudson falls into the sleep that produces the two dreams on page
384 of the novel.

The deletions seem oddly reversed, not only by their numbering
in the Kennedy Library collection, but also from their internal evidence. In the first flashback the story begins in the Alps, where
Hudson has been painting, and he and the unnamed girl have a
domestic familiarity with one another's habits and tastes (File 112);
but it is the second flashback that tells of their earliest involvement
(File 113). They are in Paris; her name is Jan; Hudson lives in a
studio like the one Gerald Murphy loaned Hemingway in 1926; and
they sometimes communicate by pneumatiques – as Hemingway and
Hadley did during the first phase of their separation. Inexplicably,
Jan asks Hudson's assurance that their tonsorial and lovemaking
experiments, which had gone on in the mountains, are not a betrayal of the way they were together in the mountains.

From Paris they begin to travel south – where they will metamor-
phose into David and Catherine Bourne and Nick and Barbara
Sheldon of *Eden*. Hudson's willingness to participate in the transformative adventures of haircutting and bleaching that make him
and Jan appear to be brother and sister in the daytime and in the
exchange of sexual positions that makes him very uneasy at night,
links him to both painter Nick Sheldon and writer David Bourne in
Eden, for Hudson and Jan's cross-dressing includes Nick and Barbara
Sheldon's hair growing, and Catherine and David Bourne's hair
cropping experiments.

The universe of *Islands,* particularly of "At Sea," is like that which Hemingway limned in choosing the title for *Men Without Women,* devoid of any of the softening influence of women.[47] And in it creativity has turned to violence that is ultimately as self-reflexive as Barbara Sheldon's suicide in the plot deleted from *Eden* – where her suicide note was initially signed "Catherine."

The second flashback culminates in Jan's obsession with displaying their androgynous grooming and garb at St. Raphael. There the sea water will keep their identically coifed heads identically light – as Catherine and David Bourne do what Jan and Thomas Hudson have planned.

These two memories are both of a time when some mediation between the masculine and feminine was still possible, and when Hudson was painting well but dangerously. They also form a web of connections among the images with which *Eden* and *Islands* explore the risk that the need to create held for Hemingway. The cross-dressing in the Alps and in Paris, like that in *Eden,* makes the male and female more alike. Hudson associates the literal high altitude of the Alps with his painting during the time when the blurring of gender roles was producing a perilous creativity. The head of the local police tells him: "Anyone can paint in the summertime. . . . But a man who paints above three thousand five hundred meters in the wintertime is a true Alpine painter" (File 113). Barbara Sheldon, one of the painters in *Eden,* is another avatar of the artist, and like the dying writer in "The Snows of Kilimanjaro," she has lived beyond her emotional and aesthetic means for too long. Barbara is able to filter out "the picturesque for the geometry" in her painting, which is "dry in the way that the snow is dry" (422.2–3, p. 11; JFK). The aesthetic assumption applied to Barbara's painting in the deleted plot of *Eden* suggests that form is separable from and superior to the emotions that create it. But Barbara becomes unable to paint, destroys her personal relationships, and commits suicide.

The removal of the two episodes contained in Files 112 and 113, which as waking memories are products of the conscious mind, obliterated the context of Hudson's two dreams of childhood which follow immediately (IS, 384), for those dreams direct the reader both backward to "Bimini," and the damage done to Roger Davis and David Hudson by knowing too much, and forward to Thomas Hudson's recognition that follows in "At Sea" that he too had a childhood over which the skin of memory has grown as over a wound. In the first dream Hudson is a boy again, riding beside a clear river where trout rise. Then Ara wakes him with the second of two identical orders, the only communications he ever receives from the Sinai-like voice at Guantanamo – "CONTINUE SEARCH CARE-FULLY WESTWARD." Hudson sleeps again and dreams that he is carrying out those orders, smiling at how far west he has gone. But the dream turns on him: his cabin is burned; his dog and the fawn he had raised are slaughtered; and Hudson wakes to continue searching carefully westward.

From the end of these dreams until the fatal ambush behind Cayo Guillermo, the natural world of the westward search reminds Hudson of the childhood he had chosen to forget and the patterns of his adult life that grew out of it. His childhood (like those of Roger Davis, David Hudson, and David Bourne) included the entrapment of pleasing an adult and becoming implicated in adult cruelty. Aground in the channel,

> He watched the shore birds . . . and he remembered what they had meant to him when he was a boy. He could not feel the same about them now and he had no wish to kill them ever. But he remembered the early days with his father in a blind . . . and how he would whistle the flock in as they were circling. (IS, 417)

This revelation is kindred to the inchoate realizations of vulnerability Nick Adams has in "Now I Lay Me," and "A Way You'll Never Be," and it began shortly before as, approaching the channel,

> Thomas Hudson had the feeling that this had happened before in a bad dream. They had run many difficult channels. *But this was another thing that had happened sometime in his life. Perhaps it had happened all his life.* But now it was happening with such an intensification that he felt both in command and at the same time the prisoner of it. (my emphasis; IS, 414)

Once they are aground, Hudson experiences his command misjudgment "as a personal wound . . . [that had] all happened before. But it had not happened in this way . . ." (IS, 416).

Hudson has no history of commanding anything other than his life until this intelligence mission began – there is, for example, nothing in the manuscripts that links him to Colonel Cantwell of *Across the River* (except the author's passionate interest in military action). He is a failed artist, a thrice-married man who buys his sexual companionship, and a parent who, when his sons were alive, did not hear their anxiety about his drinking. Therefore, Hudson's sense of being both in command of a situation and at the same time the prisoner of it can only be a reflection of his personal life. That, of course, is why the grounding comes as a personal wound. Hudson's conduct of his life until this moment has been a disaster or he would not be here, seeking to lose it in a cause from which he knows no good will come. He would be painting. And he would be with Tom's mother.

In his inability to reconcile creativity with domestic life, Hudson has fled all the places and relationships where mediation between them might have occurred. He has metaphorically followed the directive to continue searching carefully westward, which is the only sound from Guantanamo – and is as cryptic as the echo in Forster's Marabar Caves. Hudson connects what he has been doing with what has been done to him: this is clear when Henry (who has his creative basis in Hemingway's frequent hunting companion Winston Guest) asks if the wound hurts, and Hudson replies: "It doesn't hurt any worse than things hurt that you and I have shot together" (IS, 402).

Carlos Baker saw the message from Guantanamo as Hudson's "unstated and largely unplanned program of self-rehabilitation" and as Hemingway's moral directive to himself (*Writer as Artist*, 408). But his is a reading in the tradition of the Hemingway Code that can only be supported at the cost of ignoring portions of the text that are dense with meaning: the Huck Finn/Captain Marryat immaturity of Hudson's attempt to create a world of men without women; the parental failures inherent in the fact that Roger Davis and David Hudson know too much; all the sons' anxiety about the adults' drinking; the *remate* comparisons of Hudson with Ignacio Revello and Willie; Hudson's linking the childhood memory of the logs to the whisky-brown water; his dream of the burned cabin; his abandonment of his art; and his surety that no good will come of the murderous pursuit that has taken its place.

It is not easy for any Hemingway scholar to fault Carlos Baker, for without the monumental work he did on the biography and the letters, Hemingway scholarship would have taken much longer to outgrow the Code readings that were threatening to make the writing a historical artifact after Hemingway's death and before the opening of the Hemingway Collection at the Kennedy Library. However, Baker worked on the editing of this novel – Charles Scribner Jr. represents him as the dominant force in the project – and his reading of *Islands* is not part of the biography, but of his revised edition of *Writer as Artist* in 1972 (379–408).[48] In editing the novel Baker shaped the "At Sea" section to support his own inclination to see the narrative as following what he called "The Narcissus Principle"; and in doing so he treated Hudson only as an uncritical reflection of the author.[49] To do this Baker had to ignore the complex musings on the problems of gender and creativity that are embodied in the deleted episodes of Hudson as a younger artist. And he did.

Fortunately, Baker left a record of the precedence he gave westwardness and separation of the sexes over gender blurring in sustaining the creative imagination. One folder of the *Islands* manuscripts at Princeton contains discards. On it, in Baker's hand, is written: "Some Montana material near end of this batch might be rescued for Miscellany volume" (Baker-Hemingway manuscripts 0365, Box 25, Folder 3, PUL). The Montana material is from "Bimini," and in it Roger tells of a curative winter spent at Hudson's ranch – away from women, running a trap line; and on a short ration of whisky. But the folder also contains, without comment, the two long episodes about Hudson's concern with cross-dressing and creativity in his youth which I have identified as Files 112 and 113 at the Kennedy Library.

Possibly, all three of the editors were uncomfortable with these episodes; and their connection to the *Eden* manuscript, which both Baker and Mary Hemingway thought unpublishable, may have made the episodes seem extraneous. Certainly they would have given Hemingway's readers a jolt in 1970. But even without knowing of the deleted episodes of *Islands,* or of the existence of *Eden,* one cannot read this novel today as an exhortation to frontier stoicism in the face of male duty; for Hemingway created in Thomas Hudson a failed artist who has already searched so far westward that the clear trout stream is a muddy brown channel – and who has burned his own cabin three times over.

CHAPTER 4

The Garden of Eden: protecting the masculine text

Recounting for Carlos Baker the bond that he and Hemingway formed during the battle of the Hurtgen Forest, Buck Lanham said: "After that night and the next terrible eighteen days E.H. and I were locked into a species of brotherhood that both of us knew would last as long as we lasted. It did." In the public record of their relationship Hemingway has usually appeared as the more devoted of the two friends, for he inscribed his homage to Lanham in the character of Colonel Cantwell in *Across the River and into the Trees,* while Lanham's loyalty to Hemingway and his own literary inclinations remained largely unknown. Therefore, when I found the evidence that established accurately the compositional order of *Islands in the Stream* and *The Garden of Eden* in the unpublished Hemingway letters which Lanham deposited at Princeton, it seemed his tribute from beyond the grave to the brotherhood that had begun in the Hurtgen Forest.[1]

The letters to Lanham not only establish the beginning of the ur-text discussed in Chapter 3, but also identify the point at which the themes that would become *Eden* began in it; for by June 1946 Hemingway had started to inscribe in the manuscript he had embarked on the previous October the sexual experimentation that presages its split into *Eden* and *Islands* in 1948.

Carlos Baker had worked from Mary Hemingway's chronology of her husband's writing during the postwar period, and the dates that she put on letters were sometimes as much as three years awry, a fact that misled Baker when he accepted Mary's statement that the first novel Hemingway began after WWII was *Eden:* hence Baker states that *Eden* was begun in 1946. Perhaps Mary considered the part of the ur-text which Hemingway describes as dealing with fornication

Figure 23. Mary and Pauline Hemingway met in the summer of 1947 and formed a close, supportive relationship. This photo is inscribed to Sinsky (Juan Dunabeitia, an officer in the Cuban merchant marines who was often a houseguest at the Finca Vigia) (photo by Roberto Herrera, courtesy of Carrol Publishing Group).

and problems between men and women as the beginning of *Eden*. However, it is clear that Hemingway did not yet see *Islands* and *Garden* as separate works when he wrote Lanham that he intended to put the war experience and relations between the sexes in the same book in his letter of 30 June 1946 (quoted in Chapter 3).

A hairline splitting of the ur-text probably did begin in the spring of 1947 when both Pauline and Mary, the two wives from whom the character of Marita has been created in *Eden,* were at the Finca Vigia together for an extended period. By the summer of 1948, when Hemingway prescribes for Mary a haircut like that of Thomas Hudson's first wife in *Islands* and Barbara Sheldon in the deleted plot of *Eden,* the latter work is under way.[2]

Another visible trace of *Eden*'s lineage runs from the discarded "Miami" section – where Helena has Martha Gellhorn's physical traits and ambition, Roger Davis is uneasy at her plan for making him more productive by sharing his writing, and the transformative powers of absinthe are discussed at length (File 102–3; JFK). All evidence indicates that Hemingway branched off from the ur-text and began *Eden* as a separate work in the spring of 1948: Baker quotes Buck Lanham as saying that on 12 June 1948 Hemingway told him the new book was about "the happiness of the Garden that a man must lose" (460). There is no Hemingway letter of this date to Lanham among his papers at Princeton, but uninventoried papers were taken from Baker's office after his death, and that letter may have been among them; moreover, the phrase "Garden that you must lose" is used in a reference to Martha in a letter of the same date to Charles Scribner Sr. (see note 2). It is common to find the repeated use of a phrase in letters Hemingway wrote on the same day: this phrase, along with the documentation of Hemingway's directions for Mary's haircut, make the soundest dates for the composition of the *Eden* as a separate work the spring of 1948 through March 1959.[3]

Tracing the periods of Hemingway's work on *Eden* over the eleven years is problematic because the androgynous sexual activity and tonsorial cross-dressing in the novel are clearly matters that he did not feel comfortable about disclosing, and the surfacing in his letters of phrases/images from a creative work that is often helpful in dating the other posthumous narratives seldom occurs. But there are two periods when concentrated work on *Eden* can be documented. On 7 September 1948, the Hemingways – Mary with the beginning of the hair style that he had directed her to have in Havana – boarded the *Jagiello* for Italy. There, in December, Hemingway met and became besotted with Adriana Ivancich. His work on *Eden* was probably suspended then as he began a story about duck hunting near Venice. In the months that followed, he siphoned from the ur-text the material about the land war in Europe to create *Across the River,* using the duck hunting story as a frame for the novel that is his tribute to Lanham, as well as a textual consummation of his platonic relationship with Adriana.

When the Hemingways returned to Europe in November 1949, where he finished *Across the River,* he also visited Aigues Mortes and Le Grau-du-Roi, and drove the Carmargue countryside where *Eden* is set. Back in Cuba, on 7 April 1950, he began the first of the two documentable periods of concentration on *Eden* as he awaited the galleys of *Across the River* (which had been serialized in *Cosmopolitan* and was now being set for book publication in the fall). In May, depressed over his separation from Adriana, renewed in his hatred of Martha by the disclosure and events discussed in Chapter 3, and abusive of Mary to the point that she was considering leaving him, Hemingway was once again contemplating suicide. Anticipating that he might not live to finish *Eden*, he wrote a provisional ending.[4]

The second period of concentrated work on *Eden* began in late 1957, when Hemingway triumphantly told Buck Lanham that he had done fourteen chapters on a new book (the Paris sketches that became *A Moveable Feast*), and had been working steadily on another (*Eden*) – which nine months later he claimed was nearly finished (16 Dec. 1957 and 18 Sept. 1958; PUL). In his later work on the *Eden* manuscript, Hemingway discarded the events of the provisional ending (Catherine's return from a Swedish sanatorium and the suicide pact), and he continued for thirty-nine holograph pages beyond David Bourne's rewriting of the African stories. Although this continuation has been referred to by some scholars as a second ending, it seems to me more a narrative extension than a closure. Both endings will be discussed later in this chapter. In editing the manuscript for publication in 1986, Tom Jenks, working for Scribner's, chose to end the novel with the rewriting of the African stories, suggesting that David Bourne has pulled affirmation out of ashes, and making his earlier quest for a fluid gender alignment that would cross-fertilize the creative imagination irrelevant. There is no manuscript evidence that Hemingway ever considered ending the novel at the point Jenks chose.[5]

Despite the general dissatisfaction of Hemingway scholars with the novel Scribner's published in 1986, responsibility for the novel is not a simple matter, for the manuscripts of *Eden* present problems that cast doubt on Hemingway's own judgment in describing it to Lanham as nearly finished in September 1958, and that will make the establishment of a definitive text an enormous task. "Manuscripts and Typescripts for *The Garden of Eden* in the Hemingway Collection, John F. Kennedy Library" is a document of seven single-spaced pages that identifies the material according to its date of opening and by its description in Young and Mann, *Hemingway Manuscripts: An Inventory*, if it appears there. The total number of pages as of April 1990 when the document was written was 2,415. In August 1994 it is 2,409, with the reduction accounted for by the determination that six pages in Item (e) are part of Hemingway's draft of the Nobel Prize acceptance speech:

(a) Files 422 and 480: 27 pages of fragments opened with the main collection prior to 1981 (not all of which are actually part of *Eden*).
(b) Files 422.1 through 422.7: 1,903 pages opened in 1986 following the publication of the novel.
(c) File 422.8: 414 pages opened in 1988.
(d) File 422.9: 62 pages opened in 1989.
(e) Files 422.9–a, b, c: 9 pages opened in 1990.

The total, when compared with the 247 pages of the novel, suggests that a great deal of Hemingway's manuscript was eliminated, but in a sense the numbers are misleading, for the *Eden* manuscript is often more reiterative than cumulative, containing immense repetition that Hemingway seems to have been unable to control, and there is often little evidence among the variants that he privileged one text over another.

In another sense the deletions and elisions created an enormous gap between Hemingway's intention for the book that can be recovered from the novel and the meaning readers can create without knowledge of the manuscripts. Unfortunately, the androgynous sexual activities of the three major characters who remained in the novel after a mirroring plot was deleted drew the attention of reviewers, critics, and general readers away from the metafictional nature of the work. The androgyny, presented without adequate context in the published work, became a magnet for reviewers and general readers and obscured the fact that the elephant story is the objective correlative of David Bourne's independent attempt to resist the cultural constraints of family, gender, and race against which Catherine inaugurated their joint resistance in the honeymoon narrative. There the resistance is inscribed in their seeming obsession with sensual exploits which include cross-dressing and tanning, as well as attempts to satisfy with food and liquor the insatiable hunger to transcend their mortality through creation.

A conversation between Catherine and David that is an important link between hunger and creativity, and that establishes the signifying importance of the seeming obsession with drinking and eating in the novel, was elided in significant ways. In Madrid when Catherine meets Andy, the writer of the deleted plot, for the first time, she has not transformed herself into a boy for four weeks. The three-way conversation of the manuscript has been reduced to a dialogue between David and Catherine in the novel (*Garden of Eden* [hereafter GE in citations], 53–54), where his dismissal of her need to create is lost in the elision. In the manuscript she tells Andy and David, "I never wanted to be a painter nor a writer until I came to this country, now it's just like being hungry all the time, and there's nothing you can ever do about it." Ignoring David's placating response, "Andy does it for you," she continues, "There's nothing except through yourself, and I don't want to die and it be gone." But Catherine also goes on to lament the danger in moving outside herself to create, which it is clear must be the self-exposure of creating as a female in a milieu where creation is the domain of males. In the conversation that follows, David's response is just as clearly about the dialectic of masculine-feminine in the creative imagination that Hemingway was trying to resolve in this novel. He argues, "You have every mile we drove through from Vitoria to here" (GE, 53). Deleted from the novel is his response to Catherine's fear that she won't remember the landscape: he says, "I'll make it for you if you don't remember." When Catherine cries out against the absorption of her experience in an artifact she cannot create, asking, "What about when I'm dead?" David responds with a familiar and brutal riff in the masculine style that the author was trying to transcend in defense of his own waning creativity: "Then you're dead. . . . Bad luck" (422.1–6, pp. 10–13).

Catherine's return to androgyny becomes *her* creative outlet, and in an excised portion of the manuscript, David sees the lines and angles of Catherine's face, heightened by her hair style, as her creative achievement, and he thinks, "She's the sculptor with her lovely head. I see why she likes to do it" (422.1–8, p. 7).

MANUSCRIPT DELETIONS AND METAFICTIONAL INTENTIONS

And so in *Eden,* with its androgynous honeymoon narrative framing the masculine African stories, a creatively driven female and a male writer who is having trouble getting started on his third novel struggle in the honeymoon narrative over what he is writing, which – until he abandons it for the African stories – is the honeymoon narrative.

From Hemingway's 1933 safari had come two of his finest stories, "The Short Happy Life of Francis Macomber" and "The Snows of Kilimanjaro," both about the conflict between a husband and wife which reaches a climax during events of the safari and the effect of that conflict on the husband's performance – as a hunter or as a writer. From the ill-fated second safari of 1953–54, came the elephant story that was written in 1954, but incorporated into *Eden* later, and rewritten there in November 1958.[6] By the time that Hemingway began rewriting his third fine safari story to incorporate it into *Eden,* he had seen in the African book that his problems went much farther back than the marriages which he had used catalytically in "Macomber" and "Snows."

In the elephant story, David Bourne and Ernest Hemingway are removing layers of memory that shield them from what they have both heretofore avoided writing about. In the writing process each has sensed that something connected with childhood has made him able to be whole only when writing, and that this creates a barrier to human intimacy outside the metaphorical and literal locked room where the writing occurs. In the African stories David writes of the childhood events which made feeling so dangerous that writing was the only intimate relationship he could sustain; while outside the door of the room where he writes, two young women strive for an authentic relationship with him. In its postmodern structure *Eden* is closer to "The Snows of Kilimanjaro" than to anything Hemingway wrote except the unpublished African book.[7]

The three characters of the deleted plot, Nick and Barbara Sheldon, who are painters, and Andy Murray, a writer who is in love with Barbara, form a mirror image of the David, Catherine, and Marita triangle. As Catherine is the "devil" who introduces sexual androgyny and cross-dressing into the Bourne plot, and is considered crazy, Barbara has that role in the Sheldon plot. In Paris, three months before the novel opens at le Grau de Roi, the plots had been joined, and a detached narrator explains:

> None of them remembered the actual dates of commitment and none of them remembered the dates on which they had first turned in off the *rue de Varennes* to the Hotel Biron with the beautiful gardens

Figure 24. Rodin, *The Metamorphoses of Ovid,* bronze sculpture of lesbian lovers from the *Gates of Hell* series (photo courtesy of Mark Spilka).

and gone into the museum where the changings had started. One girl [Barbara] had forgotten that it had started there and, for her perhaps, it had not but she too had seen the bronze long before.

"Let's think of something fun to do that we've never done that will be secret and wicked," the girl [Barbara Sheldon] had said. (422.1–1, p. 1)

The transformational attempts of both couples have been inspired by Rodin's bronze sculpture of two lesbian lovers, from a group sometimes called "The Damned Women." It is the embrace of these lovers that Catherine is replicating when she asks David, "Will you change and be my girl and let me take you?" (GE, 17). In the manuscript David realizes that "It was like the statue. The one there are no photographs of."[8] But the metamorphic desire which took three months to affect Catherine had come more quickly for Barbara Sheldon and gone far beyond the androgynous hair cuts, dressing, and lovemaking that the Bournes explore: Barbara is obsessed with Catherine and later becomes involved with Andy. When the two couples meet again at Hendaye, she warns David to keep Catherine away from her, but she seeks them out in cafés.

The transformation seems to have ruined Barbara's ability to paint, while Nick Sheldon, with long black hair (identical to Barbara's) that makes him look like an Indian, works better than ever.[9] Nick's defense of his art is the familiar one of Hemingway's artists – separation from relationships with females. He goes off to paint for long hours – just as David will evade Catherine when he begins writing the African stories in his locked room (and as Thomas Hudson and Roger Davis have isolated themselves from women on Bimini).

David's first attempts at writing the honeymoon narrative, as well as the bargain he made with Catherine about it, have been elided where it would have appeared after "estuary of the river to Spain" on page 42 of the novel. It is a flashback to the meeting of Nick and Barbara at the Deux Magots in Paris in which David contemplates the relationship of painting and writing that Roger Davis and Thomas Hudson had discussed in *Islands*. Nick's relationship to Thomas Hudson – and Hemingway's vision of dealing broadly with the artistic imagination and the gender constraints Catherine and David are testing – is established by David's thoughts here of how writing and painting relate:

> He [Nick] painted the sea as well as Winslow Homer had painted in the Bahamas; the water colors of course. Not the set piece about the Gulf Stream. But why explain that. He painted as well as Jongkind . . . no one had ever done what he was working for; what he had already done . . . in the high alpine pictures. Why should he have to explain this? He was not an explainer. He would make Nick doing it and get what he said. . . . We have the money, he thought. Why not reproduce the pictures instead of write about them? Pictures should be looked at, not talked about or written about. What would be a better use for money? (422.1–1, chapter 5).

In Madrid, after Catherine admits that she is sometimes jealous of not being a boy, and they resume the androgynous sexual activity, one of her night roles is that of "the thief girl" (422.1–6, chapter

10), a harbinger of her later stealing David's work to destroy it after he has prevented her participation in the creative process by ceasing the honeymoon narrative. Catherine argues to David that the sexual exchanges they experiment with are natural because "We had no voice in making the rules." David accepts her reasoning, thereby making a contract for their joint participation in the creative enterprise that is under way; and he thanks her for letting *him* be Catherine (422.1–7, pp. 12–13). These events, deleted in the editing, establish David as a willing participant in the gender-blurring activities; while in the novel he appears to have been coerced by his unstable wife.

Earlier in the manuscript David had recognized that Catherine was trying to free them both from all that the old assumptions of white, Christian, European culture embody, for they see the next step in their metamorphosis as going to Africa – which is a form of sexual experimentation, as well as a continent. But the season is wrong, and they go instead to Spain where David thinks:

> Now we are going to be a special dark race of our own with our pigmentation growing that way each day as some people would garden . . . The trouble was that it will not grow at night too[.] It can only be made in the sun, strong sun against the reflections of the sanᴄ and the sea. The sun makes this sea change. The sea change [is] made in the night and it grows in the night and the darkness that she wants and needs now grows in the sun . . . . (422.1–1, chapter 4)

David recognizes here that Catherine's earliest obsession with tanning, hair cutting, and sexual exchanges, which began at le Grau du Roi, were an approach to creativity with which she hopes to cross-fertilize his creative imagination so that he will write their story; and he concludes, "She needs the sun as I need to work."

But Catherine also confesses that she cannot be a boy unless he allows her to be. Later, when being a boy encompasses her participation in the writing, he does not want this sea change to seep into his African stories, and he breaks the contract that is so clear in the manuscript, but that in the novel seems only to be her agreement to finance him while he writes. He excludes her, and she begins to lose her vitality – "I'm as old as my mother's old clothes," she says (GE, 163).

Searching for a way to effect closure in *A Farewell to Arms*, Hemingway wrote and discarded this passage: "Things happen all the time. Everything blunts and the world keeps on. You get most of your life back like goods recovered from a fire."[10] With the publication of *Eden*, the most directly autobiographical record of Hemingway's salvage attempts became public. The closure of the novel suggests that David Bourne has gotten back his life "like goods recovered from a fire" as he triumphantly rewrites the stories Catherine had burned before her departure. But in choosing to use as an ending an episode that Hemingway never intended as a closure, Tom Jenks almost obscured the pervasively self-reflexive mode of this work which Hemingway could not complete and for which the two endings that exist in manuscript are quite different than the episode Jenks has chosen. In the provisional ending that Hemingway wrote in May 1950, Catherine returns to David after some time in a Swiss asylum (422.2–1). Their relationship is more that of nurse-patient than of a renewed love affair or a marriage (and Marita has no part). Catherine notes that David can no longer take the intense sun in which they had once spent hours deepening their tans, and that he would like to protect her from it, implying that their transformative adventures failed. They agree that if her madness returns, and she asks David to commit suicide with her, he will do it.

The second termination of the manuscript, which has been treated as an ending by Robert Fleming and Mark Spilka, is closer to that of the novel in that Catherine has departed after burning the African stories, David has rewritten them, and Marita seems to be fully in charge of his future. But the narrative continues for thirty-nine pages after the rewriting, and those pages consist primarily of statements by Marita about how she will handle David like a trainer handles a big race horse, and of David's reiteration of how difficult it is for him to get out of the world of his writing and into the world of living human relationships. In these thirty-nine pages David does not sustain the confident voice he possesses in the ending Tom Jenks chose for the novel.[11]

Although the deletion of the mirroring plot containing painters Barbara and Nick Sheldon excised Hemingway's exploration of the unitary origin of creativity that had been developed in the "Bimini" section of *Islands,* it is primarily through deletions within the plot Jenks did choose that the concern of the novel with creativity has been significantly lessened. The most critical casualty of Jenks's editing is the textual coherence linking David Bourne's anxiety about the intrusion of Catherine into his writing with his reassessment of his father in rewriting the African stories Catherine has burned.

In discussing *Eden* as the only form of the novel we have – or are likely to have in the foreseeable future – I will try to restore the textual coherence of the manuscript's major concerns with creativity and gender limitations, and with families as bearers of culture, by tracing the emergence of Bourne's anxiety through use of (1) excised portions of the manuscript and (2) information establishing the autobiographical matrix of the novel. The restoration makes visible the fact that this is a novel about an unhappy childhood (which Hemingway once said was the best training for a writer), about the dichotomous sensibility such a childhood creates, and about the perils of that dichotomization for the writer and those who cast their lot with him. Further, this restoration provides from the manuscript evidence that even in its severely pruned condition, *Eden* is Hemingway's exploration of his own ambivalent attitude toward androgyny as both a catalyst and a threat to the writer and his writing.[12] It is then evident that the signifying center of the work, in both manuscript and novel, is the elephant tale, where – in its initial writing – David Bourne has inscribed and condemned the cruelty and indifference of a father who does not need to kill elephants to earn his living, and has suggested the impact of that cruelty upon the small boy who unwittingly became a party to the slaughter. But in the rewritten version, which the reader never sees, Bourne reinscribes the father and absolves him.

David Bourne writes two very different kinds of narrative in *Garden:* the first, the androgynously conceived narrative about the honeymoon he is currently taking with Catherine, is shared, for a time, by her. The second, the masculine African stories about his unresolved relationship with his dead father, excludes Catherine. Only one of the African stories, the elephant tale, is fully rendered in the novel (and in the manuscript). It is the last of the three stories written (inexplicably, David says in both manuscript and novel that he has four stories), and it is the product of using memory to gradually remove layers in the two story fragments which precede it in the novel (and in the manuscript). The fragments recount David's life with his father during the years after the events of the elephant tale in which, at the age of eight, he and his dog Kibo trailed a mythically large elephant by moonlight. Not foreseeing the consequences of his actions, David revealed the elephant's location to his father because he wanted to do something of significance on the hunt (just as Catherine seeks some significance in David's creative activity). During the tracking that follows, the child identifies with the elephant, and when his father tries to involve him in the final bloody episode, he repudiates him as a "god damned friend killer."

But trapped by the dependence of childhood (the mother's absence is not explained), David cannot prevent the slaughter; and once it has occurred, he can only resolve to never tell anyone anything again. When Catherine, whom David has begun to see in images of ivory, and who wants David to focus his creative energy on the honeymoon narrative which gives her a voice, comes too close to the African stories, David symbolically kills her by abandoning the honeymoon narrative. And when she burns the African stories and leaves, he replaces her with Marita and rewrites them. In the rewriting his father is shriven, no longer a friend killer, and David thinks, "He was fortunate, just now, that his father was not a simple man" (GE 247). In editing the novel, Jenks took this statement that David uses to rationalize his father's actions from an earlier point in the manuscript (422.1–31, chapter 39, insert 2), where the focus of David's gratitude for being his father's son is his need to have some way of coping with Catherine's resentment of his writing of things that exclude her.

BETWEEN AUTOBIOGRAPHY AND METAFICTION

If there were doubt in any reader's mind that in Catherine's destruction of the African stories Hemingway was re-enacting the trauma of Hadley's loss of the suitcase containing his manuscripts in 1922, and creating from it an exculpatory rationale for his long history of ambivalence toward women, a phrase deleted between manuscript and novel should dispel it.[13] In chapter 42, Hemingway has written three versions of a passage that appears on three pages bearing the same number. In two of these the phrase "looked into the ⟨empty suitcase⟩ trashburner" appears, with the words between angle brackets lined out (422.1–33, p. 23).

Not until the publication of Mark Spilka's *Hemingway's Quarrel with Androgyny* (1990) could readers begin to glimpse what such excisions as this mean to an understanding of the novel as the pseudoautobiography and personal metaphor it is.[14] With Spilka's work in hand it became possible to see that *Eden* is Hemingway's attempt to render aesthetic growth through sexual metamorphosis, and to recognize in this novel the most direct vision of the author's long struggle with his own androgynous inclinations. While these inclinations may have originated in a childhood in which few distinctions were made between male and female roles (either for the six Hemingway children or for their parents), there is a significant body of evidence that Hemingway was intrigued by the freedom that lesbians had achieved in their lives during his Paris years; and, wherever/whenever his interest in gender blurring as a way of evading prescribed behavior began, it must have been affected by what he saw in Paris (see Debra Moddelmog, "Reconstructing Hemingway's Identity"). Whatever its source, the single-trauma, blame-Grace silliness of several biographers has only obscured the complexity of the gender ambivalence Hemingway inscribed in *Islands* and *Eden*.

Viewing *Eden* autobiographically requires evidence of Hemingway's presence in the narrational structure beyond the unity of Hemingway and David Bourne that reviewers assumed.[15] The manuscript provides this in elided and excised passages: in the first, an interior monologue which would have appeared on page 167 immediately following "then David went in to take a shower, to shave and to change," Bourne examines his face in a mirror, noting scars, red welts, numbness, and an eye injury. These are the marks of Hemingway's injuries in the plane crashes and fire-fighting incidents of the 1953–54 safari: the voice and memory are those of the older man (422.1–23, p. 18). The second passage appears in a portion of the manuscript completely excised and in a marginal note. There David (again in interior monologue) denounces himself and "the ill smelling waste of his own recent life," which he compares to the sour mash smell of the brew at the beer shamba in the elephant tale. He comments in self-disgust about doing "what you hired out to do," suggesting the resentment Hemingway harbored toward Pauline whom he came to feel had seduced him away from Hadley and bought him – at exactly the point in his life and career where David Bourne stands now.[16] A few pages later David becomes a first-person narrator in discussing three-way sleeping arrangements identical to those that allegedly occurred with Hadley, Pauline, and Hemingway at Juan-les-Pins in the summer of 1926. Finally, in Hemingway's hand at the bottom of the page following 32, but itself numbered 26, there is written, "At this point the narrative continues in the first person." The margin of the page bears his notation, "About time, too[,] you can always go back into the third and play God again when you're up to it[.] But you're not up to it now."

Once David Bourne's relationship to Hemingway has been established, the women from whom Catherine and Marita have been invented can be recognized by their relationship to the writer and his writing – much as the juxtaposition of the women Hemingway knew in Paris was determined by the same principle in *A Moveable Feast* (which he was writing concurrently with the revision of *Eden*). Marita, the wife-to-be at the end of the novel, has her origins in a conflation of Pauline and Mary Hemingway. She shares Pauline's calculated use of her wealth (a trust fund and a wealthy, generous uncle to whom Hemingway dedicated *A Farewell to Arms* and continued to give manuscripts after he and Pauline were divorced) to secure Hemingway via her friendship with Hadley. In the manuscript Marita has a boyish haircut in an imitation of Catherine that reflects both Mary's cropped hair, and Pauline's bleaching her dark hair in order to compete with her 1930s rival, Jane Mason. Both Pauline and Mary (with light brown hair she bleached to please Hemingway) had been journalists and subordinated their own lives and talents to Hemingway's as caretakers of the man and the writer.[17]

Catherine too is a conflation, but of the women whose impact on the male's writing Hemingway mistrusted. She is Hadley, who lost his early stories in the famous suitcase incident.[18] She is the sometimes mad Zelda Fitzgerald whose demands on her husband's creative energy prompted Hemingway's famous "use the hurt" letter (*Letters*, 408), and who had herself fought male resistance to her creative endeavors in a way that is an uncanny foreshadowing (or Hemingway's literary borrowing) of Catherine's dilemma. She is

Jane Mason, the hard-drinking and slightly manic blond with whom Hemingway had a long affair while living in Key West and whose psychiatrist tried to psychoanalyze Hemingway through his sessions with her – an intrusion that (understandably) Hemingway greatly resented.[19] And, Catherine contains more than a soupçon of Martha Gellhorn, the wife whose insistence upon the importance of her own writing Hemingway called "insane" (Bernice Kert, *The Heming-way Women*, 391).

But one of the most important and frequently overlooked elements of this novel is that Hemingway also permits the writer's better self to speak as David recognizes that Catherine, in her need for creative accomplishment and her fascination with the potential of androgyny to effect it, is also a facet of himself (GE, 193), for in her introduction of tonsorial experiments and androgynous sexual activity Catherine engages them in actions that were for Hemingway the symbols of psychosexual metamorphosis.[20]

Catherine's art is conversation, and Hemingway's use of the danger inherent in silencing the female voice in *Eden* is another facet of the postmodern quality of the work, for a deadly conflict ensues when Catherine tries to give permanence to her voice through David's writing. This is clearer in the manuscript where chapter-head notations repeatedly mention "Talk," "Conversation," "Good conversation," and "Verbal flights." Marita makes this comparison: "She [Catherine] tells things in the same way you have to write them probably," and the manuscript suggests that Catherine is "feeding" ideas to David. In chapter 9, after Catherine and David have returned from Spain and he has resumed his writing, but she is bored, she makes this moving plea:

> I did what I said I'd do. I've had a fine time. I finished the Proust. I
> read *Far Away and Long Ago* and I love it. I've worked on Spanish. I
> read *Buddenbrooks*. I've confirmed what I knew[,] that I can't write
> nor draw nor even paint in water colors. I can't even draw a map to
> show how to get anywhere. Do you know if I couldn't talk I'd have no
> means of communication? So try not to mind if I talk. (422.1–11, pp.
> 11–12)

Catherine's is the most complex characterization of the novel, and she is unique among Hemingway's women because she insists upon some accomplishment of her own. While the novel offers as a red herring Catherine's failure to conceive, the manuscript makes clear not only that artistic creativity is her highest priority, but that she loathes children, and that David suspects her failure to conceive may be the result of *his* sterility. Hemingway strikes another postmodern note in this suggestion of anxiety over the paternity of texts that Sandra Gilbert and Susan Gubar set forth in *The Madwoman in the Attic*. David's awareness of the threat which Catherine's creative priorities pose to him becomes clearer when the reader recognizes that the "get" about which Colonel Boyle warns David in Madrid ("The get's no good. It's kinder to shoot the get.") becomes for David, not a child, but a text – the honeymoon narrative that Catherine shares. While the novel seems at first reading to contain only a single segment of the androgynous get (on page 78, as David writes of the trip through Spain), David's elided statement in the manuscript indicates what the reader of postmodern texts probably sensed on first reading *Eden* – that the entire novel is part of the honeymoon narrative. David simply terminates Catherine's role in the androgynously conceived narrative by ceasing to be her voice, turning his creative energy to the African stories and his sexual attention to Marita. In a passage deleted from the final chapter, Marita says, "You're going to finish it [the honeymoon narrative], aren't you? You could write it up to the fire." And David replies, "I suppose so. *It ends with the fire* [my emphasis]" (422.1–37, p. 16). Indeed at this point, which is the final chapter, David has begun successfully to rewrite the burned stories; but neither Marita nor David knows where Catherine is, and she hovers like Lilith outside their garden, for they understand fully that Catherine realizes it is not Marita but the African stories which are her rival.

David begins the African stories on the day after his first active participation in the androgynous activities Catherine has introduced – he bleaches his hair to match Catherine's. Seeking to use the creative energy for which androgyny has been a catalyst, but to keep his work safe from invasion by Catherine, he makes his writing an exclusively masculine activity, and in the manuscript, he thinks of the anxiety he feels about the developing triangle with the two women as "something outside his work[,] all that he had locked out by the work" (422.1–15, p. 3).

Everything connected with his writing (clippings, reviews, copybooks, manuscripts) remains in the room David locks as he goes to join the women each day, giving him an illusion of self-sufficiency – that he writes "from an inner core which could not be split nor even marked nor scratched" (GE, 193). In the African writing now, as in David's compartmentalized psyche, masculine and feminine do not mingle. The manuscript even establishes a difference in his treatment of the two kinds of writing that signals the primacy of the African texts before they become a source of conflict between David and Catherine. The title of each African story is printed on its copybook in ink; but the copybooks containing the honeymoon narrative are numbered, suggesting a germination that begins in memory for the masculine stories, but a five-finger exercise for the androgynous narrative (422.1–31, p. 2 insert). Feelings generated by androgynous activities feed (or starve) the languishing honeymoon narrative: David's memories of his father nourish the African stories. When Catherine burns the stories, the androgynous vision is over: it is only the masculine mode of David's creative imagination which survives in the rewritten stories.

However, exclusion of the feminine does not, as David rationalizes, make him stronger and less vulnerable to women, whose company he finds essential after the day's writing; it infantilizes him, a danger that resonates in Catherine's ridicule of the school child's copybooks in which the texts are written. Catherine's androgynous pursuits can be viewed as a form of madness from which Marita will save David only if the quasi-passive and masculine perspective from which the narration is focalized through David is not examined, for the manuscript makes clear that the "variety without perversion" which Marita offers David in the final chapter of the manuscript is lovemaking that reverses the digital anal penetration Catherine had introduced (whereby David had become "the girl"), and allows him the novelty and the dominance of making love to Marita anally, as though she were an "arab [*sic*] boy." Further, David uses the room where he writes as a place of disengagement from sexual and social involvement. But what he evades there is not the "angel-in-the-house" expectancy of companionship or service that might disrupt his writing, it is the devil of an adult sexual relationship which demands reciprocity – and he frequently calls Catherine "devil."

After Catherine's departure, Marita offers David a continuation of this state of exclusively male identification, combining sexual indulgence and domestic comfort without demanding reciprocity, for she says "Nothing that I do is important" (GE, 112). This is infantilization like that which, in the long term, was so destructive to Hemingway as he lived out the Huck Finn fantasy of evading civilization in Key West and Cuba while thinking of himself as Papa. The scene on page 140, in which Marita and David dispute his sexual access to her, has patently the tone of a mother soothing a child: "Poor David. What women do to you. She was stroking his head and smiling at him."

So David Bourne, constrained by financial dependency upon women (as Hemingway was at Bourne's age) and further constrained by emotional dependency (as Hemingway would remain until the end of his life) repudiates his earlier condemnation of his brutal and insensitive father as he rewrites the elephant tale. And at that point David forfeits for himself, and for his creator, the truth of the experience in which through the creative act, as in psychoanalysis, repetition becomes recognition. We will see that when Hemingway reached the final revisions of *Feast* in April 1961, he could no longer resist such self-insight.

WHAT DOES CATHERINE WANT?

As David has regressed, Catherine has grown; and her growth, when she is viewed apart from the burdens she bears as a facet of Hemingway's psyche and a stand-in for the women he feared and/or desired, is a striking analogue of the history of women's creative struggle.[21] Believing that she cannot write, Catherine first utilizes the feminine aspects of herself that are already acceptable to the writer in the family in order to secure his attention so that he will tell her story. She makes an art of her slightly scandalous manner of dressing, of her tonsorial experiments, of cultivating the deepest tan possible, and – in the ultimate gesture – she negotiates the services of another female to assure that David will write what she cannot. (The manuscript contains numerous references to David as a powerful race horse and Marita as his trainer.) Catherine even defines "being good" as studying Spanish every day, an echo of the touching faith Victorian women placed in the study of Latin and Greek to open doors for them in the male world.

Second, in the feminist phase, Catherine makes those creative actions of which she is master into acts of protest when she insists upon flaunting her newly tailored trousers and her and David's haircuts in Cannes after she has told him, repeatedly and articulately, how boring it is to be a girl. In the excised portion of the manuscript quoted earlier, David recognized Catherine's hair sculpting as *her* creative achievement; but in the novel even this accomplishment is denied her as the coiffeur becomes the sculptor, deferring to David's judgment and comparing his metier with David's (GE, 80). In an act of protest and defense against this appropriation and male bonding – which echoes David's assurance in Madrid that he and Andy will write what she is unable to write – Catherine attempts to create a sisterhood with Marita, making a "wife-of-the-day" agreement which leaves her free to pursue her own interests at least part of the time that David is writing. But the arrangement fails to advance her quest for significant forms of expression because Marita, with no desires of her own, repudiates Catherine as "not really a woman at all" (GE, 192) and replaces her in the feminine position, giving David the support he needs to write and taking away his motivation for change.

Sensing the imminence of her own silencing in David's neglect of the honeymoon narrative, Catherine becomes the active voice of the female phase of creativity – she seeks illustrators for the text that will tell her story. If her inclusion of Picasso among the artists she is contacting seems a riff of grandiosity, it is worth noting that she comes by it honestly, for when Scribner's was planning illustrated editions of three of Hemingway's novels in 1947, he told Max Perkins that he would like his son Patrick to do one and Picasso another (*Letters*, 617). But, like her counterparts in modern literature, Catherine is considered both dangerous and mad by her husband because, in contrast to Hemingway's other Catherine (Barkley), she wants a great deal for herself.[22] Her mistake is in believing that she can obtain it through her husband. When the patterns which establish this are recognized, Catherine's actions seem not so much madness as healthy anger.

When Catherine leaves, the reader's sense is that she is sadly undisciplined – now more a forced hybrid of Zelda Fitzgerald and Jane Mason than a conflation of those women with Hadley and Martha, both of whom found Hemingway's absence from their lives a relief.[23] But if Catherine's quest seems dangerously problematic, how much more so is the psychic state of the husband who toasts her departure with a spontaneous and remorseless "*A nous et à la liberté.*" And he is the inward voyager of this novel.

By the final page of the novel David has regressed from the protesting, masculinist vision which condemns his father to the masculine position from which he rewrites the African stories, and expresses gratitude that his father was a complex man.[24] The genesis of David's regression lies in the unresolved feelings about his dead father which will cause him to identify both himself and Catherine with the elephant – first in his desire to save her and his condemnation of the elephant killing, and then in a *volta* as he brings about her symbolic death by abandoning the honeymoon narrative and shriving his father in the rewriting of the African stories.

The pronouncement of Colonel John Boyle, the strangely prescient figure whom David and Catherine meet in Madrid, triggers this association.[25] Boyle's insouciant judgment of Catherine's potential – "The get's no good. . . . It's kinder to shoot the get." – is very like David's father's indifference to him when he asks how long the elephant and his friend that Juma killed had been together – "I haven't the faintest idea." What little can be discerned about the link between David's memories of life in Africa and his vocation as a writer is suggested by the title of his autobiographical first novel, *The Rift*, that indicates the geological depression of Africa (the Great Rift Valley), as well as the breach between David and his father that the African stories develop.

When Boyle appears to David in Madrid he reveals facts about Catherine's childhood that suggest a woman whose story is far more complex than a writer with two novels behind him and anxiety about his ability to create (with both pencil and penis) can afford to undertake. Catherine does not remember her father, raising the possibility that her delight in being taken for David's sister early in their marriage (GE, 6) may have its origin in her need to create the family she has not had. Manuscript excisions confirm this conjecture. Catherine's father was a charming, difficult, and probably childish man who lived on the edge and ended by killing himself and his wife in an auto accident – "Stupid way for a grownup to be killed," says Boyle (GE, 61). The parents were apparently not divorced, for they were killed together; but because Boyle recalls that the mother was very lonely, it seems sound to assume that the father was often absent. Her dead mother is more real to Catherine than her father, whom she seeks to recover in questioning Boyle.

However, Catherine pursues some wholeness in striving for connection with what the male principle signifies for her – no matter how destructive or trivial her attempts to do so are made to seem by the male narrating voice. She wants to paint or to write, to set fashions and to talk wittily; and she wants a love relationship with David. For him this pattern is significantly reversed. He wants simply to write; and when he can do that, David needs human companionship only as part of a menu of sensations that restore the writer – eating, drinking, making love, sun tanning, and swimming – all of which were once a part of his and Catherine's transformative endeavors, but are now merely sensations and necessary rest from the writing. As the young writer in *Feast*, from whom David Bourne was created, recognizes, writing was the only measure of himself that mattered. The woman who supplies and/or shares these sensations is not to enter into his writing or to interfere with it.

He also wants to avoid confronting the first female presence in his life, his mother. David reveals this in the elephant tale as the child, thinking about where the elephant is going, substitutes the place of the elephant's birth for the place where Juma says he killed the elephant's friend (GE, 198). The substitution is dense in significance, which I will discuss shortly.

David accepts Boyle's warning about the get, even as he argues with him, and he leaves Madrid with the genesis of the African stories and the cessation of the honeymoon narrative that will silence Catherine's voice in his unconscious. The nascent presence of the African material is adumbrated in two ways: first, David and Catherine walk in the Buen Retiro in Madrid on the day after their meeting with Boyle, and to David the scenery now is unfamiliar – a lake and trees, and the distance are quite changed (GE, 68). This is a flash-forward into the setting that will emerge in the African stories (GE, 128, 147). Second, upon their return to France shortly afterward, David acquires a separate room for his writing – a room that can be locked, at the farthest end of the building from the one that he shares with Catherine.

Catherine turns again to androgyny, her creative metier, as David's dismissal (in Madrid) of her yearning to write or paint had determined that she would. The editorial elimination from the Madrid scene of important parts of David's responses to Catherine's plea for a creative role (quoted earlier) was especially damaging to the theme of gender-bound creativity that is at the heart of this novel. In what remains of the scene, Catherine goes to their room because she has begun menstruating; thus the manuscript elision has reduced her resistance to having her story written by Andy or David to a symptom of PMS (GE, 71).

Now when the androgynous activity resumes, David's participation is active: they have twin haircuts and bleach their hair to a silvery white; and he requires only a bit of persuasion (GE, 82). After the lovemaking that follows, he is on the brink of an important recognition: looking at himself in the mirror, he thinks, "All right, you like it . . . Now go through with the rest of it whatever it is and don't say that anyone tempted you or that anyone bitched you" (GE, 84).[26] The interior monologue then continues: "You like it. Remember that . . . You know exactly how you look now and how you are . . . Of course he did not know exactly how he was. But he made an effort *aided by what he had seen in the mirror*" (my emphasis, GE, 85). The last two sentences are narrational commentary and the disclaimer is the author/narrator's attempt to rationalize what has happened in his writing and in his relationships with women since his inchoate, and ultimately repudiated, insight that an androgynous sensibility is necessary to the artist.

David acts on this insight almost immediately as the African stories come into his consciousness the next day. This is ambiguous in the novel because there he does not write on the following day, but goes on a picnic with Catherine and then to the café in Cannes where they see Marita. However, the manuscript gives to David "the best morning's work he had done in a month," as a product of the "sharp post-coital clarity" which has heretofore evaded him with Catherine. Although David begins the African stories on the day of the Cannes outing, their germination is earlier; for, as had happened in Madrid, the present landscape resembles the African terrain. Manuscript excisions deprive the reader of images of "African grass" blowing in the heavy wind and of David's assertion that this is some of the best wild country left, a statement that was not descriptive of the French-Italian border area where he is driving even in the late twenties. But enough allusions to the African terrain remain in the novel to permit the reader's understanding of what is occurring: there are references to "the high country," and to "waste country . . . that was flat and scoured by the wind" (GE, 87). These establish that it was the African material which had been in David's unconscious when he thinks later that "the story had not come to him in the past few days. His memory had been inaccurate in that. It was the necessity to write it that had come to him" (GE, 93).

David's recognition of the necessity of the androgynous sensibility to his writing is brought about by his hair bleaching – his first active participation in Catherine's tonsorial attempts to lessen gender markers – and the ability to condemn his father's exploitative and murderous actions is the fruit of this recognition in his writing of the elephant tale. But recognition is not resolution, and the wound that caused the child in the story to resolve never to tell anyone anything again is not healed. When David's writing is destroyed by the woman who brought about the androgynous insights that made possible his criticism of his father, he regresses to a position from which he no longer needs to judge his father's actions, and the father he had earlier repudiated as a friend killer becomes a complex man.

PROTECTING THE MASCULINE TEXT

Although Marita is an accessory in David's regression because her presence provides him with the companionship of a woman who is indifferent to any creativity but his own, she does not cause it. The seed of David's regression lies in Boyle's prediction about the get which, like the African stories, has been in David's unconscious since he returned from Spain and began writing in the locked room. Indeed it is the diminishment of David's early honeymoon tenderness for Catherine – and perhaps a sense that with less tenderness he is less vulnerable – which enables him to recover the "sharp post-coital clarity" necessary to enter into his writing.

David's protectiveness toward the African stories is another postmodern element of this novel, for it is a paradigm of the paternity of literary texts of which Edward Said asserts, "the unity of the text is maintained by a series of genealogical connections: author-text, beginning-middle-end, text-meaning, reader-interpretation, and so on. Underneath all these is the imagery of succession, of paternity, or hierarchy" (*Beginnings: Intention and Method*, 83). In David's writing there is no space for a feminine vision, as in his life there is no place for a woman who wants to participate in the writing. Putting his texts in a locked suitcase in a locked room is David's assertion of custody over his parthenogenetic offspring just as surely as his carelessness with the key is his recognition that his progeny needs both masculine and feminine origins. He can share his paternity, temporarily and in a limited manner, with Marita because for the present she wants nothing more than to praise his creation. But Catherine understands only too well how David is using his writing as a barrier against the feminine when she compares it to masturbation, the solitary vice. Although her prescience is presented as hysteria by the narrating male consciousness, it is clear even to David himself that he is engaged in a kind of creative onanism.[27] That David knows this too is established by his juxtaposing "creation" with "procreation" in an excised portion of the manuscript:

> If you live by the senses you will die by them and if you live by your invention and your head you die by that too. All that is left entire in you is your ability to write and that gets better. You would think it would be destroyed. By everything you have been taught it should. But so far as you corrupt or change, that grows and strengthens. . . . It is possible that the only creation that is a moral act is procreation and that is why the other kinds are suspect. It could be but it seems too simple. . . . Don't apportion blame for destruction now. It will all be apportioned in due time and not by you. (422.1–17, p. 9 and 9 bis)

All that remains of this in the novel is the final sentence which is interspersed with David's thoughts about missing the two women as soon as he finishes work for the day (GE, 132). So David feels empty and hollow after both lovemaking and writing: but after writing the African stories, the get is there – and it is good.

David's recognition that the African stories are his get occurs following a coupling with Catherine that might have resulted in conception. Just before Boyle gave David the advice about shooting the get in whose creation Catherine would have a role, he complimented Catherine on her tan – "You're the darkest white girl I've ever seen" (GE, 63). Later, when David has shifted his dependence from Catherine to Marita, and is writing well on the African stories, he looks into the mirror and notes with distaste that his hair, which was earlier described as exactly the color of Catherine's, is "silvery white." At this point Catherine, who had spoken of leaving David, returns and announces her intention of staying – although she will share him with Marita. They make love and David warns her, "Be careful [Don't get pregnant]." But as his orgasm approaches, she pleads, "Please be slow and let me keep it [Don't withdraw]." David, never hard to persuade, responds, "You have it" (GE, 169). As they lie together afterwards, Catherine echoes John Boyle's remark to her – "I'm the darkest white girl in the world." David responds, "You're just like ivory. That's how I always think. You're smooth as ivory too."

But the reader knows that both have silvery hair and that Catherine is very tan. The cessation of the honeymoon narrative and the symbolic death of Catherine, which in the manuscript David consciously links with the death of the elephant, is irrevocably decided at this moment as David, understanding Boyle's prophecy, uses the image of ivory. In a sentence that follows David's first "Maybe I can," on page 166, the manuscript reads, "Maybe I can make Catherine whole again and happy too. . . . There is nothing you can do for Catherine except to make her ⟨alive again as she was⟩ in the narrative the way she was" (422.1–23, p. 9). The phrase between angled brackets has been struck out, but it reveals that Hemingway equated the father's killing of the elephant with David's symbolic killing of Catherine through cessation of the honeymoon narrative.

A more directly lethal statement of David's intent has been excised at the point where Catherine announces that she will seek illustrators for the honeymoon narrative (GE, 188): there David thinks of the insanity of her arranging for illustrations in "something that no one knew the end of nor whether she would be alive or dead in it" (422.1–28, p. 56).

David's first perception of Catherine as ivory had occurred shortly before, during a quarrel about her access to his writing (GE, 156); but the manuscript reveals that Hemingway did not want the association of Catherine with ivory to occur until after the possibility of get. There the sentence that in the novel begins "Catherine came into the room" (GE, 168) continues, "wearing a white linen dress. Her hair was across her forehead and her cheeks were a different ivory than the dress" (422.1–23, p. 25). A margin note in Hemingway's hand has a line drawn to "ivory" and says, "fix color."

Also obscured by a manuscript deletion is the parallel David draws between his responsibility in the androgynous activities and his responsibility as a child for the slaying of the elephant. The elision occurs after Catherine has brought Marita home, but before David and she become lovers. He is contemplating the effect upon his writing of the *ménage à trois* that is imminent:

> It is going to be rough to do but so far they [the African stories] have gone well and you can thank Catherine and her disasters for them. . . . You can thank the other girl who loves you and handles you . . . or tries to when you don't impede her. You probably would have blown up with Catherine here alone. Don't go into that now. That is as useless to go into as to think what would have happened if you and Kibo had not learned to hunt at night with the full moon. How wrong that was to do. . . . What happened with Catherine goes in the [honeymoon] narrative. Don't confuse things. (422.1–23, pp. 10–11)

David last uses ivory in regard to Catherine after the final haircutting and bleaching episode on page 178, the point at which he "began to realize what a completely stupid thing he had permitted." In failing to observe his own imperative, "Don't confuse things" (which is itself untenable if his life and his art are not to be in conflict), David has permitted a trespass into the locked room of his writing. There the androgynous honeymoon narrative now threatens to mingle with the masculine African stories. Ivory next appears in the elephant tale when the child David thinks that if he and his dog had ivory, they would be killed too (GE, 197–98).

Because Catherine enters the writing through the honeymoon narrative on which she insists he work, she, like the old elephant, must be removed: and her annihilation, like the slaughter of the elephant, is rationalized after the fact as a defensive act – just as David's father rationalized the elephant's death by saying that he had killed many people (GE, 201). "I'm as old as my mother's old clothes," Catherine says (GE, 163): soon the elephant lies "in a wrinkled pile" (GE, 200); and David and Kibo are a hero and a hero's dog.[28]

David's guilt in the death of the elephant has textual echoes of Hemingway's abandonment of Hadley for Pauline – an action by which in later years he marked the end of his innocence as David's betrayal of the elephant marks his. Continuing the elephant tale the day following the lovemaking that may have resulted in get, David writes of the elephant's death: "He wished that he had never betrayed the elephant and remembered wishing that he had never seen him" (GE, 174). In *Feast*, on which Hemingway was working concurrently in 1957–59, he wrote of the remorse he felt upon returning to Hadley and their son at Schruns in 1926 after an interlude with Pauline in Paris that marked the beginning of the end of his first marriage: "I wished I had died before I loved anyone but her" (*Moveable Feast* [hereafter MF in citations], 139–40).

When David tells Catherine he has abandoned the honeymoon narrative, she cries, "That's dirty . . ." (GE, 188). Inherent in her protest are the resonances of the solitary vice that David's writing has become and the "dirty secret" David discovered about his father and Juma (the guide) when he and Kibo returned from tracking the elephant by moonlight (GE, 181). Referring to his father's native children, Catherine sees the dirty secret as the father's sexual usage of native women – analogous to David's relegating sex to sensation and making a masturbatory ritual of his writing. But David knows there are two dirty secrets: the *bibis* (married women) with whom he found his drunken father and Juma on returning from the moonlight hunt, and the skull of the elephant's *askari* (friend), whom Juma shot years ago (GE, 180). He links the orgiastic scene to his father's lust for ivory both when he tells his father, "Fuck elephant hunting," and when he imagines that Juma will probably sell his ivory and buy another wife, thereby equating the precious ivory with his treasure, which is worth symbolically killing Catherine to protect.[29]

Although David believes that his loneliness began with the death of the elephant and his resolution to never tell anyone anything again, this is demonstrably false. For some years before the elephant's death he had been lonely, a condition revealed by his asking his father how long the elephant has been alone since Juma killed his *askari*. Identifying with the elephant, David thinks: "He was alone but I had Kibo," and his father's obtusely indifferent response, "I haven't the faintest idea," establishes that David has been alone as long as he has been with his father. The dried blood that David scrapes from the severed tusk melts through his pocket, staining him with the knowledge of loneliness, but not causing it (GE, 201). When David admits that he cannot make the elephant alive again by writing of him, he instructs himself to "use the sorrow that you have now to make you know how the early sorrow came" (GE, 166). In the manuscript the "early sorrow" passage is followed by "You must show it as it came before you knew about it. You have no precedent to help you and you write about a country that has no literature where no one has written to guide you" (422.1–23, p. 9). In a stricken passage this country is identified as Africa by its topography, but *country* is clearly a metaphor, as the darkening of skin through tanning was earlier, for this is followed by:

> You must do it better than anyone ever can and never leave out anything because you are ashamed of it or because no one would ever understand. You must not let the things you must not say or write . . . because you will want to go back there affect you at all and you must not deny or forget all the tribal things . . . that are as important. . . . If you know them they will be there in the writing[.] You do not have to betray them.

"Tribal things" had long been Hemingway's term for taboos and for family matters. This is the country of childhood, and just how dangerous its terrain is becomes evident in a short time when David entertains the thought that he too could be killed – and by a parent (GE, 197–98). But it is a thought unbearable to him and he quickly denies it, substituting the elephant for himself: "Probably the elephant is going to find where he was born and they'll kill him there. That's all they need to make it perfect." But there has been no earlier mention of the elephant's birthplace, and Juma, the expert tracker, thinks he is going to the place of death – where his friend was killed years ago. That the birthplace is purely David's invention is significant, for at the place of birth there was a mother. In substituting the elephant for himself and equating the places of birth and death, David locates the point at which his childhood loneliness and adult affectlessness began.

The wounding loneliness David suffered, making the place of birth and death one, could have been the death of his mother or abandonment by her. In the novel (and in the manuscript) it seems to have been the latter. His mother turned him over to the father, who defrauded her and took him from Oklahoma (also the childhood home of Thomas Hudson and Roger Davis) to East Africa at an age so young and under circumstances so painful that he cannot or will not remember her. In the adventure story on which Hemingway drew for elements of the elephant tale and for much of David Bourne's war and flying background, the place to which the old bull elephant with the mythically huge tusks returns was the scene of its *mother's death* at the hands of hunters when it was a calf.[30]

In the story, the mythical Samburu elephant (who is also in the African book) is pursued now for his legendary tusks and lives on the fringes of the herd: he appears to the elephant hunter in a dream, just as the need to write this culminating African story had come to David in his dream. Like David, the elephant hunter of the source story is so awed by the animal's majesty that killing him is unthinkable. In substituting the old bull's *askari* for its mother, Hemingway has avoided writing of the death of the feminine, but has objectified its loss in David's dichotomized emotions. And in having David link the places of birth and death in his speculation about the elephant, Hemingway has revealed David's inchoate sense that the origin of his loneliness is connected with the absent and silenced bearer of mitigating feminine culture in his own life.

In a passage excised from *A Farewell to Arms,* Frederic Henry muses on the fact that the priest had always loved God and that Gino is a patriot because he was "born that way." He thinks to himself, "But if you were born loving nothing and the warm milk of your mother's breast was never heaven . . ." (*Farewell* manuscript, File 588; JFK). David Bourne's inability to feel – and the loneliness which is its product, a loneliness that overcomes him the moment he emerges from the locked room of his writing – is a near relative of Frederic Henry's malady. His rewriting the African stories rapidly and (to him) better than the originals that Catherine burned, and his greater appreciation of his father's complexity in the rewriting, are not a triumph over his writing block: they are a crystallization of his resistance to a feminine mode of experiencing, resistance that for a time the androgynous experiences threatened to dissolve. He has internalized a vision that can tolerate nothing which is not unalloyedly masculine, and once the catalytic power of androgyny has been spent in bringing into consciousness the experience of the

African stories, it is replaced by heterosexual novelty, "variety with-out perversion," with Marita, a subservient acolyte.[31]

David defends his father to Catherine, contending that he only defrauded himself; and he repeats his father's felony when he se-cures a wealthy and compliant young woman to replace the less wealthy and ambitious woman whose longing for achievement of her own is madness. Rewriting the elephant tale, David

> found he knew much more about his father than when he had first written this story and he knew he could measure his progress by the small things which made his father more tactile and to have more dimensions than he had in the story before. He was fortunate just now that his father was not a simple man. He wrote on a while longer now and there was no sign that any of it would ever cease returning to him intact. (GE, 247)

The rationalization that this passage inscribes is both a falsification of the experience David Bourne has had in the rewriting and a repudiation of the perceptions he had as a child in the elephant story.

Further, this passage that Tom Jenks chose for closure appro-priates an aesthetic assumption that was as deadly to Barbara Shel-don in the deleted mirroring plot as it was to Ernest Hemingway in life. It is the assumption that form is superior to and separable from the emotions which create it. Barbara is able to filter out "the picturesque for the geometry" in her painting. "It's [her painting] dry in the way that the snow is dry" (422.2–3, p. 11). The observa-tion is one of praise for the aesthetic power of her work. But Barbara immerses herself totally in the transformations, as David withdrew totally from the transformative activities into his writing. She be-comes unable to paint, destroys her personal relationships, and commits suicide.

David's fear of Catherine's intrusion into his writing (his get) and her burning of his African stories shifts his sympathy away from her, and her departure is a relief. His earlier identification of her with the beauty of ivory and with the victimized elephant changes as he rewrites the African stories. Shifting his sympathy to his dead father, David accepts the rationalization which his father gave, and which he rejected at eight – that the old elephant with the huge tusks had killed many people.

FATHERS AND SONS; WRITING AND KILLING

The implications of David's retreat from questioning the constraints of gender, culture, and family which he and Catherine were pursuing when the novel opened are far-reaching, because the father is both the mature Hemingway and his own father (a suicide in 1928, the year after this novel is set and the year that Hemingway was David Bourne's age), just as the child David is both the child Hemingway, who was taught to kill before he was four years old, and Hemingway's own three sons, whom he introduced to ritualized killing and hard drinking at an early age.[32]

David defrauds himself into believing that if he keeps his writing insulated from the feminine he can write well, truly, indefinitely. But earlier in the novel – in the middle of the second African story – he had evaluated the role of work in his life:

> You better get to work, he told himself. . . . You have to make sense there. You don't make sense in the other . . . [the androgynous *ménage*]. He had his father's ability to forget now and not dread anything that was coming. . . . His father, who ran his life more disastrously than any man that he had ever known, gave marvelous advice. . . . If you cannot respect the way you handle your life then certainly respect your trade. . . . He was not a tragic character, having his father and being a writer barred him from that. . . . He had lost the capacity of personal suffering or thought he had, and only could be hurt truly by what happened to others. He believed this, wrongly of course since *he did not know then* how one's capacities can change, nor how the other [having his father and being a writer] could change, and it was a comfortable belief. (my emphasis; GE, 146–49)

This is interior monologue: its interpolated commentary – "he did not know then" is a lamentation in other Hemingway works, a choric commentary on the inadequacy of knowledge at the time it is most needed.[33] It obviates reading the spurt of creative energy in which the African stories are rewritten as a triumph for either Hemingway or David Bourne. So also does our knowledge of the excised interior monologue cited earlier: "If you live by your senses you will die by them and if you live by your invention and your head you will die by that too." Even if it were not known how Hemingway died when he could use neither his senses nor his inventive powers, the web of images which harbingers self-violence in this novel can be traced.

With those images we can envision the relationship between the tragic character that Ernest Hemingway was and his creation of David Bourne in *Eden* as a persona with which to think of the problems that had dichotomized creativity and human relationships in his own life; for this novel goes beyond autobiography to become a text in which we watch the creative permutation of life into art.

On 30 November 1960 Hemingway entered St. Mary's Hospital in Rochester for medical and psychiatric treatment at the Mayo Clinic. On 4 December he wrote:

> To Whom it may concern:
>   My wife Mary at no time believed or considered that I had ever committed any illegal act of any kind. She had no guilty knowledge of any of my finances nor illegal acts and had only the sketchiest outline of my finances and only helped me in preparing my [tax] returns on material I furnished her. She was never an accomplice nor in any sense a fugitive and only followed the advice of a doctor friend that she trusted. (*Letters*, 909)

Although he left no note when he took his own life seven months later, at some time during the composition of *Eden* Hemingway had written for Barbara Sheldon the suicide note that could have been his own:

> Dear Andy
> Thank you very much. I know you'll write it well [Nick and Barbara's story] . . . I don't know how I was so stupid not to remember to do this before. . . . I know you will excuse it. People are so self-centered and it was kind of you to make me well so I could see what I should do. . . . This letter avoids any trouble. Nothing ever your fault. . . . I better put the date. I'm so much better really well now so I know this is intelligent and proper. I saved my legal sleep things for a month so it's truly legal. Nobody has to think about that. . . . Your friend, Barbara.

In the holograph Catherine's name is signed to this, her name has then been crossed out and Barbara's added in Hemingway's hand. A postscript adds:

> It's such a fine place really [Venice] I don't like for it to be associated with something that I undertook that turned out badly. But I must do it and not put it off in case I should get stupid again and forget. . . .

> Please Andy[,] I hate to stop talking with you but you understand
> how important it is to do a thing promptly when you must do it. . . .
> Your best friend Barbara. (422.1–7, pp. 49–50)

In this novel he could not finish, Hemingway had created a small
boy who, through his identification with the elephant, knew from
being too young how it would be to be too old (GE, 197): David's
shockingly self-referential response to watching the elephant's death
agony has been excised from the novel: "I hope that I can die as well
and as nobly as he did" (422.1–31, p. 1 and insert). And in the
African book, put aside in 1956 and still unpublished, Hemingway,
the aging writer, again watches the elephant and his *askari,* wonder-
ing why some elephants are loved long after they are impotent and
some are not. Like Barbara Sheldon, Hemingway would himself
come to know the indecisiveness of extreme depression and the
frustration of being thwarted at least three times in attempts to take
his life during the months just prior to 2 July 1961. The verbal
echoes of Barbara's letter exonerating Andy which occur in Hemingway's letter exonerating Mary and the poignant "I must do it and
not put it off" strongly suggest that Barbara's letter was a rehearsal
for the suicide note that Hemingway did not write on the day he
joined David Bourne's father and his own as a friend killer.

CHAPTER 5

The African book: an alternative life

In 1933–34 Hemingway and his second wife Pauline had taken the safari from which he crafted *The Green Hills of Africa,* a work of nonfiction that he hoped would "compete with a work of the imagi- nation." There had been much blood under the bridge by the time he set out in 1953 with his fourth wife Mary for the safari that produced the comic work of fictionalized fact that is the unpub- lished African book.[1] Pauline was two years dead, her death very probably brought on by a long-distance phone conflict with Hem- ingway. Third wife Martha had exited from his life in April 1944, leaving even her personal possessions behind; but Hemingway had spent a great deal of energy sustaining his bitterness in the years following their divorce by tracking her movements through Charles Scribner Sr. and reading her books. He lied to mutual acquain- tances about paying alimony to her and claimed a territorial viola- tion on learning that Martha and Pauline had discussed him when they met by chance in Venice, a town that he considered his own.[2]

Grace Hemingway had died four months before Pauline, and true to his belief that his mother "would be as dangerous dead as most women alive. I know I'd never go to her funeral without being afraid she was booby trapped," Hemingway had remained in Cuba when Grace was buried near her Oak Park home (EH-Buck Lanham, 30 June 1946; PUL). But now he was executor of both her estate and Pauline's, a responsibility that dredged up unwelcome memories and was complicated by the unreliability of mail in Cuba and the insouciance of the two sons with whom he shared ownership of the Key West house under the terms of Pauline's will.

Hemingway complained that he saw his oldest son, Jack, only when the latter needed a favor; he was estranged from his youngest

Figure 25. Gianfranco Ivancich, the brother of Adriana, became very dear to both Ernest and Mary Hemingway during the more than three years that he lived at the Finca Vigia (1949–52) and remained so until the end of both their lives. Shown here (with arm around Mary) at the Floridita Bar, Havana, 1951. From right: Hemingway, Taylor Williams, and Roberto Herrera (copyright Studio Paris).

son, Gregory; and only his middle son, Patrick, who had settled in Tanganyika in 1952 and was training as a safari hunter, pleased him. He now blamed Martha for his losing control of Patrick and Gregory when he left Pauline in 1939 to marry her; and he had never stopped blaming her for not giving him a daughter.

Adriana Ivancich, who from their first meeting Hemingway had invested with the status of muse, daughter, unobtainable love object, and soul mate, was in Venice now, her movements circumscribed, and her reputation protected by her family. The deep, strange merging of identities he had sought with Adriana for the past five years was the last and the most potent instance of his attempting to experience the feminine aspect of his own creative imagination through love for a woman. The power of this attraction was probably intensified by the fact that Adriana's nascent talent combined the poet and painter – and Hemingway longed to merge the two mediums (see James Brasch, "Christ, I Wish I Could Paint"). But on Adriana's side the attraction was both different in kind and alloyed by the financial advantages Hemingway could offer her and her family.[3]

Hemingway's very public and widely publicized attention to Adriana, who was eighteen when he met her in Italy in 1948, put a severe strain on his marriage of less than three years. In late 1949 he and Mary returned to Europe, and for the last two and a half months of their holiday he saw Adriana nearly every day. Before they left Venice for Paris (where Adriana was to study art), Hemingway invited Adriana and her mother to visit them in Cuba. A week later Charles Scribner Sr. arrived in Paris, met Adriana, and announced that he would use her design for the dust jacket of *Across the River and into the Trees.*

In his letters to Adriana, Hemingway often addressed her as "Adriana Hemingway", and signed himself "Ernest Ivancich." He had been experimenting with the sharing and/or exchange of identities in *The Garden of Eden* and in the fragments that connect *Eden* and *Islands in the Stream;* and in 1950 he had written the provisional ending to *Eden* discussed in Chapter 4, which leaves the twinned lovers deliberating a suicide pact. From the feeling of oneness that characterized his love for Adriana, Hemingway had conceived Renata, the young Italian woman, in *Across the River* (1950). The manuscript reveals just how consciously he saw the young woman to whom the bitter, dying Colonel Cantwell confesses as an avatar of his younger self, for on the early pages she is named "Nicola." He had created her as a female incarnation of Nick Adams, the closest approximation to Ernest Hemingway as a character in his own fiction until the four posthumous narratives. In the 1950s, watching a film made from a Nick Adams story, Hemingway claimed those stories were the best work he had ever done.[4] When he changed Nicola's name to Renata, Hemingway knew he was losing nothing of the resonance that he wanted to capture, for he also knew that "Renata" means "reborn."

Adriana and her mother – neither yet aware of rumors that the young woman in Hemingway's latest novel was Adriana – arrived in Cuba late in October 1950 and spent nearly two months at the Finca, followed by a month at a Havana hotel where Mrs. Ivancich

Figure 26. Hemingway and Mary with his sister, Ursula Hemingway Jepson, at the Finca Vigia, 1951. Ursula provided the creative basis for Littless, Nick Adams's younger sister in "The Last Good Country," which Hemingway began this year (John F. Kennedy Library).

moved them when the rumors reached her.[5] By the time Adriana left Cuba, although his marriage was in jeopardy, Hemingway had begun expanding and rewriting the "The Sea in Being" portion of the ur-text, which became *The Old Man and the Sea.*

In the years that followed he would tell Adriana repeatedly that her presence at the Finca had moved him to the creativity that produced Santiago – who is the least masculine, but the most human and serene of Hemingway's male protagonists.[6] In fact, if Santiago lived in Africa rather than Cuba, and were a Wakumba hunter rather than a Cuban fisherman, he would be a *mzee*, the status to which Hemingway aspires in the African book where he tells the reader that a *mzee* is both an elder who is still capable of deeds of prowess and an old man with mystical powers (African Manuscript [hereafter AM in citations], 513, 418).

In some mysterious way, and in the tradition of courtly love that Hemingway recognized as a literary model, the attraction to Adriana that was so destructive to his marriage allowed him to experience the androgynous balance in his creative imagination which produced *Old Man* out of the ur-text of "The Sea Book." A reviewer of the book for a major Italian newspaper grasped the essence of what happened between Hemingway and Adriana – and within Hemingway's creative imagination:

> The old man and the sea are the two terms emblematic of the history of the world: *man* who has lived long, learned much, but is substantially disarmed before the mystery if he attempts to dominate instead of worshipping it, asking to be received by it; and *nature*, which though ransacked through all its laws and forms, delivers itself only to those who make of it a path to that love from which springs everything which makes the life of creatures beautiful and precious.[7]

Old Man remains the most widely read of Hemingway's novels. Along with "El Torre Blanco," the imaginary writing partnership that he created between himself and Adriana, the novella was the offspring of their platonic relationship.

But despite the honors that *Old Man* brought Hemingway, the Pulitzer Prize in 1953, and – as he might have said – "It was a big draw for the Swedish thing too, but so were my obituaries," the Nobel Prize in 1954, he remained uneasy about it, telling his editor:

> [I am] not going to slant my stuff for those high school kids who read OMS out loud in class and write you identical, touching appreciations of it. [He then mentions plans to eventually publish] The idyllic book about the Sea [that became *Islands*] which we hope nobody will notice ends tragically. By that time maybe the younger readers of OMS will be grown up enough to read the next two. (EH-Wallace Meyer, 3 Nov. 1952; PUL)

The letter to Meyer was written only two months after *Old Man* was published and before he could have received many "identical, touching appreciations": the judgment must stand as Hemingway's own.

This then was the state of Hemingway's life; these were the visible manifestations of his writing anxiety when the second safari began like a homecoming on 27 August 1953.

Figure 27. Hemingway on his second safari watches the ceremony celebrating the slaying of a lion, fall 1953 (John F. Kennedy Library, courtesy *Look* and Earl Theisen).

RECOVERING A TEXT FOR THE AFRICAN BOOK

Although reading *The African Journal* excerpts of the African book in *Sports Illustrated* will reveal almost no evidence of the themes that connect it to the other posthumous works, the excerpts are some of the best prose in the unpublished book. And since they are all of it that the Hemingway *aficionado* has access to at the present, I recommend calling them up from the stacks of one's public library.[8]

Because only brief passages can be quoted, I intend here to proceed by summaries of the elements of the African book that relate it to the posthumous novels and establish it as Hemingway's portrait of the artist as a man who finds himself, in late middleage, trapped in the public image he once cultivated. I will not attempt to crosscut my discussion with references to the published portions because the deletions made for serial publication obscure thematic continuity. But I will occasionally refer the reader to a particularly useful treatment of some event of the safari in another work. Per-

Figure 28. Hemingway had an intense interest in elephants and refused to hunt them. Here he observes their movements during the second safari (John F. Kennedy Library, courtesy *Look* and Earl Theisen).

haps reader response to this book will revive the interest of the Hemingway estate in publishing the entire African manuscript, for it reveals Ernest Hemingway at his most human, writing of himself with sustained comic irony we have never been allowed to see. In January 1955 he writes to Adriana that he works on the African book "for enjoyment and to keep from going crazy with pain" (HRC).

Philip Percival, one of the greatest white hunters of the century, Hemingway's guide on the first safari (and Theodore Roosevelt's in 1913), came out of retirement to guide the Hemingways, and met them in Mombasa. After four days of camping at the comfortable site on Percival's Kitanga Farm, their safari supplies were ready, and Earl Theisen, a photographer from *Look* had joined them. The advance on a contract with *Look* covered expenses that for the 1933 safari had been paid by Pauline's uncle, Gus Pfeiffer. Both Mary and Theisen took photos: his would appear with the story in *Look*; and later he gave Mary and Hemingway permission to use them for a book of photos which was never completed.[9]

As the hunting began, the Hemingways and Mayito Mencal (a Cuban friend who had planned to join them) encountered Denis Zaphiro, a young, conservation-minded ranger with the Kenya Game Department who had just secured permission to open the Southern Game Reserve to hunters. Zaphiro welcomed Hemingway with the blessing of the Game Department in Nairobi, for they hoped that good publicity would encourage the safari tours (both shooting and camera) that Kenya needed, and would overshadow the horror stories of Mau Mau atrocities that appeared regularly in newspapers and magazines around the world. Hemingway's name on the cover of a popular magazine had enormous power to draw serious, mon-eyed readers eager to follow in his footsteps.[10]

In January 1954, after four months of a safari during which Hemingway often behaved more like an unruly adolescent than the *mzee* he claimed to be, Zaphiro arranged to have him appointed an honorary game warden for the Kimana Swamp region. The life in Cuba that had seemed so edenic in 1939 was deteriorating in political strife, and with Patrick in Africa Hemingway was thinking of settling there.[11] During the safari, he shaved his head, painted himself and sometimes went native in dress; and he took young Wakumba women to his tent. The complex relationship of these often foolish activities to his desire to belong in Africa has gone unrecognized by biographers. Zaphiro had argued to the Kenya Game Department for Hemingway's appointment believing that the post of honorary warden would give Hemingway direct involvement in the wildlife of Africa. It did, and he carried out his responsibility with a *joie de vivre* and pride that were evident years later.[12] When he began the African book in July 1954, Hemingway would use the experience as a way of exploring alternatives to the life in which he was judged, and could judge himself, only as a writer.

The safari was to end with a sight-seeing flight over the Belgian Congo, but ended instead with two plane crashes. The first, at Murchison Falls on 23 January, was not serious; but when the plane that was to take the Hemingways from Butiaba to Entebbe the following day crashed and burned on takeoff, Hemingway suffered injuries that can be seen in retrospect as the beginning of his decline – and the end of his dream of living in Africa.[13]

The narrator/protagonist of the unfinished African book is Ernest Hemingway the writer at fifty-five; but he is Hemingway *before*

Figure 29. Denis Zaphiro, Hemingway's guide, noted that during the 1953 safari Hemingway wanted to watch the animals but was uninterested in hunting them. Shown here with his Wakumba guide and a wild buffalo (John F. Kennedy Library).

the plane crashes. In assessing the tall-tale and wish-fulfillment characteristics of the African manuscript, as well as Hemingway's deep attachment to it, and the dead end he reached, the reader must keep in mind the physical effects of the plane crashes. The writer who stands outside the text is now, more than ever before, a prisoner of the public image he tried to live up to; but he has never been (and will never be) free of the injuries suffered in 1954.

Ray Cave's introduction to *The African Journal* excerpts in *Sports Illustrated* lists five themes in the full manuscript: (1) nature, hunt-

ing, and the hunter; (2) the Mau Mau wars; (3) religion; (4) the
graces and pleasures of age and power; and (5) the Africanization
of Hemingway. Cave says candidly that the excerpts deal primarily
with the first two themes. What he does not reveal is that the other
themes are inseparable, and that they are the objectification of
Hemingway's concern with the circumstances of his personal life
and his status as writer.

   This unfinished work of more than 800 pages, which occupied
Hemingway for two years after the safari, sets into stark and often
comic relief those concerns that are more deeply buried in *Eden* and
Islands. They are the same anxieties that will be not only buried, but
denied, in *A Moveable Feast* – the book that grew out of the impasse
he reached with the African manuscript. Hemingway was usually
reticent about what he was writing: even with Charles Scribner Jr.,
his editors, and close friends such as Buck Lanham he would claim
that in talking about his writing, he lost the creative edge. But
during the more than two years that the African book was in progress he developed a rare confiding relationship with Robert Morgan
Brown, a faculty member at Fordham University who wanted to write
a doctoral dissertation on the religious structure of Hemingway's
fiction. Since Hemingway's letters are often the best means of dating
the composition of the posthumous works, those to Brown prove
invaluable. An early letter in the correspondence also gives a
glimpse of the pleasure the African book was for Hemingway:

> I don't think it [the African book] would ever be acceptable at
> Fordham and I think maybe it would be better to wait until I'm dead
> to publish it. But it is an awfully good story and I was born to write
> stories not to please the authorities. The story is so rough and I am
> trying to write it so delicately that it is quite difficult. Miss Mary wants
> me to write it because she thinks it is a lovely and wonderful story.
> But I swear it will never be serialized in the Sunday Visitor [a Catholic
> newspaper]. (14 Sept. 1954; HRC)

   After Hemingway's Nobel Prize honor was announced on 28
October 1954, his work on the African book was disrupted by publicity interviews and the stream of sightseers who congregated outside
the Finca Vigia to "see the old elephant in the zoo" (EH-Buck
Lanham, 10 Nov. 1954). In 1955 and 1956 the interruptions continued. The emotional investment and the progenitor-like attachment
Hemingway had with the African book permeated his lament to his

editor Wallace Meyer as he put the manuscript aside for the second time in order to participate in the filming of *Old Man:*

> I have wrapped the mss. and my writing board up together and sealed them with cellophane and will try to live through the next three months without killing anyone including myself. I don't know whether a man can die from being separated from his own true work but I think it is possible. Since I started in July of '54 on this have completed 856 pages. (10 Feb. 1956; PUL)

When the African manuscript opens, the narrator, who will soon be identified as Ernest Hemingway, describes an old Wakamba man assisting his master, a white hunter, as he bathes in a canvas tub. The narrator says of the man, Wilson Harris (addressed as "Pop," and in life Philip Percival): "The white hunter had been a close friend of mine for many years. I respected him as I had never respected my father and he trusted me which was more than I deserved."[14] The older man is turning over the safari, now encamped in the Kimana Swamp Region of southern Kenya, to Hemingway, who has "recently read with distaste various books written about myself by people who knew all about my inner life, aims and motives."[15] Thus, the theme of the writer's sensitivity to the assumptions of readers and critics enters the narrative matrix early. In the middle of the narrative, a book by Leicester Hemingway arrives. After some ironic commentary on his brother's bravery, Hemingway borrows Mary's typewriter to write a response to the critics who reviewed it badly. However, his tirade is not a catharsis; he simply loses all desire to write and decides that he "would exchange the chances of attaining literary immortality for a few words with my fiancée at the *shamba* and the possibility of doing away with half a troop of baboons" (AM, 411).

As Harris instructs him on the responsibilities he will face as game warden, Hemingway thinks how difficult it is for the experience of males to be passed on because of the inadequacy of male language, especially in peacetime.[16] He wishes that Pop did not have to communicate with him in

> that odd short-hand of understatement which was our legal tongue. There were things I wished that I could ask him that it was impossible to ask. I wished more than anything that I could be instructed fully and competently as the British instruct their Air men.[17]

One of the problems the game warden regularly faces is that elephants damage the native *shambas* (settlements with land cultivated for food crops) and must be killed or driven off into unsettled areas. Pop and Hemingway discuss an old bull elephant and his *askari* (friend or male comrade) that are likely to appear. This is the elephant who, in the elephant story that is part of *Eden,* signified the powerlessness of the writer as a small boy. By the end of the African manuscript the elephant signifies the burden his reputation has become to the aging, unproductive writer.

Hemingway's first safari had produced not only *Green Hills,* but two of his finest short stories: "The Snows of Kilimanjaro" and "The Short Happy Life of Francis Macomber." If one is the same person at fifty-five as he was at thirty-five, he has probably wasted twenty years, and Hemingway was often a time waster. In one sense he had come a long way in the two decades between the safaris; but in another he had not grown at all. "The Snows of Kilimanjaro" (which Darryl Zanuck had made into such a dreadful film that Hemingway ever after referred to it as *The Snows of Zanuck*) is about an unproductive writer, dying of gangrene on safari, and blaming the softening effect of his wife's money for his failure to write the stories that he now writes in his mind as he waits for the plane that will take him to Nairobi. The African book is also about a writer searching his personal history for the events that have thwarted his creative imagination. Hemingway's advance is that he no longer blames a woman. Instead, he scrutinizes his midwestern childhood and muses on the fact that what were treated as absolutes then and there are not absolutes now and in this place where he yearns to belong. What was unthinkable in his culture is (or was) natural in Africa: animism, polygamy – even cannibalism. Forgetting what he had so confidently pronounced to Scott Fitzgerald in 1934, "If you take real people and write about them you cannot give them other parents than they have (they are made by their parents and what happens to them) you cannot make them do anything they would not do" (*Letters,* 407), Hemingway wonders how it is that one generation and one culture can proscribe the practices that are accepted without question in another.

But in the matter of male-female relationships, Hemingway has not moved beyond his other great safari story. "The Short Happy Life of Francis Macomber" sets in opposition the hunter/warrior virtues and domestic harmony. The white hunter in the Macomber story, who shares half a name with Wilson Harris in the African book, assumes every woman is a predator – ready to bed with him and willing to put her husband (and him) out of business. Although the authorial voice shrives Margo Macomber by saying, "She shot at the buffalo," it does not allow the reader to see her intentions in firing the shot that kills her husband. On the surface of the African book, the tension between male and female that fuels self-destruction or (perhaps) murderous hostility in "Snows" and "Macomber" is handled with mild ridicule of Miss Mary; but the dichotomy of hunterly and husbandly virtues remains very much present as Hemingway begins his game warden tour hoping to do something spectacular and "thus become beloved as a hunter by my lawful wedded wife" (*African Journal* [hereafter AJ in citations], 1).

There are also some significant patterns of association where more long-standing anger at past wives shows through the veneer of Hemingway's detachment from the world outside Africa. In one he sits by the fire drinking whisky, which makes him feel that he is almost at home in Africa. His boots, he thinks, are most certainly at home – for they are made of ostrich hide. But he then begins to remember who chose the leather (Martha) and where they were made (Hong Kong, on their honeymoon trip). A riff of anger at "true bitches" and "bitches [that] only hunted men" follows.

In an image configuration that works by association, Hemingway thinks of the anger of his wives, first of Miss Mary's, then of Mary's accusing him of "atrocities against a former wife" (Pauline, with whom she had become close friends). These atrocities "did not fade nor pale as the atrocities of the first war did . . . they were as fresh as the first launching of the bayoneted Belgian babies" (AJ: 2). And so here the two wives who were Hemingway's best caretakers, but who could not produce the daughter he wanted, are juxtaposed with an old propaganda image of dead infants that works in unexpected ways, enabling the reader who knows Hemingway's personal history to feel a knowledge he cannot think. His continuing search for an offspring will become a major concern that, near the end of the manuscript, is inseparable from his identification as a writer.

The weakest part of the African book is Hemingway's attempt to construct a religious mythology that resembles nothing so much as the hilarious, irreverent South African film *The Gods Must Be Crazy*.[18]

Reading the randy nuttiness of the way the writer will rid himself of the barren white wife who says he might win the Nobel Prize if he wrote more, and take as a new wife the fruitful Wakumba girl who doesn't know what is a writer, one understands why Hemingway became so fond of the book. Often the flashes of comedy have all the kinetic energy of a Faulkner story like "Was."

He takes over as game warden on the "last day of the next to the last month of the year," a torturous way of saying, "November 30th" but a locution that also suggests the burlesque of a myth to follow. The myth is soon reported by the Informer, a weasely character descended from Garrick in *Green Hills*. His story, which has wide credence, is that

> the Bwana occupies a position in America similar to that of the Aga Khan in the Muslim world. He is here in Africa to fulfill a series of vows he and Memsahib Lady Mary have made. One of these vows deals with the need for the Memsahib Lady Miss Mary to shoot a certain cattle killing lion before the birthday of the Baby Jesus. It is known and believed that a great part of the success of all things known depend on this. I have informed certain circles that after this vow has been performed the Bwana and I will make the visit to Mecca in one of his aircraft. It is rumored that a young Hindu girl is dying for the love of Bwana Game.

Here the young game ranger, G.C. (Denis Zaphiro, nick-named "G.C." for gin-crazed), tries to stop the Informer's disclosures, but he continues:

> It is rumored too that if the Honorable lady Miss Mary does not kill the marauding lion before the birthday of the Baby Jesus the Memsahib will commit suttee. Permission, it is said[,] has been obtained for this from the British Raj and special trees have been marked and cut for her funeral pyre [the trees Mary was considering for their Christmas tree]. These trees are those from which the Masai make the medicine which both of you Bwanas know [a ginlike intoxicant]. It is said that in the event of this suttee, to which all tribes have been invited, there will be a giant N'goma [festival with much dancing] lasting a week after which Bwana Mzee will take a Wakumba wife. The girl has been chosen. (AM, 135)

In the buffoonery that follows the Informer's departure, G.C. comments that this expectation "puts a little heat on Miss Mary."

Hemingway concedes that suttee always does. The rumors spur Miss Mary's lion hunt, but the details the Informer reports have other resonances too: they put the responsibility for losing her husband (and her life) directly on Miss Mary, as Hemingway had blamed Hadley when he left her for Pauline, and Pauline when he left her for Martha. But now the wife possesses the only typewriter.

The Wakumba "fiancée" is Debba, who receives little attention in the *African Journal* excerpts, but whose portrait appears there. Drawn from photographs taken by either Mary or Hemingway, the artist's rendering of her reveals a masculine-looking, sturdy young woman – short of hair and square of face. Hemingway's intention for Debba, and the therapeutic role she was playing in his escapist fantasy, are laid out in one of his confiding letters to Robert Morgan Brown, written just a few weeks before he put the manuscript away for the last time:

> And there [in Africa] you do not have to be a literary character nor Robert Graves the Graves Robber. And I can pray to the Mountain, we have an illegal *shamba* at its foot, and to the trees, the special trees, and keep the customs and the laws and break them as the young men do and pay fines and Miss Mary who can't have children can have Debba to help her as a second wife. Debba can have children and they can be doctors, soldiers or lawyers as they decide. This all was cleared with elders. N'gui who is my blood brother . . . has probably had to marry Debba since I could not return in time. [In his cups Hemingway claimed he had impregnated a young Wakumba woman. Denis Zaphiro said this was nonsense.][19] If he wants to keep her as a wife or not share her that is o.k. (and you think you have trouble with canon law. Imagine Carlos [Baker] with this. Shades of Wordsworth and a field of waving daffodils). I am legally (Kamba law) the protector of a widow [Debba's guardian, and the Informer's consort]. Since neither N'gui, Debba or the widow can read or write[,] communication is difficult.[20]

Debba functions not only as the young, fertile woman who will replace the barren wife, but as a device for evoking memories of the narrator's early food preferences that foreshadowed his mature affinity for African life: he loved milk, game, fish, and wild berries, would eat no vegetables except corn roasted in the ashes of an open fire, and he rolled fish in corn meal before frying them. Now he reflects that corn meal is the posha of Africa, and Debba brings him a gift of mealies (corn).

Debba is protected by tribal law that forbids him to make love to her, and returning from an unsatisfactory visit to the *shamba* where she lives with the widow, Hemingway and N'Gui fantasize taking over the *shamba* "where the men are worthless and the women are beautiful." With self-mockery rare in Hemingway, he says, "N'Gui and I were engaged in that characteristic occupation of men; planning the operation which will never take place."

Since Miss Mary has killed her lion, she is not going to be a good sport and go up in smoke; but once she is safely removed to Nairobi, Hemingway and Debba evade the chaperoning of the widow, defy the Elders, and make love. Later, with the widow and Debba back at the *shamba,* Hemingway thinks of the strangeness of moral strictures in different countries and of who has the power to make an act a sin. The child that he is confident has been conceived will have choices not mandated by a culture of absolutes: if it is a daughter, she can come to Cuba and live with him; or he will give her a dowry and she can marry a warrior. If it is a son, he also can come to Cuba, where he can be any number of things, among them a doctor or a lawyer. Being a writer and public figure is never mentioned. Then, as if to remind himself of what he liked to call his metier, Hemingway recalls how lowering courtships and threatened misalliances are handled in the novels of Henry James and John O'Hara. He decides to give a gift of beer to the protector of Debba's guardian, calculating that would be the equivalent of a Cadillac in an O'Hara novel.

Between Debba and the narrator there is a ritual action and refrain: at every opportunity Debba presses "the carved leather pistol holster hard against her thigh and then places her left hand where she wanted it to be." Neither subtle nor very effective, Debba's gesture is both a sexual invitation and an expression of the narrator's wish that the gap between them could be bridged by a kind of symbolic imprinting that requires no reading on her part, and no writing on his. But Hemingway knows that living without the mediation of the intellect and out of the matrix of a culture is impossible, and to this and other insurmountable obstacles, he comments, "No hay remedio" (There is nothing to be done about it).[21] After Debba has returned to the *shamba,* he (like Thomas Hudson) lies in bed with the pistol in the leather holster between his legs, and dreams of "the wife I loved first and best and who was the mother of my oldest son."

Earlier Hemingway flew with Willie, the pilot who had come to take Miss Mary to Nairobi, in order to survey the movement of elephants who have been damaging the *shamba*. The old bull elephant and his *askari* that Wilson Harris (an authentic *mzee*, it now seems) had told him to expect are on the fringes of the herd; and he notes that the right tusk of the big elephant drags on the ground when he is tired. The elephant is a bridge between the older writer of the African book and his younger counterpart in *Eden*. The elephant story that is part of *Eden* was written shortly after Hemingway returned from Africa and was incorporated into the novel during the big rewriting drive of 1958 when he worked alternately on *Eden* and *Feast*. In *Eden,* the small boy realizes that "his own tiredness . . . had brought an understanding of age. Through being too young, he had learned how it must be to be too old" (GE, 197).

When the old elephant appears in the African manuscript, his condition has become a metaphor for the heavy and destabilizing burden that the expectations of the writer's public are creating for the prematurely aging Hemingway. It is a burden as inescapable, but as essential, to the writer as tusks are to the elephant; and Hemingway knew that *mzee nodofu* means "old elephant."[22] Lying in bed alone after Mary has gone to Nairobi, taking with her the only typewriter, he muses:

> In the night I thought about the elephant . . . and about the long time he had lived with so many people against him and seeking to kill him for his two wonderful teeth that were now only a great disadvantage to him and a deadly load for him to carry. . . . I knew finally in the night . . . the slow[,] terrible effort the elephant made to lift them high . . . I wondered, in the sharp coldness of the night[,] listening to the talking of the animals, how great a trouble the huge weight of his tusks were to him and whether he was impotent and what sort of comradeship he had with his askari. I knew that old bulls were driven out of the herds long before they were impotent but I did not know why some were still loved after they had gone by themselves and why others were not. (AM, 442)

With Hemingway-the-character alone in his tent, his pistol between his legs and dreaming of his first wife, Hemingway-the-author does not seem to know how to end this book in which he has written so lightly of matters that weighed so heavily. Instead of creating an ending, he arrived at another beginning as dreams of Hadley lead to memories of the days in Paris – of cafés where one could work undisturbed; of Ezra Pound playing tennis in white flannels; of Ford Madox Ford as a monumental liar; and of an imperfectly remembered line from Scott Fitzgerald's *The Crack Up:* "In a real dark night of the soul it is always three o'clock in the morning, day after day." The Paris book that became *A Moveable Feast* begins to take its form here.

Buoyed by the sustained comic tone so foreign to him, and dis-tanced by the fantasy of it all, Hemingway wrote openly of the lasting anxieties affecting his writing that are rendered only symbolically in the other posthumous works: the inescapable power of childhood, his dependence on and conflict with women, and his writing as his offspring. But here there is a twist – he is indifferent to Mary's taking the typewriter to Nairobi and has happily traded it for the opportunity her absence gives him to beget a living child. Fantasiz-ing about taking over the *shamba* where Debba lives, the place of worthless men and beautiful women, Hemingway had recognized earlier that he and N'Gui were engaged in "that characteristic occu-pation of men; planning the operation which will never take place." But in the African book he had considered for the first time drop-ping out of the world of writers – an alternative life that must have been both tempting and frightening. That escape is the true subject of this text. Although the writer hunts game and protects a *shamba* against the Mau Mau in good Tom Sawyerly fashion, he is seeking – if only in comic fantasy – a culture and a woman that harbor no expectations of writers because they do not know writers exist.

In addition to not knowing how to end the African book, Hem-ingway may have been unable to imagine that after the critical reception given to *The Torrents of Spring* (1926) he could be sympa-thetically reviewed as a comic writer, and he was probably right. In the manuscript, his discussion with Mary of the fiction writer as liar has an eighteenth century ring as he compares the efforts of *his* critics to prove him false to the wrong-headedness of calling *Robinson Crusoe* a bad book because Defoe was not on Crusoe's island. But even the seriousness of this theoretical dialogue is touched with levity as Hemingway launches into an appreciation of the dark blood

mysteries in D. H. Lawrence's fiction, and an allegedly unlettered
Mary directs him to the *shamba* of his Wakumba girl.[23]

When Hemingway left Cuba early in August 1956 his destination
was Africa: he had with him a list of details to be checked for the
African book – from the names of a bookstore and streets in Nairobi
to the way that branches grow on a certain tree. And he was also
searching for a place to resettle. But practical considerations inter-
vened: Egypt closed the Suez Canal; Hemingway's health, which had
been problematic since the plane crashes, deteriorated; and medical
advice he received in Spain became unignorable when the itinerary
that was to take him through the Suez Canal to Mombasa became
instead a more arduous trip around the Cape of Good Hope.

In returning to Africa, Hemingway hoped to rescue himself from
the impasses he had reached earlier with the manuscripts that became *Islands* and *Eden*. The need to go back to Africa in 1956 was
the pursuit of a rainbow he would repeat with more lethal results
when he returned to Spain in 1960 in an attempt to complete *The
Dangerous Summer*. It is now clear Hemingway hoped that if he got
the country in Africa right, the aging writer who dwelt in and
created it would again triumph. But the changed travel conditions
combined with his health problems to send him back to Paris, where
he stayed at the Ritz Hotel from mid-November 1956 to late January
1957.

THE BIRTH OF THE PARIS BOOK

Ill and in a state of mind that made any artifact from his earlier
years in Paris precious evidence of a time in his own creative past
that he now needed desperately as a counterbalance to his yearning
for escape from the burden that his role as a writer had become,
Hemingway recovered manuscripts from the 1920s – perhaps *at* the
Ritz Hotel, but most certainly in Paris.[24] His account of the found
manuscripts lists three complete holographs, "Fifty Grand," "The
Undefeated," and "Big Two-Hearted River," the latter "in the copybooks I used to write it in the café." The first of these was intimately
connected with memories of Scott Fitzgerald, whose presence in the
Paris book constitutes nearly one-third of the work (and on whom
Hemingway wrote an additional unpublished chapter). Whatever

else the Ritz Hotel trunks contained, they connected with Hemingway's memories of Paris near the point where he had suspended
work on the African book.

The complete holograph manuscripts were probably sold for
Hemingway by Lee Samuels, the friend he had informed of the find;
but the four-page fragment of "Fifty Grand" now at the Kennedy
Library (File 388) shows how the African-Paris connection was
made. A portion of the first page has been torn off, but is in the file,
and Hemingway has written on it: "lst 3 pages of story mutilated by
Scott Fitzgerald with his [illegible]." On the margin of page 2,
Fitzgerald has written, "D[?] yourself." Hemingway's self-described
"rat trap memory" would have quickly returned to the conflict and/
or horseplay with Fitzgerald which resulted in the mutilated fragment of "Fifty Grand" that is now at the Kennedy Library. In their
connection, the Paris manuscripts evoked a *belle époque* he had
known, and confirmed for him that there had been a time when,
despite personal problems and depression, his ability as a writer had
seemed infinite.

Five months earlier in Cuba, the middle-aged, rapidly aging writer
had been trying to finish a book inscribing a life in which he could
be something other than a writer.[25] In Paris, in the winter of 1956–
57, he found a temporary reprieve that allowed him to continue
writing. Hemingway began the Paris book early in 1957 and for
nearly four years was able to imagine that he was a *mzee* rather than
a prisoner of the myth he helped to create. I can find no evidence
that he ever worked on the African book again.

CHAPTER 6

A *Moveable Feast:* all remembrance of things past is fiction

The physical and emotional state in which Hemingway returned to Paris from Spain in November 1956 after his trip to Africa had been cancelled combined with the evocative power of the manuscripts he recovered in Paris to create exactly the conditions under which he could comfortably turn to the memoirs he had once claimed were the last resort of a former writer – but had often threatened to write. A quarter of a century before he deposited the manuscript of the Paris book with Scribner's for its first reading, Hemingway had written in the *Transatlantic Review,* "It is only when you can no longer believe in your own exploits that you write your memoirs." But over the years he had related many of the incidents that he would incorporate into his final work, sometimes accompanying the anecdotes with the promise or threat that they would appear in his memoirs.

THREATS AND PROMISES OF A RAT TRAP MEMORY

In 1933, when Gertrude Stein's the *Autobiography of Alice B. Toklas* was being serialized in *Atlantic,* Hemingway had written Max Perkins, "I'm going to write damned good memoirs when I write them because I'm jealous of no one, have a rat trap memory and the documents" (*Letters,* 395–96). He also had that ability to hold a grudge forever which informs so many lively memoirs.

In 1949, when Hemingway was inscribing his attraction to Adriana Ivancich in the manuscript of *Across the River and into the Trees,* several things happened that again brought the matter of writing memoirs to the fore and he proposed to begin them. Alice B. Toklas and Gertrude Stein were the godmothers of Hemingway's oldest son. Stein died in 1946, but when Jack (Bumby) was married on 25 June 1949 in Paris, Toklas was present. In August, Hemingway agreed to the publication of his letters to Stein as long as he could reserve the copyright.[1]

A few weeks earlier he had written Charles Scribner a scandalous anecdote about Sinclair Lewis (part of which is used in *Across the River*), concluding his letter with a reference to the things he would write if he weren't so inhibited, and "Now I know the copywrite remains with me am liable to write you god-damn near anything. And I don't even have to count the words" (*Letters*, 661).

On 28 July 1949, Hemingway asks Scribner to buy a "talk machine" for him, and he will write all kinds of memoirs which Scribner can "hold till the womens are dead." Scribner must then have suggested that Hemingway write of his early years; for on 3 August he told Scribner that he could not write of Oak Park while his mother and his Uncle George are alive. On 16 August, he recounted to Scribner the Fitzgerald anecdote that would be featured in the "A Matter of Measurements" chapter of *A Moveable Feast*.

Just before his next letter to Scribner (on 25–26 August) the tape recorder had arrived, and Hemingway wrote, "Have some lovely topics to speak into the talking machine. How do you like *The Things That I Know* [emphasis added] as a title? Have always been able to get a better title than I started out with; so don't worry. It will only be what I know and say in extremis . . ." (*Letters*, 667). The title he suggests is very close to one Hemingway lists and rejects in April 1961 as he does his last work on the Paris book.

By spring 1957, the work that became *A Moveable Feast* was definitely under way as a collection of Paris sketches which raised questions even before the publication of the book in April 1964:[2] (1) When was it written? Had it really begun as Leonard Lyons and, later, Mary Hemingway claimed – in papers from the late 1920s that Hemingway recovered at the Ritz Hotel in 1957? (2) Had Hemingway intended it as fiction or memoir? (3) How much was Hemingway's work, how much was Mary's? If Mary *had* completed it, to what extent had her editing changed or obscured his intentions?[3] The

third question is particularly relevant because the Paris book had
been on Scribner's forthcoming list in 1960 and 1961, but Mary did
not submit the final manuscript until 27 July 1963. Her letter of
transmittal to Harry Brague, Hemingway's last editor at Scribner's,
was found at Princeton in September 1992:

> Here is the Paris book as revised by Papa from the first draft he left
> with you and *lightly, slightly, edited by me* [my emphasis]. This is the
> only corrected copy. He had titled some chapters and I have tenta-
> tively titled the rest.
>
> The preface I made up from notes he left about the book, notes
> which you are welcome to look through, if you would like to verify my
> impression of his original intentions for the preface.
>
> The small note I've written about the book you may or may not
> wish to publish. . . . If you think this draft is an improvement over the
> original, I'd love to hear.
>
> Bests – Mary

Long-standing skepticism among Hemingway scholars that *Feast*
could have had its genesis in his retrieval of old manuscripts in Paris
has found its strongest support in the fact that Hemingway himself
had apparently never recounted finding the manuscripts to anyone
except, allegedly, Leonard Lyons.[4] Although I can now lay to rest
that objection, I do so without offering a definitive answer to the
vexed question of what – if anything – the Ritz Hotel papers contributed to the text of Hemingway's last work. Because I know that from
as early as 1933 Hemingway had intended to write his memoirs, and
had related a number of the incidents that are central to *Feast* in his
letters, and that his state of mind when he ceased working on the
African book and then recovered papers from the 1920s in Paris
made the memoirs a salvational venture, my sense is that what have
become known as "the Ritz Hotel Papers" were evocative rather than
substantive in his creation of the text of *Feast*. Moreover, it is now
clear that the memories of Scott Fitzgerald which were stirred by the
Ritz papers were catalytic, for Fitzgerald, who was as flamboyantly
self-destructive as Hemingway and had died in 1940 at forty-four,
had long been Hemingway's Dorian Gray.[5]

At this distance of years it is unlikely that we will ever know all of
the papers that Hemingway retrieved in Paris; however, the partial
list Hemingway gives in his letter of 19 January 1957 to Lee Samuels

suggests the course that his "rat trap" memory followed.[6] Written on the pale blue letterhead of the Ritz Hotel it reads:

> I found stuff here that has been in storage for 30 years. Good stuff for you and Mss. of The Undefeated, Fifty Grand, most of In Our Time and Men Without Women all holograph and Big Two Hearted River in the copybooks I used to write it in the café. Plenty stuff to make the trip worthwhile. Bough[t] some good Vuitton bags and packed the stuff all day yest. . . . Some is pretty exciting to see again.

Samuels was an important figure in Hemingway's business life, and a declaration made to him of found manuscripts was likely to be the beginning of a contractual commitment. He came from a Havana tobacco family, and was Hemingway's sometime banker, as well as a book collector and the compiler of a Hemingway bibliography.[7] It was Samuels who arranged the microfilming of manuscripts that Hemingway put in the bank vaults in Havana in the 1950s; and during the late 1950s he was the courier for manuscripts that Hemingway was removing from Cuba.

After Castro came to power, foreign currency regulations were imposed and American funds were frozen in Cuba. It was Samuels who devised a scheme whereby the Hemingways (in Idaho) purchased Canadian dollars for paying their Cuban obligations, which included rental on two bank storage facilities where manuscripts remained in 1961 (Samuels-E. and M. Hemingway, 3 Mar. 1961; JFK). Samuels also bought and sold Hemingway first editions and manuscripts, and he arranged the insurance that Hemingway carried on his literary assets, personal property, and real estate.

Jacqueline Tavernier-Courbin, whose careful scholarship on the manuscripts of *Feast* is indispensable to discussing its genesis, dismissed the rumors of recovered manuscripts as Hemingway's beginning a myth that would allow him to write the memoirs he had said he would do only when he could write nothing else. However, Hemingway's letter to Samuels commits him to following through, for Samuels would be involved in the disposal of the manuscripts he reports finding.[8]

The letter to Samuels is also noteworthy for what it does not say: Hemingway's list makes no mention of the manuscript of *A Farewell to Arms*, which Leonard Lyons had reported in 1957 as part of the

Ritz Hotel papers, and which Samuels (and Hemingway scholars) knew Hemingway had given to Gus Pfeiffer (Pauline's uncle) in 1930. One can't know what Hemingway *did* say to Lyons, but they were old acquaintances and often communicated in settings where a great deal of drinking was the main event. Neither does Hemingway suggest that he has found material he intends to use in a memoir of the Paris years; or that what he found was *at the Ritz* – only "I found stuff here," which may well mean *in Paris,* since when Hemingway married Pauline in May 1927, his papers were scattered among three apartments.[9]

There is some redundancy in Hemingway's list, because "Big Two-Hearted River" and "The Undefeated" were published in *In Our Time,* while "Fifty Grand" was the lead story in *Men Without Women.* However, he seems to be saying that he has found full holographs of the three short stories. Holdings at the Kennedy Library do not include full holographs of any of the three, and only two of the three short story holograph manuscripts that Hemingway mentions have formats similar to items now in the Kennedy Library: one of these is the four-page typescript of "Fifty Grand" with holograph corrections discussed in Chapter 5 (File 388, JFK; Young and Mann, *Hemingway Manuscripts,* no. 38).[10] What Hemingway had laid hold of in the Ritz papers included the full holograph of this story. We know that he had also been writing of Fitzgerald in the African book. Since the first-written as well as the most extensive portions of *Feast* concern Fitzgerald, the contact point of the evocation by which the Ritz Hotel papers triggered the creation of the Paris Book seems to be Hemingway's relationship with Scott Fitzgerald. The centrality of Scott and Zelda Fitzgerald to *Feast* bears this out.

Neither Matthew Bruccoli's *Hemingway at Auction 1930–1973* or extended RLIN data-base searches provide a clue as to where these holographs went. The phrasing in Hemingway's letter, "Good stuff for you . . . ," suggests that Samuels had ready buyers for Hemingway holographs, and the scarcity of his holograph manuscripts in auction catalogs prior to 1957 supports such a market assumption. If Samuels sold the mss. directly, there may be no trace. (I am presently attempting to locate his business records.) Moreover, in November 1959 Hemingway mentioned a 1957 tax liability of $51,000 on which he still owed $18,000, indicating that in 1957 his income was substantial.[11]

When *Feast* finally appeared in April 1964, five months after the death of John F. Kennedy, it had been anticipated for four years and repeatedly mentioned in gossip columns as Hemingway's memoirs of the time in Paris during which he had trained and established himself as a writer.

Reviewers and critics were divided, all curious about, and many grateful for, what we thought was the final gift from the man whose death had sent a shock through America that now seemed to have been a harbinger of President Kennedy's death. Some reviewers did not question the genre of *Feast*, even as they praised or damned it. Marvin Mudrick found the book "a fresh beginning . . . and an honest recounting of youth and love"; while Geoffrey Wagner wrote that "for all the good it is likely to do Hemingway's reputation [it] could have stayed in Cuba permanently." Lewis Galantiere, who had been in Paris during the same time, was one of those untroubled by fiction–autobiography distinctions and called *Feast* "a true triumph of Hemingway's art." But another of the literary detectives whose comments regularly annoyed Hemingway quickly grasped that this was fiction done in memoir form, depicting the growth and development of a writer. Alfred Kazin's judgment predominates today.

In fact, by March 1961 Hemingway had himself admitted that what he was writing was fiction, and had tried to convey this to the reader. File 122 at the Kennedy Library contains seven pages of attempts to create a preface or an insertion to be "(Put in later chapter)" that would establish the book as fiction. The variant phrasings in his preface are: "This book is fiction . . ." (nine times); "It was necessary to write as fiction . . ."; "This book is all fiction . . ."; "[C]all it all fiction as it is." The statement that the book is fiction is never qualified in these fragments. Further, the phrase that is marked for insertion in a later chapter expands to say that "all remembrance of things past is fiction." The preface Mary Hemingway created is a pastiche of fragments from Files 122–124, some of which Hemingway was writing in an attempt to create either a final chapter that satisfied him, or an epilogue. The most misleading aspect of the published preface, "If the reader *prefers* [my emphasis], this book may be regarded as fiction," is that it offers the reader an interpretive option the author did not intend. During the difficult weeks of February and March 1961, Hemingway never wrote other than that the book was fiction. Further, a Hemingway letter of 26

March 1961 to Lee Samuels indicates that he and Mary disagree over the state of the manuscript they are sending to Samuels, she calling it "incomplete," and he clearly feeling otherwise (HRC). On 18 April 1961 Hemingway wrote Charles Scribner, telling him that the book should not be published. Mary withheld the letter and it was eventually misfiled with the Ezra Pound papers at Princeton, where it surfaced twenty-nine years after the publication of *Feast*.

For more than a year it had been Hemingway's fear of lawsuits that had made him indecisive about allowing any of the Paris book to be published serially. Scribner's was urging some serial releases of the sketches, probably afraid that the manuscript they thought would create "a fine controlled thermo-nuclear reaction" would be relegated to the limbo where what we know today as *The Garden of Eden, Islands in the Stream,* and the African book were languishing.[12] However, we now know that in April 1961 Hemingway's motivation for withholding the manuscript changed but that Mary's determination did not.

There are three indications that Mary Hemingway was dissatisfied with the Paris book she turned into *Feast:* first, and most dispositive, is her July 1963 letter to Harry Brague quoted earlier, which acknowledges her changes and indicates that she feels she has improved the work. Second is the disagreement between her and Ernest which he mentions in a letter of 26 March 1961 to Lee Samuels, and which suggests they were at odds about how the book should end. Third are comments she made in the summer of 1959 when the Hemingways were house guests of Bill Davis in Malaga as he began gathering the material that became *The Dangerous Summer*. The remarks in Malaga were made shortly after Mary had typed the manuscript of the Paris book, which Hemingway had with him and showed to Davis (among others) before leaving it with Scribner's as he passed through New York on his return. Correspondence between Hemingway and Davis shortly after his return to Cuba indicates that Mary had criticized the Paris sketches in Davis's presence – an action on her part for which there is no parallel.[13]

American literature would be much poorer if Mary Hemingway had been less dedicated to gathering her husband's literary remains or less determined that they be housed in a manner that would make them accessible to scholars, for there is no other major modern author whose compositional process is so minutely documentable as Hemingway's now is. Further, the posthumously published novels have extended the range of our ability to understand Hemingway's art far beyond what could have been imagined when he died in 1961. However, an informed examination of *Feast* and of the thematic unity of the posthumous works requires both recognition of the changes Mary made in the Paris Book and some informed speculation about why she made them.

"ALL MAN'S PROBLEMS COME FROM HIS INABILITY
TO BE ALONE"[14]

Among Hemingway's four wives, Mary Welsh alone came from a rural, working-class background. Bill Walton speculated that feelings of inferiority may help explain why she remained with Hemingway when, within less than three years of the marriage, he became so publicly indifferent to her feelings. Although Mary's memoir romanticizes her origins, she had fled them early, choosing to work as a journalist (*How It Was*, 1976). Walton recognized that she was rewriting her own past when he and Mary Welsh worked together for *Time* in England during the war. He sensed that she lost much of her authenticity as the revision continued, and that after her marriage to Hemingway, she lived in circumstances where she had forfeited her identity as well as her independence. Mary had less education than Hadley, Pauline, or Martha; and Walton recalls that when he visited at the Finca and talked of art and literature with Ernest (Walton is a painter), Mary simply could not participate in the conversation.[15]

But Hemingway had an almost psychotic inability to function as a writer when he was alone. He had explored it in the time and setting of his Paris years in [Philip Haines was a Writer . . .] an untitled ironic short story (File 648a; JFK) that may have been written while the African book was in progress and intended as part of *Feast* before Hemingway settled on the elegiac and tragic tone that pervades the Paris book.[16]

Although even his sons felt that his behavior had driven Martha Gellhorn away, Hemingway was derelict, angry, and shaken when she left him in April 1944. Further, when he met Mary Welsh in London in May she was involved with Irwin Shaw, a factor which appealed to his competitive spirit.[17] In what can now be seen from his letters as a combination of panic at being alone and a manic state that was probably stimulated by his being headed toward a real area of combat after two years of playing at espionage, Hemingway turned his emotional and then his domestic life over to Mary Welsh just as quickly as she would accept the responsibility.

We now know how quickly the marriage deteriorated. Among the many expectations of the narcissistic personality to which Mary became subject in marrying Hemingway was his insistence that she give up her reporting job.[18] Unlike Hadley and Pauline, who had independent incomes; or Martha, who had made it clear that she would continue supporting herself, Mary did not ask the critical question – "What are you charging me for this?" – when she contemplated the position she imagined she would have as Hemingway's wife. She accepted the lifestyle Hemingway offered her, which in fishing, hunting, and living near water resembled the life of her childhood in northern Minnesota; and since Mary was an only child, Hemingway agreed to support her dependent parents.

Mary paid a high price for her determination to be the last Mrs. Hemingway. Her letters that have been opened at the Kennedy Library and the accounts of friends, particularly those who were house guests at the Finca Vigia or traveling companions of the Hemingways, reveal much about their life together that cannot be glimpsed – even between the lines – of her memoir.[19] But Mary wanted to hold on to that life: she did so by cultivating a high level of denial; by living on the surface; and by refusing, as she has said, to analyze why Hemingway behaved as he did.[20] She also drank. By the time her memoir was published, Mary had begun her terminal descent into alcoholism.[21]

One of the ways Hemingway controlled Mary was through her dependence; and since her training was as a journalist, he discouraged, denigrated, and sometimes tried to interfere with her writing. Although Mary wrote later that in the editing of posthumous works she had made the decision that "no one was going to lay their cotton picking typewriter on Papa's work," by the time she sent the manuscript she called *A Moveable Feast* to Scribner's, she had done just that. And as she did, she may have felt that she was getting a bit of her own back.[22]

Mary Welsh Hemingway's biography remains to be written. Perhaps it will reveal a more complex woman than her memoirs did.

Figure 30. Mary Hemingway, Sun Valley, 1954. By the early 1970s Mary's drinking had become a serious problem (John F. Kennedy Library).

Although Hemingway scholars write in her debt, the reality relevant to *Feast* is that by the time she parted with the manuscript, Mary knew what she had begun to suspect at least four years earlier – when, at the end of the summer of 1959, she had again contemplated leaving Hemingway, and with the help of those who understood just how dangerous this would be for him, had negotiated some positive changes in her life. Mary had rebounded from Hemingway's death with energetic determination, and three weeks later was in Cuba preserving his literary remains. The following year she sat on President Kennedy's left, representing her husband at a dinner honoring Nobel Prize recipients.[23] Eighteen months later, when Mary Hemingway submitted to Scribner's the Paris book manuscript she had edited, she knew that it was much easier to be the keeper of a national monument than the wife of an extremely difficult man.[24]

MARY'S TURN

Although the reasons for Mary's changes in *Feast* will probably never be fully known, some explanation can be found in her habitually unanalytical approach to the version Hemingway had given her of his life and in her refusal to contemplate his past as an explanation for the ongoing difficulties in their relationship and his declining ability to create. Living on the surface was essential for Mary in sustaining the high level of denial at which she had chosen to exist in order to remain in the marriage; and later it was essential to fending off self-blame after Hemingway's death.[25] All this certainly limited her ability to see what Hemingway was about in the Paris book. Fortunately, the extent of her changes is more easily determined than her motives.

In arranging his short stories Hemingway was always aware of the effect created by juxtaposition; and his chapter ordering in the Paris book established thematic patterns that were obscured by the rearrangement done after his death.[26]

Mary told Carlos Baker that when Hemingway gave her the first three sketches for typing, she was disappointed that they contained so little about him and said, "I thought it was going to be autobiography." To which he responded that he was working by *remate*, a jai alai term for a double-wall rebound (Baker, *A Life Story*, 540).

In *Feast* the rebounding walls struck by the dangerous missile that Hemingway's early years had become to him by 1957 are the same surfaces he had hit in 1948 as he began writing in *Eden* of the year that followed Paris: the writer's inability to be either alone or part of an intimate relationship, and at the same time sustain his creativity.

The African stories framed within *Eden,* particularly the elephant tale, probe the writer's childhood for the point at which this dichotomous vision of creativity and tenderness began. In fragments written as he tried to complete *Feast,* Hemingway says:

> I wrote about Pauline. That would have been a good way to end a book on those days except that it was a beginning, not an ending. I wrote it. I left it out. It is intact and it starts another book. You can only write it in fiction of course. It has the most happiness in it and it is the saddest book I know. But it comes later. (File 124; JFK)

This "saddest book," which will tell what happened after Paris, is of course, *Eden;* and the sadness is David and Catherine Bourne's realization that writing is the only intimate relationship David needs.

Hemingway began revising *Eden* in 1957 as he was writing *Feast.* He worked alternately on the two books throughout 1958–59; and by 1959, with eighteen chapters of the Paris book finished (although he would initially show only thirteen of those chapters to Scribner's), he had already inscribed in *Eden* the tragic irony of his phrase "There is never any end to Paris." Hemingway's late recognition of the tragedy set in motion by the circumstances under which he ended his first marriage in *Feast* and began the second marriage in *Eden* is revealed in a letter of 15 October 1959, where he writes Mary that after putting her on the plane in Paris, he drove to Malaga, and made

> good notes on country for the novel which is in Hendaye and in Spain. Have driven and made notes over every place these *unfortunate kids* drove [my emphasis] .... (JFK)

The tragedy of these "unfortunate kids," who for eleven years Hemingway had been creating from the *remise* of his past, was that neither knew in 1927 that writing was the only intimate relationship Ernest Hemingway could sustain. It is that discovery which lies just beyond the final page of the Paris book – but has already been inscribed in the *Eden* manuscript. One of the pages in File 123 at the Kennedy Library bears evidence of Hemingway's attempts to create a closure for the Paris book alongside a list of names and episodes in *Eden,* suggesting that in these last weeks of struggle with the Paris book, Hemingway recognized that he was closing the circle he had begun to circumscribe eleven years earlier in *Eden.*[27]

AUTOBIOGRAPHY BY *REMATE*

In *Feast* the vertical surfaces for the writer's *remate* are good or bad women and good or bad writers; and the momentum of the rebound can be calculated from their impact on Hemingway's development as a writer. Dangerous families, whom one is never completely able to escape, can be seen mingled with the author's configurations of women, writers, and painters:

> With bad painters all you need to do is not look at them. But even when you have learned not to look at families nor listen to them and have learned not to answer letters, families have many ways of being dangerous. (MF, 108)

Mary and the Scribner's editor(s) almost certainly did not recognize the conjunction of rebounding surfaces Hemingway had created when they shuffled his chapter arrangement. Literary concealment and multilayered irony akin to the relationship of author to text in the African book are the result of editorial failure to realize the literal aptness of Hemingway's *remate* metaphor. As in the African book the author, who is suffering from the plane crash injuries of 1954, stands outside the text while writing a comic fantasy of his life in Africa before the crashes, a life that he cannot sustain in his present condition, so in the textual arrangement of *Feast* the wife/editor stands outside the text, suffering from the accumulated injuries of the marriage and her own limitations. And with the author's unmailed letter of withdrawal concealed behind her back (so to speak), she moves pieces to convey a vision that the dead author himself could not sustain.

The evidence of Kennedy Library Files 188–89 indicates that Hemingway had settled on the following arrangement for the nineteen chapters he intended to use:

(1) "A Good Café on the Place St.-Michel"
(2) "Miss Stein Instructs"
(3) "Shakespeare and Company"
(4) "People of the Seine"
(5) "A False Spring"
(6) "The End of an Avocation"
(7) " '*Une Génération Perdue*' "

(8) "Hunger Was Good Discipline"
(9) "Ford Madox Ford and the Devil's Disciple"
(10) "With Pascin at the Dome"
(11) "Ezra Pound and His Bel Esprit"
(12) "A Strange Enough Ending"
(13) "The Man Who Was Marked for Death"
(14) "Evan Shipman at the Lilas"
(15) "An Agent of Evil"
(16) "There Is Never Any End to Paris"
(17) "Scott Fitzgerald"
(18) "Hawks Do Not Share"
(19) "A Matter of Measurements"

The editor(s) rearranged some chapters, added "Birth of a New School," and positioned "There is Never Any End to Paris," a pastiche of Hemingway's proposed chapter 16 and the fragments from Files 122–24, as the final chapter. Hemingway himself was not certain if the book should have a final chapter and was tormented by what was becoming clear as he wrote and rewrote chapter 16 in late March and early April 1961. In *Eden* there is a good deal of focus on how writing something truly frees the writer of the emotional weight of the experience (e.g., 422.1–33), but the clarity of Hemingway's vision as he labored to complete *Feast* became unbearable, for the writing was compelling him to face truths that resulted in his letter of withdrawal. When Hemingway referred to his typewriter as his only analyst, as he often did, he called it a "portable Corona #3," even when it was not. We will ultimately see just how prescient his metaphor was, for as Hemingway tried to end *Feast*, the writing process did indeed become his analyst.

"IT SEEMED SO EASY WHEN IT STARTED. AND THEN YOU
FOUND MISTAKES AND ERRORS"[28]

Hemingway wrote most of *Feast* with the protective grandiosity of his narcissistic personality intact, telling Buck Lanham in a letter of 18 September 1958 that he had written "a book, very good, about early earliest days in Paris, Austria, etc. – the true gen that everyone has written about and no one knows but me" (PUL). Despite his recognition in 1959 of "these unfortunate kids," as he checked the route David and Catherine Bourne drove in *Eden,* he seems to have sustained the enamel of self-idealization he had inscribed in *Feast* until late winter 1961. Although, as we shall see shortly, it had begun to crack during the summer of 1960.

The young writer who sits in the good café of Chapter 1, segueing between his writing and observing a pretty girl with a fresh face, is the immediate ancestor of David Bourne. His writing, like Bourne's, is a symbolic sexual act and the text is his parthenogenetic offspring:

> I was writing . . . A girl came in the café . . . I looked at her and she disturbed me and made me very excited. The story was writing itself . . . and I watched the girl . . . I've seen you, beauty, and you belong to me now, . . . You belong to me and all Paris belongs to me and *I belong to this notebook and this pencil* [my emphasis]. Then I went back to the writing . . . and was lost in it. . . . Then the story was finished and I was very tired. . . . then I looked up and looked for the girl and she had gone. . . I felt sad. . . . I closed up the story in the notebook and put it inside my pocket . . . After writing a story, I was always empty and both sad and happy, as though I had made love. (MF, 5–6)

After the excitement of the writing, the surrender to it, the finish, and the fatigue of the activity, comes a postcoital triste when the writer takes custody of text. The creative tension relieved for the moment, he can return to a less important cohabitation with the wife who exists to praise and agree.[29]

Between one session and another, Hemingway tells us, he did not think about writing, but instead walked the streets of Paris, looked at paintings and visited bookstalls so that

> my subconscious would be working on it and at the same time I would be listening to other people and noticing everything, I hoped; learning, I hoped; and I would read so that I would not think about my work and make myself *impotent* [emphasis added] to do it. (MF, 13)

The author's account of how he spent his time away from writing ironically cancels his assertion, for it demonstrates that everything he does is valued only as it increases his stock of material and renews him for the next writing session. Because factuality is not the measure of *Feast,* the truth of the author's account here lies not in his imperceptive assessment of how he spends his time when he is not writing, but in the fact that so many of the Paris scenes he observes when he is not writing existed in his letters and anecdotes long before the book began. (See Tavernier-Courbin, *Making of a Myth*, chapter 4.)

Feast may be the account of how Ernest Hemingway learned to write, but it is also his admission that from the beginning the need to write was an obsession that cannibalized and subordinated all other activities and relationships. And, as Hemingway admitted in middle age, it became a vice – the isolating and onanistic act that Catherine Bourne charges her husband with in *Eden*.

The Nick Adams story being written in the good café is "The Three Day Blow," identifiable by the "wild, cold, blowing day" of the action. It is about staying unattached, wanting a girl, but breaking with her because, as Nick's friend Bill says, "Once a man's married, he's absolutely bitched."[30] Nick Adams is not yet a writer in the story: he and Bill are naive readers, amateur drinkers, and avid hunters. But as he closes the notebook, the young Hemingway makes plans to leave Paris. Away from Paris, he thinks, maybe he can write about it, just as, far from Michigan, he has written the "Three Day Blow" – and as the author, in Cuba and Idaho, wrote of Paris in the book we are reading.

The pervasive sense of Paris that has made *Feast* a guidebook for so many readers never wanes; but in the cycle of Hemingway's portrait of the artist, invoking Paris is a controlled search through the *remise* of his memory for a time when he was innocent and his creative future was infinite; a time when the test of everyone he now remembers was their ability to see in him an adept soon to become master.

JUXTAPOSITIONS *PERDUE* – THE STEIN AND BEACH CHAPTERS

Hemingway's chapter arrangement had juxtaposed Gertrude Stein's inability to see the young writer apart from her own needs and theories with Sylvia Beach's unqualified acceptance and support. But the resonance this arrangement created has been obscured in the published work. The chapters he gave to Stein (two, seven, and twelve) present a woman seen through the scrim of another woman she physically resembles. Stein is "big, heavily built . . . [with] beautiful eyes . . . and lovely, thick, alive . . . hair . . . put up in the same

Figure 31. Bumby Hemingway with Gertrude Stein (his godmother), Paris, 1924 (John F. Kennedy Library).

way she had probably worn it in college" (MF, 14). Like the mother who introduced Hemingway to the literature that first shaped his vision, to the music for which he concealed his love, to the Impressionist painters in the Art Institute of Chicago, and who had herself become a competent painter in middle age, Gertrude Stein has much experience and knowledge to give him; and she gives it.[31] But like Grace Hemingway, Stein is solipsistic, controlling, prudish, and finally, condemning. And, like both Grace Hemingway and her son, Stein is full of herself.

Stein wants to be published in the *Atlantic,* a magazine young Hemingway had accused his mother of having around the house as an intellectual prop. She tells him how to spend his money – no clothes, save for pictures. She is too lazy to revise and uses him to gain recognition for her own work when he arranges to serialize *The Making of Americans* in the review he is tending for the absent Ford Madox Ford. She tells him that another of the Nick Adams stories is *inaccrochable* – in a literal translation, "unhangable," but from the root word *accroc,* "a stain on one's character" – because of its frank and rather brutal sexual episode. And she warns him, "You mustn't write anything that is *inaccrochable.* There is no point to it. It's wrong and it's silly" (MF, 15).

File 799 at the Kennedy Library reveals that after gleaning what was useful from Stein's teachings, Hemingway gave them about the same weight he accorded his parents' platitudes. The manuscript of "Up in Michigan" bears Stein's editorial attempts to efface the language she found offensive: Hemingway has crossed them out and written: "Pay no attention." (See Paul Smith, "Impressions.")

Hemingway's father had returned *In Our Time* to the publisher, and when *The Sun Also Rises* appeared in October 1926, Clarence wrote his son:

> You are now a famous writer and I shall trust your future books will have a different sort of subject matter . . . You have such a wonderful ability and we want to be able to read and ask others to enjoy your works. (22 Oct.; JFK)

Six weeks passed before the first words were heard from Grace, and they read a bit like the Widow Douglas lecturing Huck Finn. After complaining that she had been too ashamed to attend a discussion of the book at the Nineteenth Century Club, Grace warms to her subject:

> Don't you know any words other than "damn" and "bitch." [Apparently a rhetorical question, for Grace was careful in her punctuation.] It is a doubtful honor to have produced one of the filthiest books of the year. . . . Have you ceased to be interested in loyalty, nobility, honor and fineness of life – I have found *my* heaven here – in the opportunity to create beauty and exalt the nobility of life . . . [She closes with] I love you dear, and still believe you will do something worthwhile to live after you. (2 Jan. 1927; JFK)

In placing the second Stein chapter, "*Une Génération Perdue*," as number seven, Hemingway had compelled the reader to contrast Stein with Sylvia Beach of "Shakespeare and Company." Although both women have lesbian unions, the author omits that fact about Beach, who is physically less formidable than Stein (or Grace) and wants to help the young writer, not control, use, or shape him. Lively, with pretty legs and short hair, Beach trusts him, worries if he is eating properly, and provides access to the writers he has not been exposed to in his family home – and whom Stein dismisses – writers like Lawrence ("a sick man"), Huxley ("a dead man"), early Anderson, Joyce, Tolstoy, and Turgenev.

Like Grace Hemingway, Stein is determinedly cheerful, wanting to know only "the gay part of how the world was going; never the real, never the bad" (MF, 25). And she recommends a diet of sentimental fiction and mystery stories. Further, Stein's solipsism allows for no distinctions. If a phrase pleases her and an auto mechanic or writer does not, everything equals everything else: "Don't argue with me, Hemingway. . . . All of you young people who served in the war. You are a lost generation" (MF, 76) sounds very much like Grace making dire predictions in the birthday letter with which she evicted her obstreperous son from the family home.

Hemingway had placed the second Sylvia Beach chapter, "Hunger Was a Good Discipline," as he had the first – so that it would comment on the Stein chapter which preceded it. Only Beach and Stein address the young writer as "Hemingway": Beach's utterance of his name is a benediction, for no sooner has she assured Hemingway that his writing will sell than a check for a story materializes in her hands. Using the check, he first feeds his physical hunger, then, instead of going home as he had planned, asks himself "What did I know best that I had not written about and lost? What did I know about truly and care for the most? There was no choice at all" (MF, 76). Hemingway sits in a corner at the good café and begins one of his greatest stories, "Big Two-Hearted River," the story that in 1957 he told Lee Samuels he had found in Paris, "in the copybooks I used to write it in in the café."

But Stein's appellation is a curse. She utters "You are a lost generation," and it is a harbinger of Hadley's losing the manuscripts – a disaster related in the chapter Hemingway had intended to follow. The loss she conjures seems for a time fatal to Hemingway's talent, for he says, "I did not think I could write any more then"; and her curse is lifted only when Edward O'Brien breaks his own rules by choosing for *The Best Short Stories of the Year* an unpublished story that is one of the two Hemingway had left after the manuscripts were lost. The other, he tells us meaningfully, was "Up in Michigan" – the story Stein had found *inaccrochable.*

THE LOST MANUSCRIPTS AND PROTECTING THE TEXTS

The wound of Hadley's losing his manuscripts in December 1922 reverberates throughout the posthumous novels and is one of the links that joins the three Fitzgerald chapters to the rest of the book; the other is Hemingway's repeated contrasting of himself and Fitzgerald. The explanation he gives Fitzgerald of why Zelda would say that her husband's penis is too small to satisfy a woman ("A Matter of Measurements") is that she is trying "to put you out of business" (MF, 190).[32] It was a phrase Hemingway used in life and in fiction for a woman's power over a man: Robert Wilson in "The Short Happy Life of Francis Macomber" fears that Margo will report his hunting violations to the licensing board in Nairobi and he will "be out of business." When Pauline insisted on payment of the $500 per month the court had granted her in the divorce settlement, and Hemingway was intent upon writing *For Whom the Bell Tolls,* she was trying to "put [him] out of business." Thus, "sexually inadequate because of size" and "unable to do one's work as a writer (or a safari hunter)" had been synonymous with impotency in Hemingway's parlance from very early on.

Recalling the way the young writer felt when he returned to his apartment after learning that the suitcase containing his manuscripts had been stolen from Hadley's train compartment and found that she had packed even the carbons, Hemingway writes, "I remember what I did in the night after I let myself into the flat and found it was true" (MF, 74). The cryptic sentence has given rise to much speculation on the part of readers and scholars who most often answer their own questions by imagining an act of infidelity to Hadley or a bout of heavy drinking. But Hemingway wrote "in the night," rather than "that night," his locution suggesting something done *throughout* an interval.

He has inscribed the loss of the manuscripts in each of the four posthumous narratives. A passage from "Miami," the deleted section of *Islands* which contributed to *Eden*, revealed that the troubled, much-married, heavy-drinking writer Roger Davis experienced the loss of his manuscripts like a castration and spent the night with a pillow between his legs. In Hemingway's metaphorical equation of the loss of texts and the inability to write with castration in the "Miami" fragment, in his explanation of Zelda's motives to Fitzgerald in *Feast*, and in his choice of "impotent" to indicate both David Bourne's initial inability to rewrite the burned stories in *Garden* and his own inability to create if he has not restored himself between writing sessions in *Feast*, he has conveyed fully and frequently the power he believed women to have over male creativity. These assumptions explain why the text must be protected from the woman who serves the writer – in life and in fiction – far better than the simple label of misogyny.

MORE DANGEROUS WOMEN: ZELDA AND THE BOOK SELLERS

Zelda Fitzgerald reigns as a succubus in Hemingway's pantheon of the women in Paris who seek to appropriate the writer's talent and put their own mark upon it, or who have no idea how to judge writing, or who would like to put the writer out of business. This was a role in which he had cast Scott Fitzgerald's wife for years in his letters to Max Perkins, occasionally understudying her with the wives of poet Evan Shipman, painters Waldo Pierce and Mike Strater, or of other creative men.[33] Scott Donaldson's biography of Fitzgerald, *Fool for Love*, tells a very different story of the struggle for possession of the writing in the Fitzgerald marriage; but in Hemingway's mind Fitzgerald's self-destructive behavior became a paradigm of the power of woman to destroy the creative male.[34]

With Hemingway's chapter arrangement, "People of the Seine" came after "Miss Stein Instructs" and "Shakespeare and Company," allowing the author to enlarge his tour of Paris while continuing his exposure of how shallowly writing could be judged. The two book venders whose conversations he recounts are both women, which might be irrelevant despite the historical fact that both sexes ran these stalls. However, the author makes a point of identifying the second vender as "a woman stall-keeper"; and both value a book by its prettiness – pictures and a leather binding are the hallmarks of a good book. Fitzgerald's books are "bound in light blue leather with the titles in gold" (MF, 179).

THE LAST STEIN CHAPTER AND THE COMPANY OF MEN

The editor(s)' movement of Hemingway's final Stein chapter, "A Strange Enough Ending," from number twelve to number thirteen is less disruptive to thematic unity than the earlier rearrangements were because the reader has already seen the young writer take his own measure against a liar and time waster, Ford Madox Ford, who like Stein was his early patron, and has seen him recognized and "adopted" by Ezra Pound.[35] Her patronage no longer needed, Stein's company is not worth the social effort required because "there is not much future in men being friends with great women . . . usually even less future with truly ambitious women writers" (MF, 117). The other truly ambitious women Hemingway had known were a voice teacher turned painter – his mother; and the writer who had been his third wife – Martha Gellhorn. We know how dangerous he considered his mother; and in 1953 he had written to Bernard Berenson of Martha: "M. was the most ambitious girl I ever met. That doesn't mean much because I have not met many ambitious girls as they frighten me and I dislike them" (27 May 1953; JFK).

Pascin, like Pound, has also recognized the young writer's talent and offered his hospitality; but there is an ominous quality in their affinity. Pascin's dark-haired model resembles the girl who excited the writer in the good café (MF, 5); and she reveals that Pascin's painting, like Hemingway's writing, becomes a sexual frisson. Pascin explains that he "bangs" her to keep his head clear for painting; and the writer in the café feels "empty," as though he had made love when he closes his notebook after a good session (MF, 6). The painter and the writer recognize their shared darkness: Pascin takes leave by warning Hemingway not to fall in love with his typewriting paper. Hemingway's epilogue to the encounter at the Dome speculates that "the seeds of what we will do are in all of us" and reports that Pascin committed suicide (in 1930).

Chapters 13 and 15 relate thematically to the Ford chapter, but while Ford is remembered as a pompous and foolish liar who never listened, Ernest Walsh's lies are those of a true corrupter; and Cheever Dunning has destroyed his talent as a poet with opium, a parallel with Fitzgerald's inability to handle alcohol, but less tiresome. Dunning speaks in *"terza riruce"* (a typist's faulty transcription of *terza rima*) when he is under the influence, compelling the care of altruistic poet Ezra Pound; and he amuses the pure, humble poet Evan Shipman with his other stoned antics.

FITZGERALD'S EARLY WINTER AND HEMINGWAY'S FALSE SPRING

The three Fitzgerald chapters are the culmination of Hemingway's *remate* technique. Thinking of Scott as a "rummy" and a failed, self-indulgent writer who had let a woman destroy his talent had been a favorite pastime of Hemingway's for years. And as suggested earlier, it was probably the duration and intensity of his own feelings about Fitzgerald that had been evoked by the Ritz Hotel papers in 1957 and prompted Hemingway to begin creating the Paris book around anecdotes he had previously told.

Fitzgerald had had one wife, who Hemingway believed was jealous of his writing and had finally put him out of business.[36] Hemingway had had four, and as the Paris book progressed, he clung to the belief that he was still very much at the top of his tree and that the Paris book would prove it. But the chapters which on the surface are about racing – "A False Spring" and "The End of an Avocation" – harbor just beneath the surface irrefutable evidence that during the Paris years Hemingway had done what he had excoriated Fitzgerald for doing. He had put his writing talent at the mercy of his marital,

extramarital, and domestic affairs. And the tragic irony of his statement that "there is never any end to Paris" is that as he aged
prematurely and his creative powers waned, Hemingway saw his
original sin as his having listened to the piping of Pan during the
false spring.[37]

   The first of the racing chapters, "A False Spring," introduces the
assumption of the young writer that a safe zone existed between
himself and Hadley and the other people whom the aging author is
preparing to blame for the destruction of their edenic union: "People were always the limiters of happiness . . . the only thing that
could spoil a day" (MF, 49). These destroyers of happiness are
quickly identified as "the rich" – the pilot fish and others whom
Hemingway needs to hold responsible for the end of his first marriage in order to shrive himself. But there is a concealment here, for
the chapter opens with, "When spring came, even the false spring,
there were no problems except *where to be happiest* [emphasis
added]." In young Hemingway's life, the locations of happiness at
this time had not been indoors writing or outdoors at the horse
races; they were with Hadley *or* with the unnamed young woman
who is his companion at the bicycle races in the next chapter.

   The secret "racing capital" which he keeps "apart from all other
capital" is not only the winnings of horse racing; it is the emotional
horde that he tries to divide between Hadley and Pauline (keeping
twice as much for himself as the two share!). Similarly, "gambling" is
not simply the betting on both kinds of races, it is the risking of his
own peace of mind that the older Hemingway now believes was a
mortgage on his creative ability. The danger in which he placed
himself is conveyed by the reiteration of the word "remember" as he
and Hadley play a game that he ultimately loses, for she can remember everything; but he cannot remember a story about a wisteria
vine. The game itself, which has no nuance of competition between
the pair, is a running account of the adventures they have had
during their five years together. Her triumph, seven years in the
future, will be her happy marriage to Paul Mower – an event that
Hemingway refers to repeatedly in the fragments of the preface to
Feast (File 122; JFK).

   Returning from the races, the couple is hungry with what he
thinks is simply hunger for a fine dinner, but which Hadley warns
him is more complex – "Memory is hunger," she says. They use their
winnings to dine at Michaud's, but the hunger is still there. They

make love in the dark and the hunger is still there. When he awakes in the night, the hunger is still there. And as the aging author writes, the hunger is still there and Hadley was right. Memory is indeed hunger; hunger for a time before he had any need to divide his winnings and keep some a secret; hunger for a time when "life had seemed so simple . . . [before] I had wakened and found the false spring and heard the pipes of the man with his herd of goats and gone out and bought the racing paper" (MF, 57–8).

In the second racing chapter, "The End of an Avocation," Hemingway had at one point intended to reveal Pauline's presence, for what is now simply a mention of seeing the fatal accident of "that great rider Ganay," read in three manuscript versions "Pauline and I saw the great rider Ganay fall [in August 1926]." But instead of including Pauline, Hemingway inscribed her in the complex feelings he had about horse racing – it is a false friend, beautiful, exciting, time-consuming, demanding and profitable; and it gave him material for writing (MF, 61).[38] Later in the chapter he introduces his turning from the horse races to the bicycle races with a passage in which the subtext is the peace of mind he regained as he settled into his second marriage:

> That was a new and fine thing that I knew little about. But we did not start it right away. That came later. It came to be a big part of our lives later when the first part of Paris was broken up. (MF 65)

It is only in these two chapters, where racing becomes an indirect way of talking about his first and second marriages, one ended and the other begun in Paris, that Hemingway is not focusing on his writing or making *remate* comparisons between himself and other writers. A story mentioned earlier suggests the reason for this silence: [Philip Haines was a writer] (File 486a; JFK) is about a writer separated from his wife of five years, waiting out a complicated divorce while the woman he plans to marry is in America, and who is put out of the writing business by the loneliness of having left one woman for another and having neither with him.[39]

TRYING TO END THE PARIS BOOK

Hemingway had begun the Paris book confident that he was creating a testimony to his own virtue and dedication. And he had chosen a form that allowed him to seal off, by closure or elision, what did

Figure 32. Hadley Hemingway and Pauline Pfeiffer at Gaschurn, Austria, in January 1926 as the romance which would end Hadley and Ernest's marriage was beginning (John F. Kennedy Library).

Figure 33. The pilot fish and the rich whom Hemingway blamed in *A Moveable Feast* for the destruction of his first marriage. Front row: Gerald and Sara Murphy with Hadley. Rear: Ernest and John Dos Passos. Schruns, Austria, March 1926 (John F. Kennedy Library).

not support the vision of himself he was trying to sustain: saying, for example, of his discovery of Gertrude Stein's peccadilloes, "That was the way it finished for me"; concealing the presence of Pauline; praising Ezra Pound who was now mad and could be pitied; creating the false impression that Scott Fitzgerald, safely dead, had never given him good advice about *Sun*.[40] Further, by structuring the Paris book in vignettes from a limited and involved point of view that demanded no narrative continuity other than setting, Hemingway was initially able to evade any consideration of similarities between himself and those he presented as weaker, less dedicated, and contagiously corrupt.

Energized by the project he began in the late winter or early spring of 1957, Hemingway had one Fitzgerald sketch done by May. Seven months later, he wrote Buck Lanham that he had 14 chapters of a new book done; and, nine months following, that the work had been typed by Mary, and he was "ready to give it a final going over." He also reveals that he has been working steadily on another book that is nearly finished and that he hasn't "taken twenty days off in eight months" (18 Sept. 1958; PUL). This is the big rewriting drive on *Eden*.

In "There Is Never Any End to Paris," Hadley is again the strong presence she was in "A False Spring," and the chorus-like use of "I remember" that marked the earlier chapter resumes. *We* need to remember that Hemingway was unsure about using the "There Is Never Any End" chapter and that Mary added to it fragments from Files 122–24. Some pages of these files are dated: the earliest date, 18 February (1961), is in File 122; the latest, 27 March (1961), is in File 123. Thus we can establish that "There Is Never Any End to Paris" is the last chapter of the Paris book on which Hemingway worked.

The truth that Hemingway saw as he labored to complete the Paris book during the difficult months between his first treatments at the Mayo Clinic (1 Dec. 1960–22 Jan. 1961) and his return there on 23 April is *the* truth of this beautifully wrought work of fiction. It is this truth which supplies the penultimate link between *Eden* and *Feast* and reveals fully the tragic irony of Hemingway's lovely, oft-repeated judgment that "there is never any end to Paris." The link is visible in the locution Hemingway chose to render his betrayal of Hadley and young David Bourne's betrayal of the elephant in the story the mature Bourne writes. In both instances, the young writer's culpability is constructed through memory and inscribed in the text he is writing years after the act. In the elephant story, written in 1954 just after Hemingway's return from Africa and incorporated into *Eden* during the rewriting drive of 1958–59 (when Hemingway was also working full-steam on the Paris book), David Bourne thinks of how he has betrayed the location of the old elephant that his father shoots: "[H]e wished that he had never betrayed the elephant and remembered wishing that he had never seen him" (GE, 174). In the winter of 1961, searching for an ending to that which could never end while he was alive, conscious, and haunted by remorse over the betrayal of himself as a writer and a man that he had inscribed in *Feast,* Hemingway wrote of what he felt upon seeing Hadley and Bumby waiting for him at the train station in Schruns as he returned from New York in March 1926 after an interlude with Pauline in Paris: "I wished I had died before I loved anyone but her" (MF, 210).

Figure 34. Hemingway and Matador Antonio Ordonez whose father had dedicated a bull to Hadley in 1925. During the summers of 1959 and 1960 Hemingway dissipated the creative momentum with which he had begun the Paris sketches as he followed Ordonez on the bullfight circuit in Spain (John F. Kennedy Library).

The final conjunction among the boy, the elephant, and the young writer in *Eden* and the aging author of *Feast* appears in the self-reflexive passage edited from *Eden:* thinking of how the elephant had died that day, of the elephant's age, and of how difficult it must be to die well when one is so old and tired, David resolves, "I hope that I can die as well and as nobly as he died."[41]

During his last efforts to bring closure to the Paris book, betrayal

Figure 35. In Spain during the summers of 1959 and 1960 Hemingway was the houseguest of Bill and Annie Davis at their estate in Malaga where Mary held Hemingway's sixtieth birthday party on 21–22 July 1959. Hemingway at ringside with Bill Davis (left) and Dr. George Saviers. Saviers was Hemingway's physician in Ketchum, Idaho, and Hemingway had flown him and his wife Pat to Spain for the birthday party. In November 1960, he and Mary would use Saviers's name at the Mayo Clinic in order to avoid publicity (John F. Kennedy Library, courtesy Paco Cano y Guerra of Fotografo Taurino, Madrid).

and dying well became the contact point between the two Hemingway personae, the young writer in *Feast* and *Eden,* and the ill, aging writer who stands outside the text he is creating and understands finally why there is never any end to Paris.

ANOTHER DETOUR ON THE ROAD TO THE PAST

The surety and sense of renewal with which Hemingway had completed fourteen chapters of the Paris book and revised much of *Eden* between May 1957 and March 1959 was dissipated as he became involved that summer in gathering information for, and then writing, the bullfight piece for *Life.* Trying to provide himself with a secure permanent residence in the face of the political changes in

Figure 36. Buck Lanham, another guest at Hemingway's sixtieth birthday cele-
bration, with Valerie Danby-Smith (John F. Kennedy Library, courtesy Paco
Cano y Guerra of Fotografo Taurino, Madrid).

Cuba (where Castro had taken over after the fall of the Batista
government in early January 1959), Hemingway purchased a house
near Ketchum, paying $50,000 in cash, before returning to Cuba
that Easter. It may have been the anticipation of this expense and
his erratic penurious tendencies that had prompted Hemingway to
make the agreement with *Life* in February when he was working so
feverishly on both *Feast* and *Eden*. In late April he sailed for Spain,

taking the manuscript of the Paris book. When he returned more than six months later, Hemingway had lost much of his momentum on the work, and his behavior had once again destabilized his domestic life. He had ignored or criticized Mary through most of the summer and had humiliated her by his attentions to several young women who had joined their party in Spain. With one, Valerie Danby-Smith, he had also become infatuated. Mary returned to Cuba ten days earlier than he, and unpublished correspondence shows that she had insisted upon the rental of an apartment in New York and had delineated the limits of her domestic duties before agreeing to go back to Cuba.[42] They remained in Cuba for only two weeks, and in Ketchum, on 27 November, Mary fell, breaking her elbow while hunting. Finding Hemingway unsympathetic to her limitations and need for help while it was healing, Mary agreed that Valerie Danby-Smith should be hired as his secretary, and Bill Davis (in Spain) immediately set about finding a way to get Danby-Smith to Cuba.[43]

Scribners' reaction to the Paris book, Hemingway's first long manuscript since *The Old Man and the Sea* (seven years earlier), was one of high praise, and they were eager to get the publication started, even as serialization. On Hemingway's promise that he would begin going over it as soon as his income tax was organized, they put the Paris book on their list for fall 1960. However, by the end of March, mired in the bullfighting book that seemed to be expanding beyond his control, Hemingway told them to cancel plans for the fall publication, and he arranged to follow the bullfight circuit again the coming summer.[44]

Hemingway's return to Spain in 1960, in an effort to complete the book that became *The Dangerous Summer,* was a reprise of the actions that marked the end of his work on the African book four years earlier. But now there were no manuscripts from the 1920s to be found in Paris and evoke a *belle époque* he had known: those evocations had been inscribed in the Paris book that he could not return to until his obligation to *Life* was satisfied. Mary went with him only as far as New York, where she settled into the apartment at 1 East 61st Street that had been part of the conditions of her returning to Cuba the previous October after that dangerous summer in Spain.

Mary had health reasons for remaining in New York: her need of

Figure 37. Even Buck Lanham tried to point out to Hemingway his insensitivity to Mary during the summer of 1959. In 1960 she refused to return to Spain with him. Shown here in Valencia, July 1959, are Lanham and Hemingway with Valerie Danby-Smith and Mary behind them (Princeton University Library, courtesy Paco Cano y Guerra of Fotografo Taurino, Madrid).

physical therapy for the elbow broken in November, and a sinus condition that had been aggravated by the dust in Spain the previous summer, where she had also broken a toe – as she had twice broken her ankle skiing in Italy when Hemingway's attachment to Adriana was new. (The accidents may be part of the price Mary paid for choosing to live beyond her emotional means.) But the correspondence between the Hemingways during the summer of 1960 makes clear that Mary was distancing herself in the marriage. His letters have lost their braggadocio and truculence and become the cry of a man who is physically and emotionally deteriorating: her responses, when they acknowledge his cries at all, are off-hand. She thanks him effusively for a cash present of $8,000 he gave her at the airport when he departed, flatters him in ways she had not done since 1944–45; and when problems concerning the upkeep on the Finca Vigia are discussed, Mary is positively servile, referring repeatedly to her loyalty to him and her commitment to caring for his property, even at the risk of being detained in Cuba. She reports in chirpy detail the pleasures of life in New York – the fresh raspberries, the variety of cheeses, the plays and galleries she has enjoyed, and the ease of purchasing furniture for the apartment. She also considers getting involved in the Kennedy presidential campaign, which their friend Bill Walton was running in the city.

It is the disparity, bordering on blindness, between Hemingway's letters and Mary's responses during this dangerous summer that led me to seek out Bill Walton for an interview in 1992 because I sensed that Mary was trying to put down roots in New York and making plans to end the marriage. Walton thought not, but said he sensed that Mary realized she was going to be a widow sooner than actuarial tables would predict. I remain uncertain because Walton's point – that Mary enjoyed being Mrs. Ernest Hemingway too much to give it up – is well taken, for some of the double-edge of her flattery to Hemingway in the correspondence of that summer is reporting the awe his name evokes when she writes a check that reveals her as Mrs. Ernest Hemingway; or when *Summer* begins to appear in *Life*.

Whatever else brought on Hemingway's despair during the dangerous summer, he was also peeling away the layers of denial about his actions that had allowed him to sustain the vision of himself he had inscribed in the Paris book.[45] On 15 August he wrote to Mary:

> [T]he whole bullfight business is now so corrupt and seems so unimportant and I have so much good work to do . . . If there was any way to do it would take the next plane. But every time I've ever been this bad have pulled out of it into a *belle époque* and will try to do it again. . . . Rupert (sober) is more repetitive than Sinsky drunk – and Sinsky will be at Bilbao. Everybody is as egotistical as Sinsky at his worst.

Sinsky (Juan Dunabeitia) was an officer in the merchant marine who had come to Cuba from Spain after the Civil War and had regularly stayed at the Finca for extended periods. Hemingway had recounted with gusto in letters to Buck Lanham, Harvey Breit, Hotchner, and other male friends the drunken, talent-wasting time he, Sinsky, and the other Finca habitués spent together. Two revealing photos of Sinsky as the Finca's harlequin appear in Norberto Fuentes's *Hemingway Rediscovered* (150–51). Hemingway's insight into the company he had been keeping was a long overdue epiphany.[46]

On 18 August, Hemingway wrote Mary, "I understand all the things and people you hated last year." But most revealing of what was happening to Hemingway is his reaction to the superb photo of himself (by Loomis Dean) that appeared on the cover of *Life* when the first installment of *Summer* was published: "[T]he horrible face on the cover made me sick (literally)."[47]

In the summer of 1960, Hemingway was beginning to lose his notorious and protective ability to blame others for whatever went wrong in his own life. Now in a state where he could not depend on his own judgment, unable to remember if he had written something to Mary or just thought it, Hemingway must have sympathized a good deal with Ezra Pound, who had been released from St. Elizabeth's in 1958 and was now living with his daughter in Italy, for he left a check with his host, Bill Davis, to cover the expenses of relocating Pound in the South of Spain. Pound did not go (Brigit Patmore to Joyce and Geoffrey Bridson, 8 Jan. 1962; Lilly Library, Bloomington, Indiana).

Hemingway returned to New York on 8 October, and by the 22nd he and Mary were in Idaho, where his condition continued to deteriorate. On 30 November he checked into the Mayo Clinic, using the name of his Idaho physician, George Saviers, in order to avoid publicity. There he chose electroconvulsive therapy over the tricyclic drugs (stelazine, thorazine, compazine, etc.) that were offered to him.[48]

Discharged from Mayo on 22 January 1961, Hemingway returned to Ketchum and began trying to write; but with his short-term memory impaired by the treatments he had received during the hospitalization, he could no longer sustain his claim that the truth of the Paris book was truth that only he knew. Instead, he saw with blinding sight the part he had played in destroying the two personal relationships that he now believed had been the most sustaining of him as a writer and most indicative of his integrity as a man. He admitted, perhaps for the first time, his culpability in the ending of his early marriages, and he saw how dishonestly he had blamed the pilot fish and the rich for destroying his first marriage in the manuscript he was trying to bring to closure. He saw also how he had compounded his guilt by suggesting in the Paris book that all that occurred in his second marriage was corrupted by a conspiracy of these rich whom he had blamed. And at this point Hemingway admitted to himself not only that he had postured in the role of a naif manipulated by the rich into actions that ended his first marriage, but also that the cycle had been repeated a decade later with Martha Gellhorn playing the role Pauline had played in 1926.

Hemingway's earlier anxiety about publishing the Paris book had been focused on fear of lawsuits; but now he was experiencing remorse for what he had done to others. The man who in 1927 had become a Catholic out of opportunism had now become capable of perfect contrition.[49] He wrote Charles Scribner, withdrawing the manuscript that became *Feast*. In the letter he says: "[T]ried as many as fifty times to end properly as I did in A Farewell and kept *feeling* [my emphasis] day after day."[50] This sentence follows closely on Hemingway's admission of the wrong done to Hadley and Pauline, and its context leaves no doubt that the word he consciously intended was *failing*, not *feeling*. But the parapraxis leaves no doubt that the remorse of perfect contrition originated in Hemingway's recovery of emotions connected with the end of his first and second marriages, which he had long suppressed.

Among Hemingway's medical records at the Kennedy Library is a "Do Not Disturb" notice printed in block letters on a sheet torn from a shorthand tablet. It is dated (by Mary) "January 1961" and appears to be a draft of the notice (also in the file) circulated to the staff of the Mayo Clinic regarding the response to be given to requests for information on Hemingway. The letter "g," occurring thrice in words of the twelve short lines, and the "x," used twice as a period, establish the "Do Not Disturb" notice as the work of Hemingway's hand: it begins with words predictive of the dirge for which it is the overture – "FORMER WRITER."

In 1957, Hemingway had seen in the Ritz Hotel papers a commutation of the self-imposed sentence he had considered at the terminus of the unfinished African book – the abandonment of writing, the only activity by which he defined himself. But the Ritz Hotel papers were only a stay. By April 1961 his metaphorical analyst, the eponymous portable Corona no. 3, had done what a living analyst strives to do – to take the patient through the past in order to alter the present. However, Hemingway saw the past so clearly that in his

Figure 38, (a) and (b). In Idaho, during the winter of 1959, the aging writer asserted that there was never any end to Paris. The following year he would fully understand what the young writer had set in motion when he ended his first marriage and began his second in the city of light (John F. Kennedy Library).

diminished state he could neither bear the present, nor see a future that he was willing to endure – and the writing process as self-analysis provided no safety net. He wrote the letter of withdrawal to Charles Scribner on 18 April – three days before his first suicide attempt and five days before a second suicide attempt resulted in his return to the Mayo Clinic. But Mary Hemingway did not post it. After editing the manuscript, and choosing *A Moveable Feast* as the title, she forwarded the manuscript and Hemingway's letter to Harry Brague on 27 July 1963. His final words on the Paris book were found by Don Skemer, Princeton's curator of rare books, as he prepared in September 1992 for the new openings in the Scribner's Archives.

Attached to Hemingway's withdrawal letter is the list of titles we have come to expect as the final evidence of Hemingway's intention when a work was nearly ready to leave his hands.[51] *A Moveable Feast* is not among them. The title he chose was "The Eye and the Ear" (from Eccl. 1:8) – just three verses beyond the passage from which he had chosen the title for *The Sun also Rises*. The verse reads:

> All things toil to weariness;
> Man cannot utter it,
> The eye is not satisfied with seeing,
> Nor the ear filled with hearing.

Notes

A FRAME FOR HEMINGWAY'S PORTRAIT OF THE ARTIST

1. *A Moveable Feast* (1964), *Islands in the Stream* (1970), *The Garden of Eden* (1986).
2. Hemingway's ambivalent interest in Proust spanned many years, and his narrative techniques, as well as his meditations on the past as a way to understand the present, became more attractive to Hemingway as he tried to write of his own early years. (Proust died in 1922, Hemingway's first year in Paris.) He had endorsed John Dos Passos's complaints about Proust in May 1933 (*Selected Letters,* 390); but he may not have read Proust's long work by that time, since in a letter to Max Perkins the following year he discusses writing a trilogy and writing a novel about his childhood in Oak Park (after his mother and his father's brother, George Hemingway, are dead), and then asks Perkins to send him the "4 volume Proust" (30 Nov. 1934; PUL).

    By 1953, *remembrance of things past* had become shorthand for Hemingway's writing about his early years, and mentions of Proust in correspondence with Buck Lanham indicate that he was re-reading him. He also complains to Wallace Meyer, his Scribner's editor, that the "literary detectives" (at this point Philip Young and Charles Fenton) who want to probe into his past "destroy all possibility of your own Remembrance of Things Past where Albertine was really a girl and not your chauffeur" (15 March 1953; PUL). Just how much his agitation is linked to the intent of using his early years in fiction is indicated by the fact that Hemingway began the first draft of "The Last Good Country," the posthumously published story of Nick Adams and his tomboy sister Littless, on the back of an angry letter to Philip Young that is at the Kennedy Library. Ironically it would be Young who edited the story for publication nearly 20 years later.

    By 1959, when Hemingway's mental and physical deterioration were becoming manifest in his obsessive attention to detail, he objected to A. E. Hotchner's editing the manuscript of *The Dangerous Summer,* on the grounds that what he had written was Proustian, cumulative in its effect, and eliminating detail would destroy it.

By the spring of 1961, ill and trying to complete the Paris book that Mary Hemingway titled *A Moveable Feast*, he wrote: "[R]ightly or wrongly all remembrance of things past is fiction," and indicated that the book should be so read (File 122; JFK).

3. Hemingway's editors at Charles Scribner's were: Maxwell Perkins, 1926 through mid-June 1947; Wallace Meyer, 1947 through April 1957; and Harry Brague, 1957 through the publication of *A Moveable Feast* in 1964. The two Scribners who were his publishers were Charles Scribner Sr. (1890–1952), and Charles Scribner Jr. (1921–). The present representative of the family firm (now merged with Macmillan) is Charles Scribner III (b. 1951).

4. EH-Lanham, 30 June 1946; PUL. Unless otherwise noted, all letters to Buck Lanham are cited from Princeton University Library holdings.

5. Hemingway seldom discussed what he was writing, even with his publisher or editor, and in January 1951, when Charles Scribner, Sr. began pressing him about "the big book," joking that he would have to bribe Mary to tell him about it, Hemingway became angry and protective of his working privacy, asserting that unless he revised certain sections it could not be published at all. In May 1952 (three months after Scribner's death) Hemingway tells Wallace Meyer that he will have to "leave here [Cuba]" when the next two books come out. He is referring to the works that became *Islands* and *Eden* (PUL). Several times he declined to tell Buck Lanham what he was writing, but said that it might be publishable only after his death. In the summer of 1956, working on the African book, he told Robert Morgan Brown:

> I don't think it would ever be acceptable at Fordham and I think maybe it would be better to wait until I'm dead to publish it. But it is an awfully good story and I was born to write stories not to please the authorities. The story is so rough and I am trying to write it so delicately that it is quite difficult. Miss Mary wants me to write it because she thinks it is a lovely and wonderful story. But I swear it will never be serialized in the Sunday Visitor [a Catholic newspaper]. (HRC)

6. In fact, one might reasonably think of the novel Robert Jordan plans to write as the Nick Adams stories which Hemingway had already written, or as some permutation of the elephant story that David Bourne writes.

7. The beginning of self-knowledge that would culminate in Hemingway's attempt to withdraw *A Moveable Feast* is evident in his letters to Mary during the late summer and early fall of 1960. They were opened in 1992 at the Kennedy Library and will be quoted in Chapter 6.

8. Nick's statement was originally an interior monologue deleted by Hemingway from the end of "Big Two-Hearted River," and appears as "On Writing" in *The Nick Adams Stories*.

9. Bill Walton was Chairman of the Commission of Fine Arts throughout the Kennedy and Johnson administrations, and later a trustee of the Kennedy Library. He now lives near Stone Ridge, New York, and in New York City.

10. Quoted through the kindness of Bill Walton.

RECOLLECTIONS WITHOUT TRANQUILITY

1. I list these alphabetically by author: Carlos Baker, *Ernest Hemingway: A Life Story* (1969); Matthew Bruccoli, *Scott and Ernest* (1978); Peter Buckley, *Ernest* (1978); Jose Luis Castillo-Puche, *Hemingway in Spain* (1971, English translation, 1974); Scott Donaldson, *By Force of Will* (1978); Norberto Fuentes, *Hemingway in Cuba* (1984); Peter Griffin, *Along with Youth* (1985), *Less than a Treason* (1990); Gregory Hemingway, *Papa* (1976); Leicester Hemingway, *My Brother, Ernest Hemingway* (1962); A. E. Hotchner, *Papa Hemingway* (1983); Kenneth Lynn, *Hemingway* (1987); James Mellow, *Hemingway: A Life Without Consequences* (1992); Jeffrey Meyers, *Hemingway: A Biography* (1985); Madelaine Hemingway Miller, *Ernie: Hemingway's Sister "Sunny" Remembers* (1975); Constance Cappel Montgomery, *Hemingway in Michigan* (1966); John Raeburn, *Fame Became Him* (1984); Michael Reynolds, *The Young Hemingway* (1986), *The Paris Years* (1989), *The American Homecoming* (1992); Marcelline Hemingway Sanford, *At the Hemingways: A Family Memoir* (1962); Mark Spilka, *Hemingway's Quarrel with Androgyny* (1990).
    See also: Gioia Diliberto, *Hadley* (1992); Mary Hemingway, *How It Was* (1977); Bernice Kert, *The Hemingway Women* (1983); Carl Rollyson, *Nothing Ever Happens to the Brave: The Story of Martha Gellhorn* (1990); Alice Sokoloff, *Hadley, The First Mrs. Hemingway* (1971).

2. Clarence's tendency to think of himself as a pioneer endured long after the physical and emotional strain of this cyclical pastoral had caused its charm to fade for Grace. As late as 1920 his letters show that even in Oak Park he thought in the terms of a farm wife; and that he was frequently tired and irritable from pursuing his domestic frugality into the hot summer nights when he remained in Oak Park while the family was in Michigan. His letter of 21 July 1920, Ernest's twenty-first birthday, makes no mention of that event, but records:

    I have another one hundred pounds of extra good granulated sugar all in one bag (#25.00). So you see I am looking out for next winter. You know the philosophy . . . "Most natives lay up for the Winter, even the chipmunks and deer mice." (HRC)

    On 27 August he reports that it has been "an ideal harvest day. I long for the fields and the open life," and that he has made twenty-seven quarts of pickles (HRC).

3. Hemingway's medical records at the Kennedy Library, opened in 1991, establish that the diagnosis of his hemochromatosis had been made in January 1961.

4. Muscular Christianity was an approach to living idealized in nineteenth-century British popular novels, where fortitude and vigorous activity were combined in a hero from the business middle class to create a literary character with the piety, grace, and social responsibility of the "good" aristocrat of earlier literature. The ideology provided the plot/character basis for a whole series of nineteenth-century novels, including Dinah

Craik's *John Halifax, Gentleman*. Clarence and Grace read *Halifax* together during their courtship and early marriage, and their letters show that it became a blueprint for their life together (see Mark Spilka, *Hemingway's Quarrel*, chapter 1). Further, they tried to stamp their identification with the sentimental vision on the lives of their children, as some of their letters to Ernest quoted later in this chapter will reveal. At Christmas in 1900, Clarence gave Grace stationery imprinted with an arrum lily, the flower that young Guy Halifax gives to Lady Caroline in the novel. The "crest" that Grace designed for the art glass door insert in their new home in 1906 bore the same lily. When their third child was born in 1902, they named her Ursula for Ursula March Halifax, the wife of Gentleman John; and when they purchased a small farm across the lake from Windemere in 1905, they named it Longfield after John Halifax's country retreat.

5. Just how long this stance of moral righteousness endured for Clarence is evident in a letter to his youngest daughter Carol on her eighth birthday:

> We planned a long time before you were born that our children should have good healthy bodies and some good food and a nice place to live and grow up without all the naughty people of the cities to bother them. (16 July 1919; HRC)

6. The scrapbooks are unpaginated. I remain skeptical of this yoking of nature and God to the destiny of Grace Hemingway's first son because letters between her and Clarence which are at the Humanities Research Center indicate that on 25 August 1899 (when Ernest was four weeks and four days old), Clarence was in Michigan making arrangements with carpenters, and Grace was at home in Oak Park, consulting by mail on the details. On that date she writes her father that she has encouraged Clarence to stay a few more days, and makes no mention of joining him. The contract for the house was signed by Clarence alone on 8 September. The trip from Oak Park to northern Michigan was a strenuous one, involving steamboat, train, and carriage. That Grace made this journey with a toddler (Marcelline) and a small baby when all details had been arranged by mail seems improbable.

   These letters contain some insight into the accusations of extravagance that have been leveled against Grace by some biographers (e.g., Lynn, *Hemingway*, 36–37), for she tells Clarence that if the house plans are too pretentious, they should build the shell and add on later.

7. What Hemingway chose to remember about his childhood became fact for him, and in a letter of 13 September 1945, this version is given to Mary:

> My father married the daughter [of the Halls, who lived across the street] and as long as my English grandfather was alive it was all right because he exercised all discipline and controlled the daughter and her terrible selfishness and conceit. But I can remember when he died very clearly

and how the pain of what he died of was unbearable and he wished to shoot himself and my father removed the cartridges from his pistol (which he had under his pillow) and he was allowed to shoot himself with an empty gun. I was a very little boy (six) but it still seemed to me the cruelest thing I could imagine, much worse than what God who they were always spooking us with, would do. My father was very proud of it. I could never forgive him for that nor for any of his other cruellnesses [sic] nor weaknesses . . . .

I think both my father and my mother were very cruel (not to me and have no kick ever because I was armoured after about eleven). My father did such good kind things and so many people worshiped him, but I think he was worn out by over-work almost into a state where cruelty, against the habit of goodness, was almost like the pleasure of a drink.

Looking back I can't see where my Mother was ever good. . . . I think my mother's main fault was spoiling from her Mother dying when she was a girl [Grace was twenty-two when her mother died!] and her sense of the loss of a career (she made her debut with Schumann Heink in Madison Square garden . . . and never forgave my father for she haveing married him altho she could *never* have been a great opera star but never relinquished the idea). She was just phony enough, though, to have made a certain success. And absolutely without conscience and absolutely ruthless and absolutely justified to herself. (JFK)

There is nothing in the family records to confirm or disprove Hemingway's version of his Grandfather Hall's last days. Perhaps most relevant to an understanding of the postwar years of Hemingway's life is that if he believed what he had written in this letter – as he frequently came to do with other tales he had told, then by the time he took his own life, he also believed that he was the third generation of suicidally intent men, and that they had come from both sides of his family.

8. Clarence's comments on Grace's symptoms (numbness of face and pain in smiling, along with an inability to grasp or hold, and pain in arms and hands) are strange. He contends that "the reflexes for the arms are not in the back, but in the brain," and advises that the masseuse who is treating her may not know that (Grace to Clarence, 4 Aug., and Clarence to Grace, 12 Aug. 1917; HRC).

9. The Hemingway children had been born in two groups: Marcelline (1898), Ernest (1899), Ursula (1902), and Madelaine (1904), Carol (1911), and Leicester (1915). This complicated the parents' overseeing of the older children's activities when the younger children needed their constant presence. In the summer of 1917 Clarence, with one household helper, had the responsibility for a two- and a six-year-old, and for four teenagers.

10. The manuscript versions of *At the Hemingways* were given to the Hemingway Museum in Oak Park by Marcelline's children. Draft C recounts Clarence's bringing home illegal brook trout and railing against regula-

tions that made them illegal, an incident that may have provided the creative basis for the purloined logs in "The Doctor and the Doctor's Wife." Another incident recounts Mrs. Dilworth's carrying out Clarence Hemingway's request that Ernest and his friend Harold Samson be required to work for their keep at the Dilworths when they had gone there after Grace ordered Ernest out of the house for bad behavior. Marcelline speculates that it was Ernest's anger at the long arm of his parents' discipline reaching to the Dilworths which prompted him to use their names in "Up in Michigan." Her manuscript continues:

> My father could be terribly stern when he felt a principle was at stake. . . . The trouble for us, as children, was that the things he'd felt were matters of principles were so confusing to us. Punishment was swift and severe when we were "bad" but how to know which thing or action of ours would bring on a whipping was the problem, at times.
>
> Being on time, to the minute, was important, we learned. Coming home *instantly* when Dad or mother whistled the penetrating "Bob-White" which was our family whistle summons was another. Being rude or talking back to parents or not doing what we were told immediately brought an immediate punishment. Punishment varied from being put to bed on bread and water to being whipped with a razor strap (Daddy), a hair brush back (Mother) or being deprived of some trip or pleasure we'd looked forward to expectantly.

In another typescript version Marcelline describes the humiliation of being compelled to pull down her undergarments, even into her teens, when her father spanked her. She then recounts the events that ended the twinning:

> Our parents were conscientious, not cruel, but the repeated and frequent physical punishments were not as hard to bear as the psychological ones. One I remember was given to me in the second grade. The summer after we, Ernest and I, finished the first grade, while we lived temporarily in the rented house near the library on North Grove Avenue [#169], Mother decided that I should have a boy's cropped haircut like Ernest's. We had been dressed alike as little children, both in fluffy girl's dresses and picture hats. Later we'd both had Buster Brown haircuts and had worn overalls alike each summer and had even had winter boys' coats in keeping with Mother's wish to have us be twins. I'd been kept in kindergarten until I was seven and a half waiting for Ernest to be six, so Mother could start us in school together. She was determined that we should be as much alike as possible.
>
> I hadn't minded too much before but now I was almost eight and I resented having my hair cut off like a boy. [There is a discrepancy here, for if Marcelline, who was born on 15 Jan. 1898, had remained in kindergarten until she was seven and a half, and then spent a year in first grade with Ernest, which he began in 1905, she would have been eight

and a half when the events related here took place.] I cried and begged to keep my hair. I felt people laughed at me – I didn't want to look like a boy. It wasn't too bad after we got to Walloon for my short hair was easy to dry after swimming. Nobody talked about it and my hair grew out all summer at the cottage. In September we came back from Walloon to our newly finished house on Kenilworth Avenue. When September came the grown out hair was long on my neck and two long side burns looked particularly repulsive to me. One of my new playmates from Holmes School, in the new neighborhood, came up to my bedroom after school to play. I remember standing in front of my little grey dresser and looking in the mirror. "I just hate my hair," I said. "Oh, it will grow out," my new friend said. "It wouldn't look so bad if you didn't have those long side pieces hanging down in front with your ears showing." "I know it," I said. "I just hate looking like this." "Why don't you cut them off?" my friend asked. "Oh, I don't dare," I remember saying quickly. "Oh well, if they were even at the ends instead of hanging down so long, they'd look a lot better," she said indifferently. "I'll get some scissors and you show me," I said. "Oh, no, it's your hair. You cut it yourself," she insisted. "Just even it a little. It will hardly show." I went into Mother's room and borrowed her gold-handled scissors shaped like a stork, and in fear and trembling I cut off a bit in front of one ear.

"That looks much better," said my playmate. I cut off a bit on the opposite side. It wasn't even with the first. I cut a bit more from the first side then more on the second side to even that. The first thing I knew both sides were cut off even with the middle of my ears and I looked like a boy again!

"Now you look worse than ever," my frank little friend remarked. "Well, I've got to go home, good-bye." She left. I was left alone with my butchered hair. I stayed in my room in fear until my father insisted I come downstairs to supper.

Mother saw my hair and let out a shriek. "What have you done to your hair? You look a fright. I am ashamed of you. Eat you supper and go right up to bed. You shall be punished."

I tried later to tell Mother how badly I felt, how I'd only meant to cut off a little on the ends to even the wisps, how the girls from school said it looked awful the way it was. I wept, I begged forgiveness. Nothing helped.

The next morning when I got up Mother met me with a white nain-sook baby bonnet in her hand. "You will wear this from now on all day long until your hair grows out. I think you'll remember not to cut your hair again." She tied it firmly under my chin. "But I can't wear it to school," I said. "Yes, you can and you will," Mother said. "I'd rather be spanked," I said, "don't, *please* make me wear a baby bonnet to second grade, please."

It was useless. I wore the white bonnet. The children jeered. Mother went to school with me to explain to the teacher that I was to keep the bonnet on all the time "to remember." Even the teacher protested, though feebly, and I wore that badge of shame for days. Finally the teacher asked Mother if I hadn't worn it long enough and Mother relented and the bonnet was removed.

I was grateful to the teacher but I never felt at ease with the children in that grade again. I was very glad when the teacher suggested that I skip the rest of second grade and move on to the third grade, which was in another building on the same grounds.

Ernest stayed in second grade. I don't know what that humiliating punishment taught me that was useful excepting that if adults cut your hair it's all right but if you do it it's wrong. I can't believe that publicly humiliating a child ever did anything but make the child feel hurt and inferior. But I feel sure my mother thought she was doing the right thing.

My parents often disagreed about methods of raising us. Although my father was not in accord with my mother's theory of the baby bonnet humiliation as an effective discipline, as I learned much later from his reference to it as "that silly baby bonnet business," my father said nothing against it at the time. He insisted on quicker, more, to his mind, effective punishments, which Mother often resented. (Sanford, *At the Hemingways,* manuscript draft C, 48-52.)

Marcelline was sixty-four years old when *At the Hemingways* was published, and as the various drafts were written (apparently beginning in 1955), she had silenced her own voice more with each. For the published memoir, she invented a playmate who had done the haircutting that caused her so much humiliation.

11. In a photo of Marcelline, Ernest, and Ursula, dated October 1904, Ernest is dressed as a boy (and the girls as girls). There are no later photos of him in clothing that is unmistakably feminine (Scrapbooks, volume 2; JFK).

12. Marcelline's oldest son, John Sanford, told me at the Hemingway/Fitzgerald Conference in Paris in 1994 that he had fond memories of Grace, but believed Ernest disliked Marcelline so intensely because she was like her own mother – "very bossy."

13. Leicester Hall, Grace's older brother, had visited the Hemingways at Christmas 1918. His letters to Grace, beginning with that of 1 January 1919, indicate that she was under a great strain when he was there, and that there was tension between her and Clarence which was related to her resignation as choir director at First Congregational Church under the threat of being forced out. Leicester asks Grace if her mail is read by others and suggests that she bring the two younger children and come to him in California for a long visit. In 1920–21 Grace did so, taking only Leicester who was five, and entering him in kindergarten in California for a few months (HRC).

14. See Michael Reynolds, *The Young Hemingway,* 81, and n.26, 266; and Max Westbrook, "Grace Under Pressure." The Westbrook essay includes letters documenting Grace's stance on the eviction of Ruth Arnold.

15. Evidence from Clarence Hemingway's hand shows that as early as 1903 he suffered from "nerves" that required a rest cure; and at least twice between 1909 and 1920 he wrote his wife the details of financial provisions he had made for his family in the event of his death under suspicious circumstances. In the most detailed of these, the letter of 26 October 1909, which is reprinted and discussed in Michael Reynolds, "Hemingway's Home," he instructed her in the creation of a consistent and convincing story for a coroner's hearing. Throughout the spring, summer, and early fall of 1920 Clarence wrote of his need to have some relief from the family so that he would not be so irritable; and when he went north to close Windemere, he included in a letter to Grace a check for $1,000 and keys to a safety deposit box "in case of some unforseen accident I should not return" (2 Oct. 1920; HRC).

16. Perkins, who was responsible for Scribner's publishing Zelda's novel *Save Me the Waltz*, wrote to Hemingway:

   Scott and Zelda seem to be settling down in Baltimore, and I hope that they will stick with it, and be compelled to be quiet. . . . [I]f Zelda can only begin to make money, and she might well do it, they ought to get into a good position where Scott can write. (11 June 1932; PUL)

17. Now that the letters of Charles Scribner Sr. and Hemingway (as well as those of Perkins and Hemingway) are open, their complex relationship can be recognized as the contact point of a great deal of Hemingway's enmity toward James Jones, enmity that was inexplicable when one could read only what was published in *Selected Letters*. The projective and abusive references to Jones in Hemingway's unpublished letters were born of the resentment Hemingway harbored toward Perkins and Charles Scribner Sr. for the constraints they imposed on the language of his fiction. Throughout late 1950 and into 1951 Hemingway piled up scurrilous judgments and predictions about Jones in his letters to Scribner and to Wallace Meyer. Some were childishly and simply scatological; others – for example, the hope that Jones would make $20,000,000 for Charles Scribner and then hang himself – were more complex and probably self-reflexive. Finally, when *From Here to Eternity* was praised by the same reviewers who had dismissed his war novel the previous year, Hemingway's jealousy of the attention and the freedom of language usage Scribner had allowed Jones poured out in a torrent:

   Boy I can remember when Scribners cut Go Fuck yourself out of A Farewell to Arms and all the different times when blanks were left in soldier talk. Then I had to learn how to make those words clear without useing them. Then along comes this boy and he is allowed to use them all and the critics say[,] "This is the first man with the courage to write as a soldier's talk. etc." They should say this is the first man Scribner's allowed to say "Go fuck yourself . . ." [T]hanks to the courageous Jones and the fact that his book, with an absolute license to use them (I can use them). In fact I wouldn't be courageous if I didn't. So God bless courageous Jones the liberator of the American language and God bless his publisher. (4–5 May 1951; PUL)

18. The picaresque narrative was first called *A New Slain Knight* and is the "Jimmy Breen" manuscript that is closed at the Kennedy Library. Two fragments from it were published as "A Train Trip" and "The Porter" in *The Complete Short Stories* (1987).

19. The letters of Grace and Clarence Hemingway show that they both used the blessing "May the Lord watch between me and thee while we are absent the one from the other," which Robert Jordan attributes to his father in *For Whom the Bell Tolls*, but Clarence's letters to his son remain those of a father talking to a child long after Ernest is grown. In 1918 he wrote to Ernest, who was in New York waiting to go abroad with the Red Cross: "May a great success always follow you and keep you pure and a hundred percent a Christian gentleman, willing to fight for the Right" (19 May 1918; JFK). Two years later Clarence counseled, "I want you to represent all that is good and noble and brave and courteous in Manhood, and fear God and respect Woman" (4 June 1920; JFK). Six months earlier he had pleaded with his son: "[S]urely you want to continue as my chum and keep me in your confidence" (16 Dec. 1919; JFK).

Clarence had returned *In Our Time* (1925) to Three Mountains Press because he thought it "filth," but Hemingway may not have known this, or if he did, may have assumed that his mother was exercising her position of literary arbiter through Clarence. Grace had lectured Ernest at length on the tone and language of *The Sun Also Rises*. Although Grace and Clarence held in common the very language of dangerous and sentimental abstractions that Frederic Henry rejects, the critical difference for Hemingway may have been that his mother attacked his work, while his father, as far as Ernest was aware, attacked only his personal life.

20. Just how clearly Mary Hemingway recognized Hemingway's intentions toward Valerie Danby-Smith is documented in a letter she wrote to Ernest on 13 July 1960 trying to avert his taking Valerie to Ketchum with them on his return from Spain. One of her arguments is "Perhaps you should include an estimate of how much use you will make of her as secretary, and the cost of equipping her for life out there . . . it would seem uselessly extravagant to spend much on teaching her to shoot" (JFK).

21. In mid-January 1940, Hemingway was alone and lonely at the Finca Vigía (with Martha away on assignment), and had no one to read his daily writing on *For Whom the Bell Tolls* because, as he wrote Max Perkins, "Pauline hates me, and she has the best judgment of all" (PUL).

In June 1933, Hemingway had written Pauline from Havana asking how to get his hair from red (which it had become in the bleaching process) to blonde. She replies:

About your hair, don't know how to turn red to gold. What about strong peroxide – or better what's the matter with *red* hair. Red hair lovely on you, and you lovely yourself, and it will be so nice to have you again. I was thinking at lunch sick of not having you here. (JFK)

22. Martha had become involved with Bertrand de Jouvenel (the step-son of Colette) in 1930 and had returned to her home in St. Louis fleeing a commitment to him in 1931. In St. Louis she took up an earlier relationship with Joseph Stanley Pennell, a former classmate at the John Burroughs School who was working for the *St. Louis Post Dispatch*. In September 1931 she left Pennell (who had written a sonnet sequence to her), saying she planned to marry Jouvenel. Yet only a few days after their parting, she wrote Pennell that she doubted her ability to commit herself to any person. In 1943 she helped to get Pennell's Civil War novel published at Scribner's.

Martha and Jouvenel lived together but did not marry – despite the fact that an announcement of their marriage appeared in St. Louis newspapers. In a letter of October 1933 Martha told Pennell that she would stay in Paris and raise Jouvenel's son by an earlier marriage, yet a year later she was back in the United States alone.

This fleeing of commitment was a pattern that would be repeated, even with the men that Martha Gellhorn did marry: Hemingway, Nathan (Bill) Davis, and Tom Matthews. It is also observable in love affairs: for example, in the early 1950s Martha fled an intense relationship with Dr. David Gurewitsch that she had described to a friend as having finally helped her to overcome the fear and mistrust which had remained since her marriage to Hemingway. She seems to have been incapable of sustaining love that tied her to one place. This information comes from several sources: Bernice Kert, *The Hemingway Women*; Carl Rollyson, *Nothing Ever Happens to the Brave*; Emily Williams's 1980 interview with Martha Gellhorn (Franklin D. Roosevelt Library, Hyde Park, NY); Scribner's Archives IV, PUL; Baker-Hemingway Papers, PUL; letters in a private collection; and the author's interview of September 1992 with Bill Walton.

23. *The Trouble I've Seen*, stories of people uprooted by the Depression, was published by William Morrow and Company. In 1940, Scribner's would become Martha Gellhorn's publisher.

24. It is clear from correspondence that Pauline had been tolerant of the affair for a long time, and that Hemingway was making *her* draw the line that would free him. In a letter of 8 July 1939 she says, "My God, Papa, but you have made things complicated with this Einhorn [Gellhorn] business. Next time I see you we'll have to work something out. Can't go on this way" (JFK).

25. The Charles T. Lanham Papers contain his view of Martha and of events in the Hurtgen Forest which was written for Carlos Baker (PUL). Leicester's innuendoes are distributed throughout *My Brother, Ernest Hemingway*.

26. Gellhorn broke her long silence to write "On Apocryphism," for the *Paris Review* in 1981. There she demonstrates the absurdity of Stephen Spender's and Lillian Hellman's tales about Hemingway's morbid interests in

the carnage of the Spanish Civil War. A recent piece, "Cry Shame," is about press treatment of the Clinton administration and appeared in the *New Republic* on 27 June 1994.

27. In late 1949 or early 1950 Charles Scribner recalled in a letter to Hemingway the visit he had made to him and Martha more than a decade earlier:

> My first view of Marty was in the corridor of the hotel in Havana when she advanced on me with an open door behind her through which the sun was pouring and setting her hair aflame. It was a sight for the Gods . . . . (PUL)

28. Bernice Kert recounts Joris Ivens's judgment that Martha "was doing most of the courting" (*The Hemingway Women*, 305). It is a perception shared by Archibald MacLeish, who wrote Carlos Baker on 9 August 1963:

> I watched Miss Gelhorn [sic] conduct her amazing and quite shameless attack on that marriage. I have always suspected that his subsequent detestation for her was in part the consequence of his own sense of disloyalty [to Pauline, who is discussed earlier in the letter]. (Carlos Baker Papers; PUL)

The Ivens and MacLeish evaluations are shared by Herbert Matthews and Josephine Herbst, who also knew Martha and Hemingway in Spain.

29. The unpublished correspondence at both the Kennedy Library and Princeton suggests that Hemingway was sometimes resentful of Charles Scribner's attention to Martha's career before and during their marriage. For example, his particularly truculent and abusive cable of 11 September 1941 to Scribner, which seems to be motivated solely by Scribner's defending a plagiarism action against Hemingway without telling him that the charge had been made, has another dimension. When the firm was bringing out Martha's book *The Heart of Another*, which Hemingway wanted published under "Martha Hemingway," Charles Scribner had visited them in Cuba and done something Hemingway considered preemptive regarding Martha's contract – exactly what is not clear; but at that time Hemingway was already resentful of Scribner's influence over Martha. On 23 April 1942, he closes a letter to Scribner with, "Martha's fine and sends you her love, whatever that means."

As the marriage of Hemingway and Martha deteriorated, her letters to Charles Scribner Sr. became more confiding, making it clear that she had sought and received emotional support from him during the difficult period when her marriage was ending. Several thank him for orchids sent to her hotel in New York or London, but a letter of late 1949 or early 1950 provides the strongest evidence that Scribner felt some sense of regret or betrayal as Martha changed from the "sight for the Gods" he had considered her at their first meeting (in Havana, 1939) to a flesh and blood woman, exhausted after a trans-atlantic flight with a small child. In a letter to Hemingway, Scribner reports that Martha has adopted an Italian child:

> She [Martha] phoned me yesterday from Englewood having landed from Italy the day before. She is off for Mexico Friday. She is now the proud but exhausted mother of a 19 mo. old son. She says it is all completely legal, though unnatural – so doesn't blame either of us. (PUL)

The letter ends with "Well F – - or S – - on all this or whatever you would say – only I thought it might intrigue you." It was almost unheard of for Charles Scribner Sr. to use expletives – even in their deleted form – and even in his letters, to Hemingway.

30. Hemingway's retrospective description, to Buck Lanham, of the intelligence operations (22 Dec. 1948; PUL).

31. Although the recent biography of Gellhorn (Carl Rollyson, *Nothing Ever Happens to the Brave*) contends that the characters who appear in the novel Martha was writing during this period are based on people she encountered on the Caribbean assignment, *Liana* is far closer to an allegory of the end of her marriage to Hemingway.

32. The now-sealed letters of Martha to Ernest (which Mary Hemingway returned to Martha) document her desire to make the marriage satisfy both their needs. These efforts have frequently been overlooked by those critics who feel that Martha abandoned Hemingway. See Bernice Kert, *The Hemingway Women*, chapters 22 and 23.

33. Ironically, Martha probably arranged Duran's assignment to the Cuban operation during her recent stay with Eleanor Roosevelt. He had been a lieutenant colonel in the Loyalist army and led the forces of the Spanish Republic at the decisive, losing battle of Teruel. Years later, in letters to Buck Lanham, Hemingway would recount in convincing detail having himself led forces at Teruel, his information coming from Duran.

34. Edna Gellhorn's reply to Scribner's letter is dated 15 February 1945. She is well informed about Hemingway's attachment to Mary Welsh, having been told of his poem to Mary by visiting Bill Walton, who had tried to have a copy made but found it difficult as the poem was written on toilet paper and bits of brown wrapping paper. She seems neither surprised nor disappointed by the demise of the marriage, concluding her letter with the prediction that Ernest will do a fine war novel when he settles down to writing again (PUL).

35. Biographer Michael Reynolds obtained the file under the Freedom of Information Act and shared it with Jeffrey Meyers, who promptly published it in the *New York Review of Books* without acknowledging his source.

36. Hemingway and Hadley had one son, John (Bumby), born in 1923. After his parents' divorce Bumby lived with his mother, first in France, and later in the Chicago area, spending school holidays with his father, Pauline, and his two half-brothers. Pauline had two difficult labors that culminated in caesarean deliveries – of Patrick in 1928 and Gregory in 1931. Following the birth of Gregory, they were warned that another pregnancy might be life-threatening.

After Hemingway had left Pauline and Martha had left him, he would

contend that Pauline's refusal to practice contraception ruined their sex
life. However, Pauline's letters to Hemingway – who was absent so often
and so long that she took to calling him "Mr. Home-and-away," – present
the picture of a woman quite strongly attracted to her husband, and
frequently yearning for his presence in her bed.

37. The exact date on which Scribner made his disclosure is not clear, for that
letter is missing from the correspondence; but on 15 May 1950 Hemingway responded to the news with this:

> She [Martha] told me she had an abortion by Bernard de J. but she never
> told me anything about it making her sterile and she always used contra-
> conceptives [sic]. You don't think I ought to lose my blind and shining
> faith in womens do you? What do you think about marrying a man and
> swearing to him you were not Jewish and to conceal from the man she
> was going to marry, who was giveing [sic] up a damned good wife and
> the control and custody of children and paying punitive alimony, the fact
> that she was definitely sterile from cause. (PUL)

On 12 October 1950, Mary wrote Charles Scribner a long letter detailing
the abuse, both physical and psychological, that Hemingway has inflicted,
concluding with:

> I won't bore you with my attempts at analysing all this, and I have nothing
> conclusive in the way of analysis anyhow. Ernest has doubtless had these
> periods before, although it looks like the disintegration of a personality
> to me.

Mary was, as she indicates here, not a very analytical person, but in this
letter she also links Hemingway's abuse of her to her own sterility, as she
continues:

> I don't know if he ever told you but last spring in New York, after
> thorough examinations, I discovered definitively that my one remaining
> reproductive tube is congested and I can't have a baby. When I married
> Ernest I had no faint idea that this was or would be true . . . He taunts me
> with this. And it may be one of the basic reasons for his behavior. (PUL)

In her chirpy, unreliable memoir, *How It Was*, Mary gave quite a different
version of the problem, saying that Ernest never recriminated with her
over her barrenness.

38. Announcing Bumby's birth to Ezra Pound in 1924, Hemingway said that
Hadley still liked him "better than the baby." And in an early letter to
Mary he explains that children aren't very interesting until they become
old enough to do things with their parents.

39. The first mention of wanting a child with Martha occurs in the mid-
January 1940 letter to Max Perkins in which Hemingway also complains
that Pauline, his best critic, won't read his work on *Bell* (PUL). This is
about a month after Pauline had left Key West with their two sons.

ISLANDS IN THE STREAM

1. I use "ur-text" here to indicate "a reconstructed proto-text set up as the basis of variants in extant later texts" (*American Heritage Dictionary*), for although "The Land, Sea, and Air Book" never became a reality, the interconnectedness of the narratives discussed in this chapter establishes that proto-texts existed – not simply in Hemingway's mind, but in the 1,600 pages of manuscript that Lee Samuels had microfilmed for Hemingway in late June or early July 1951 (EH-Charles Scribner Sr., 4 July 1951; PUL). On 6 August 1951, Samuels sent Hemingway a receipt (#3517, 17 July 1951) for the deposit of this microfilm in the Havana branch of The First National Bank of Boston, saying, "This receipt covers the microfilm. It can be delivered only to you or to your order" (JFK). In *Hemingway: A Life*, Carlos Baker, working from Mary Hemingway's remembered chronology of her husband's writing, had indicated that *The Garden of Eden* was the first postwar writing and was begun in 1946 (454). However, at a later point Baker refers to *Eden* as "begun ten years earlier [hence 1948] and partly used in the development of *Across the River and into the Trees*" (540). While it is true that *Eden* began as a separate novel in 1948, both *Eden* and *Across the River* branched off from the ur-text: *Eden* was not a source for *Across the River*.

2. Hemingway to Charles Scribner in explaining his taking time off from "The Land, Sea, and Air Book" to write *Across the River* (24 Aug. 1949; PUL).

3. In response to Charles Scribner's comments on *Across the River*, Hemingway writes from the Ritz Hotel in Paris, where he is finishing the manuscript:

   In reserve I have the poems which have all of everything I know in them; and which I distilled to preserve that when thought it was doubtful if I could complete a novel (1944–45–49). Then there is 87,000 (it was 187,000) of another book. I boiled down, and distilled 100,000 out of it to make 17,000 for this book [*Across the River*]. I have not touched the sea, nor the air, but I've thrown in most of the land in this one. (28 Nov. 1949; PUL)

   The manuscripts of *Across the River* and *Old Man* that are at the Kennedy Library are almost clean typescripts. While Hemingway makes direct statements about where he saw the old fisherman material fitting in (as the fourth volume of The Sea Book), there is no clue as to how one of the two main characters in "Bimini" was transported (or was going to be transported) to the European theater in WWII to provide for the land portion of the novel's covering seven months of the land war in Europe, which is how he describes it. The closest that the ur-text approaches this logistical problem is Roger's thinking (in the deleted "Miami" section) that he should be in Spain reporting that war as he drives north and west toward Montana in September 1936.

4. In a letter to Charles Scribner that makes clear he is not talking about "The Sea Book," Hemingway says that if he knows he is going to die he will burn "the big book" because he doesn't want anyone else editing it. He had written a provisional ending for *Eden* approximately three months earlier and was probably returning to work on *Eden* after revising the galleys for *Across the River* (26 Sept. 1950; PUL).

5. Letter on Samuels' microfilming (EH-Charles Scribner, 4 July, 1951; PUL). Letter on status of bank vault rentals (Mary Hemingway-Lee Samuels, 18 Feb. 1961; HRC). Letter suggesting arrangements for paying rental on vaults after Cuba froze bank accounts of non-citizens (Samuels-Ernest and Mary, 3 Mar. 1961; JFK).

6. **(a)** On 2 February 1944, while preparing to leave Cuba to work for *Collier's*, Hemingway wrote to Ramon Lavalle, whom he had known from his Paris years (when Lavalle was a boy) and had seen most recently during his Far Eastern trip with Martha in early 1941. Lavalle's four-year-old daughter Wendy, who had prompted Hemingway to declare how much he wanted a daughter when he visited the family in Hong Kong, had died in a Japanese internment camp in 1942. Hemingway has just learned of the death, and he advises Lavalle to join the Marine Corps, where he will be able to fight against the people he hates most:

   > It is a great happiness to kill those we hate (not supposed to be said) but it is. I have always tried not to get to like it too much because it is very narrowing for you as a writer and always I am a writer sooner or later. But still think it is very good to do. . . . It is good to hear from you and be angry about things in particular. *I have just been angry in general like a fire under a boiler* [my emphasis]. Remember that you can only allow yourself the luxury of getting killed if you have your family well provided for. (2 Feb. 1944; Baker Collection, PUL)

   (b) Two eye-witness accounts of Hemingway's conduct under fire also point to his seeking a witnessed, heroic death. The chronology Buck Lanham prepared for Carlos Baker in the early 1960s describes Hemingway's refusal to leave the table when others took cover in the cellar as the lethal, silent 88 shells were fired into Lanham's command post while the men were eating a celebratory meal in October 1944 (Baker-Hemingway Collection; PUL). Bill Walton, then a *Time* correspondent, told me of Hemingway's throwing himself protectively on top of him as they were strafed in December 1944 (author's interview).

7. *Men at War,* the preface for which was the only non-journalistic work Hemingway published in the decade between *Bell* and *Across the River,* lists him as editor for the volume; however, it originated in a proposal by William Kozlenko; and several times while he was writing the preface (aboard the *Pilar,* in the midst of the Crook Factory) Perkins, who was editing the preface, chided Hemingway about its tone.

8. The deleted "Miami" section of *Islands* presents Helena (named Audrey in *Islands*) as a young journalist who has Martha Gellhorn's physical appear-

ance, and is seeking a fiction-writing mentor in the apprehensive Roger Davis (File 102; JFK).

9. For a further account of the writing conflicts between Martha and Hemingway during this period, see Gregory Hemingway, *Papa* (90–92). All of the considerable primary evidence I have seen supports Gregory's analysis of the matter.

10. As what would be their last summer together passed with Hemingway either absent at sea (with his two younger sons) or surrounded by his male entourage at the Finca, Martha could see no end to her stewardship, and she wrote to Charles Scribner of how sick she was of having her time consumed by such things as hinges for doors, cement bases for water tanks, salaries, and nails (27 Sept. 1943; PUL).

Two years later, Hemingway was faced with completing these renovations and other repairs as he awaited a visit from Buck Lanham and his wife. (Mary, who had come to Cuba in May and helped to plan the changes to be made and/or completed, was in Chicago getting her divorce.) After enumerating the domestic concerns that reduce his time to write and exercise, he writes: "Feel like an old bear that used to kill cattle on the open range and now has to live off the garbage dump behind Old Faithful Inn in the Park" (12 Sept. 1945; JFK).

11. Although Hemingway told Martha that seats on the plane were solely for military personnel and combat reporters, the record shows that two actresses (Gertrude Lawrence and Beatrice Lillie) were on the flight. Martha described her passage to Europe in a May 1944 letter to Charles Scribner Sr. which is riddled with a censor's excision of all mentions that would give the route of the convoy's travel or the time that it was at sea. Only her departure and arrival can be documented (PUL).

12. Mary had made her living by writing all of her adult life, and Hemingway's efforts to separate her from that source of income and recognition were unrelenting and devious. See Chapter 6, note 22.

13. Hemingway gave a label to his technique, which is the jai alai term for a double-wall rebound, when he told Mary in 1958 that the Paris sketches were autobiography by *remate* (Baker, *A Life*, 540).

14. The "Lost Leader" was General Raymond ("Tubby") Barton whom Hemingway felt had treated Lanham unfairly and behaved like a coward in the Hurtgen Forest. The Hemingway-Lanham papers at Princeton give Lanham's version, which verifies Hemingway's.

15. All quoted Hemingway letters to Lanham are at Princeton unless otherwise noted.

16. When Hemingway first offered *Old Man* to a magazine (*Cosmopolitan*) for publication he described it as "20,000 words or close to" (EH-Mary, 7 July 1951; JFK). He identified the published novella as 26,531 words and sent the longer manuscript off "just before the 10th March [1952] revolution here" (EH-Harvey Breit, 23 June 1952; JFK).

17. See Chapter 4, note 2 for evidence of the point at which *Eden* seems to begin.

18. On 3 March 1951 Hemingway had written Scribner that he had just done "1578 words on another long section of the sea book [which] should come out in the fall of 1952." On 18 May he says:

finished third book of the four books that make up the Sea (not a title but a designation). . . . If anything should happen to me ever I am sure you could publish the third and fourth parts with only corrections in spelling. It is written as cleanly as the part you read. (PUL)

What Scribner had read during his February visit was the manuscript that became *Old Man*, but it was not the 26,531 words that allegedly (I have not done a word count) make up the published novella, for on 8 July 1951 Hemingway turned down *Cosmopolitan*'s offer of $10,000 for a version of *Old Man* that he refers to in a letter to Mary as "20,000 or just under" (JFK).

19. Carlos Baker indicates that magazine publication for *Old Man* was suggested to Hemingway by Leland Hayward in February 1952, citing Hemingway's letter of 4 and 7 March to Wallace Meyer. But whatever Hayward had suggested, Hemingway was being disingenuous with Meyer, since more than six months earlier he had already rejected *Cosmopolitan*'s offer.

20. In "Miami" (1) the Helena/Audrey character wants both to write and to "be good for" Roger so that he will write more; (2) Roger remembers Helena's mother and her husband's suicide, as well as his own dark tendencies and his "bitch of a mother"; and (3) he tells Helena of the lost suitcase.

Other elements which form a link between "Miami" and *Eden* include Roger's belief in the transformative power of absinthe, Helena's having been married to a gay man (as Marita was in the manuscript of *Eden*), and Helena's desire to become caretaker of the writer's creativity (File 98, pp. 864–72; JFK).

21. Hemingway gave what he described as the first typescript of *Old Man* to Gianfranco Ivancich, Adriana's brother, expressing the belief that Gianfranco could sell it to pay debts on his finca. I have not be able to locate the typescript (EH-Adriana, 28 Oct. 1952; HRC).

22. **(a)** A fragment in File 99 at the Kennedy Library reveals that an early title for "Bimini" was "The Happy Summer." Files 103–110 contain the Bimini re-writes, with File 108 (a 466 page typescript) dated "May 1–Aug. 6, 1951." **(b)** An undated note from Malcolm Cowley, File 101, indicates that the marlin episode may be too much like that in *Old Man*. Cowley also remarks that "Thomas Hudson is still Roger" and that Hudson is becoming a painter, George Davis a writer. Cowley does not see here that George Davis becomes the painter Thomas Hudson, and that his surname is given to the writer Roger Davis. While Cowley's comments on "Bimini" are undated, File 110–3 contains his comments on "Cuba" that are dated 9 April 1965, indicating that either Carlos Baker or Charles Scribner Jr. (perhaps both) asked him to bring some kind of order to the manuscript of "The Sea Book." **(c)** See also Robert Fleming, "Roger Davis of *Islands:*

What the Manuscript Adds." (d) The puzzlement some critics expressed at Hemingway's giving the sons to Hudson in the manuscript revisions indicates they did not see that Hemingway had split the artist and the father, and that the children are trapped between them. See, e.g. Earl Rovit and Jerry Brenner, *Ernest Hemingway*, 170; and Philip Young, "The Writer in Decline." Young seems to sense the *doppelganger* nature of Davis and Hudson, but he does not explore it. (e) Narrator writes and paints (Baker-Hemingway manuscripts 0365, Folder 2; PUL); Hudson as a writer (File 98.10, p. 452; JFK); Roger as a former painter (File 108.4, p. 7; JFK).

23. "Bimini" had originally ended with the departure of Roger and his sons on successive days, and George resigned to the loneliness that has reclaimed his life.

24. For example: Phil in "The Sea Change," Philip Rawlings in *The Fifth Column*, and the writer in a fragment at the Kennedy Library [Philip Haines was a writer . . .] (File 648a; JFK).

25. On 12 October 1950, shortly after "Cuba" had been completed, Mary wrote Charles Scribner that she planned to leave Ernest:

> The reason I have to leave Ernest – not easy for me since I have no other home and no money – is that in his program of being a tough guy, he has destroyed what I used to think was an inexhaustable supply of devotion to him. He has been truculent, brutal, abusive, and extremely childish. (PUL)

26. (a) In a deleted fragment Thomas Hudson thinks:

> I would rather love a good house and the sea and my work than a woman, . . . He knew that would never be true. But he could almost make it go. . . . He was still trying and he was painting very well. (File 104, p. 16; JFK)

(b) Marjorie Kennan Rawlings, a Scribner's writer who visited on Bimini in June 1936, wrote Max Perkins:

> There is, obviously, some inner conflict in Hemingway which makes him go about his work with a chip on his shoulder . . . He is so great an artist that he does not need to ever be on the defensive. He is so vast, so virile, that he does not need ever to hit anybody. Yet he is constantly defending something that he, at least, must consider vulnerable. It seems to me that there is a clue to it in the conflict between the sporting life and the literary life; between sporting people and the artist. That life on the water, with its excitement, which almost nothing that I have experienced can equal, is a self-containing entity. When you are a part of it, nothing else seems valid. Yet occasionally a knife would go through me, and I became conscious of treachery to my own . . . [T]he sporting people lave your soul [but] when you leave them you are overcome with the knowledge that you are worlds away from them. You know things they will never know. Yet they wear an armor that is denied you. They are somehow blunted.

Hemingway is among these people a great deal, and they like and admire him – his personality, his sporting prowess, and his literary prestige. It seems to me that unconsciously he must value their opinion. He must be afraid of laying bare before them the agony that tears the artist ... of lifting the curtain that veils beauty that should be exposed only to reverent eyes. So, as in *Death in the Afternoon*, he writes beautifully, and then immediately turns it off with a flippant comment, or a deliberate obscenity. His sporting friends ... are the only people who are pleased by the things in his work that distress all the rest of us. (PUL)

Rawlings's letter is reproduced in full in John Delaney, "The Archives of Charles Scribner's Sons" (175–77).

27. It is surprising how many general readers and fine, sensitive critics assume that the death of his oldest son causes Hudson to give up painting. A closer reading of the text rules out such a simple explanation.

28. Although Roger does not appear in the novel after "Bimini," in discards from the "At Sea" manuscript the captain of the ship is at one point Roger Chapman, and his first mate is Mike. Their relationship resembles that of Davis and Hudson in "Bimini" (Baker-Hemingway manuscripts 0365, Box 25; PUL). In the novel, Willie's exhortation to the fatally wounded Hudson, "Don't die, you bastard, [j]ust hold it and don't move," elicits a single word from Hudson: "Roger," which may be a cryptic pun acknowledging his double who has gone missing (IS, 465).
There is an extended treatment of the death and burial of a flyer named Roger in a passage deleted from *Eden*. Despite the fact that the *Eden* passage refers to WWI, this episode may provide a clue to where that portion of the ur-text which became *Across the River* once fitted.

29. On the night of 1 October 1951, Pauline and Hemingway had argued long distance over Gregory's involvement in a drug incident in Los Angeles, and a few hours later Pauline died on the operating table as the result of an undiagnosed pheochromocytoma, a rare adrenal tumor, which had sent her blood pressure soaring and then plunged her into a fatal shock. Jinny Pfeiffer, Pauline's sister, who had witnessed her reaction to the phone conversation, blamed Hemingway. The following summer he told Gregory that *he* had killed his mother. It was the last time Gregory saw his father alive, although Hemingway continued to support him, writing a check for his medical school tuition in May 1961 during his last confinement at the Mayo Clinic; and, ironically, it was in his medical studies that Gregory learned that the adrenalin release which triggered the fatal rise in his mother's blood pressure was probably the anger generated by her phone conversation with his father. See Baker, *Hemingway: A Life*, 496; and Gregory Hemingway, *Papa*, 6–8.

30. Robert Fleming's *The Face in the Mirror: Hemingway's Writers* is an important extended consideration of Hemingway's concern with the artistic and ethical dilemmas of his artist protagonists.

31. Hemingway owned all of Joyce Cary's novels. See James Brash and Joseph

Sigman, *Hemingway's Library*. Bill Walton, himself a painter of recognized stature, recalls that during one of his annual visits to the Finca Vigia Hemingway asked him to read a piece of *Islands*, and that when he told him the portrayal of Hudson as a painter was unconvincing, "the weather became rather chilly" (author's interview). Walton remembers that Hemingway also considered making Hudson a sculptor, an alternative that may have been related to the importance of the Rodin statue in *Eden*.

32. Three weeks after his leaving Key West for good, but at the point where Pauline had finally forced him to choose, Hemingway wrote Max Perkins: "[W]ould like to have a daughter. I guess that sounds funny to a man with five of them but I would like to have one very much" (mid-Jan. 1940; PUL).

33. It was the boys' second summer in the enterprise. Hemingway's view of what he was adding to his sons' development, and the resonance of his own early years, can be glimpsed in a letter of 7 September 1942 to Max Perkins:

> I have to send Patrick north this week to go to school. He feels it is sort of like haveing the gates of Eden shut. We have had a batchelor house here all summer and have had fine times. . . . What we've been doing this summer has given them the same sort of grounding the kids got in Marryat's time. The sea is a marvellous discipline for kids because you have to be neat, orderly, economical and unafraid to enjoy it. (PUL)

34. Charles Scribner, Mary Hemingway, and Baker edited *Islands*. Baker saw Hemingway's work in the novel as "The Narcissus Principle" and believed that "to his original impulse to transform his personal past into material for art was added an ulterior and perhaps mainly subconscious determination to exploit it as a means of justifying himself and his actions in the eyes of the world" (*Writer as Artist*, 384–85).

35. Torpex is a highly explosive powder used in torpedoes, mines and depth bombs.

36. W. H. Auden.

37. Jack (Bumby) had been taken a prisoner of war near Montpellier, France, in October 1944 and came to the Finca to recuperate in June 1945 after more than six months of imprisonment.

38. Note that Bobby, the bartender at the Ponce de Leon, asks Roger if he and Thomas Hudson are related, and adds, "You look like quarter brothers and the boys look like both of you" (IS, 154–155).

39. During the writing of "Cuba," Hemingway wrote Lillian Ross that he had dived very deep into the Gulf Stream the previous day, and was tempted to stay down, giving us a splendid example of the way in which incidents in life and fiction merge in his work – often leaving the reader with no sound basis for determining where one ends and the other begins (Baker, *A Life*, 485).

40. In deletions from "Bimini" Roger tells of a winter spent in Montana

running trap lines and says that he never felt so much like a fascist as when he was trapping. George responds,

"Hell, Roger, you don't have to explain to me. When I was a kid I liked to kill everything. Now I don't like to kill anything." (File 98–6, p. 324; JFK)

Roger's memories of trapping in Montana and his repudiation of killing animals when it is not necessary to sustain one's life are akin to David Bourne's challenge to his ivory-hunting father in the elephant story; and both Denis Zaphiro (Hemingway's guide on the 1953–54 safari) and A. E. Hotchner (who hunted with Hemingway in the fall of 1960) testify to the fact that, after 1953, Hemingway wanted more to watch animals than to kill them.

41. There is an interesting slip here which suggests the enduring quality of the early years in Cuba when Hemingway's sons were often with him, and the blurring of that time into the novel. Hudson's sons were killed at the end of the summer of 1936, yet he remembers them as being with him at the bar in Cojimar on Christmas morning of the first year of the war (IS, 209).

42. Through the period when this part of the manuscript was being written for the first time (1945–46), Hemingway reports several times dreaming that Buck Lanham has become "a rummy." The material of these dreams seems self-reflexive, for there is no evidence that Lanham ever drank excessively.

43. By the time Hemingway became involved with Mary Welsh in London, he was, like Jake Barnes, sexually dysfunctional. In a letter of 19 September 1945, he wrote her: "Since met you at low ebb of my fortunes, have recovered Mr. Scrooby [the name he used for his penis]" (JFK).

44. "Up on the porch Thomas Hudson kept on painting. He could not keep from hearing their talk" (IS, 190).

45. During the return voyage from Africa there is much talk of making love in a lifeboat (the Princess doesn't want to). On a side trip, Hudson and the Princess sit in the back seat of a car while her husband and the driver share the front:

He had not slept with the Princess on the ship . . . [but] they had both reached a sort of ecstasy of desperation . . . Thomas Hudson saw the back of the Prince's head . . . and he remembered now that the road from Damascus to Haifa, where the ship was anchored . . . runs down a river. There is a steep gorge in the river but it is very small as it would be on a small-scale relief map and in the gorge there is an island. He remembered the island better than anything on the trip. (IS 226)

"Cuba" was being written while Hemingway was revising the galleys of *Across the River,* and the labial, vaginal, and clitoral images of the gorge, river, and island are nearly identical to those in the gondola passage in that novel: "[U]nder the blanket . . . [Colonel Cantwell's] ruined hand . . . searched for the island in the great river with the high steep banks" (*Across the River and into the Trees* [hereafter ARIT in citations], 152–153).

46. Lying on the deck, Hudson reflects that "there was no use thinking about the others. He had lost them, too, and there was no use thinking about them. He had traded in remorse for another horse that he was riding now" (IS, 383).

47. Hemingway explained to Perkins the world he was representing in *Men Without Women* (1927): "[I] want to call it Men Without Women [because] in all these [stories], almost, the softening feminine influence through training, discipline, death or other causes, [is] absent" (14 Feb. 1927; PUL).

48. One cannot be certain how much voice Baker had in the editing, but Charles Scribner Jr. indicates in his memoir that "The laboring ore in publishing *Islands in the Stream* was wielded by Carlos Baker." (*Among Writers*, 80). Furthermore, Baker's comments suggest that he was not entirely satisfied with the results: in *Writer as Artist* he says, "[T]he published novel gives grounds for the belief that the cutting [of "Bimini"] was not carried far enough" (389, n.20).

49. In each of the five extended treatments of *Islands* besides Baker's there is some insight into the complex nature of Thomas Hudson's self-destruction, but no critic truly hears the sons' anxieties; and none sees alcohol as a significant factor in the depression that has overtaken Hudson by the time "Cuba" begins. **(a)** Joseph DeFalco recognizes that Thomas Hudson is a painter only "in superficial matters of color and detail," that the sea is a symbol of the cosmos, the background against which Hudson's "contracted ego deludes itself into believing that it knows itself," and that therefore the two sea episodes involving David define Hudson early in the narrative (" 'Bimini' and the Subject of Hemingway's *Islands in the Stream*"). **(b)** Richard Hovey concludes that machismo destroys the masculine self it professes to support since Hudson "lives by and exemplifies the famous code and . . . is the most miserable of the Hemingway heroes" (*"Islands in the Stream:* Death and the Artist," 261). **(c)** Gregory S. Sojka hears the echoes of Nick Adams in the novel and sees *Islands* as a transition between the Nick Adams stories and *Old Man;* but he gives Hudson greater status as a painter than the text can support ("Art and Order in *Islands in the Stream*"). **(d)** Arthur Waldhorn is more sensitive than any other critic to Hudson's inadequacy as a parent; but in matters of Hudson's merit as a painter, he has taken the assertion for the accomplishment (*A Reader's Guide to Ernest Hemingway*, 200–211). **(e)** Earl Rovit and Gerry Brenner, in holding to Baker's view that Hemingway was trying to deal with personal anxiety by assigning it to Hudson, do not see the instances in which he is treated with irony (*Ernest Hemingway*, 168–73).

THE GARDEN OF EDEN

The citation of manuscripts for *The Garden of Eden* has been done in the manner that I believe will make the material easiest to find at the Kennedy Library. The series is cited first: e.g., 422.1. A dash then follows to designate the folder: e.g., 422.1–2. Following the folder designation I have inserted p. or pp. before citing pages to avoid confusion of folder and page. Not all of the manuscripts have page numbers, and when this occurs, I have cited the chapter. Users should be aware that the folder number does not signify the chapter that it contains, for in the main series, 422.1, there are forty-six chapters stored in thirty-seven folders.

1. The papers of Charles Trueham Lanham (1902–1978) and of Carlos Baker at Princeton University reveal that Lanham not only provided Baker with what Hemingway would have called "the true gen" about the period they had been together in Europe; he also read the drafts of each chapter of the Baker biography, used his own information network to locate Hemingway correspondence and, in 1962, tried to persuade Mary Hemingway to deposit at Princeton the material that forms the Hemingway Archives at the J. F. Kennedy Library. This was a period when she was being courted by Columbia University, the Library of Congress, and the New York Public Library. Baker dedicated *Hemingway: A Life Story* to his wife and to Lanham. The biographical sketch which Lanham provided to Baker says:

> General Lanham has written extensively for military publications and, in his younger years, for national magazines and other periodicals throughout the United States. As a young officer he achieved a considerable reputation as a poet. Several of his better known poems are still being republished after more than twenty-five years.

   While finishing the first draft of *Across the River*, Hemingway wrote Lanham that "the hero is a combination of Charlie Sweeny, who used to command a regiment in the Foreign Legion, me, who never could command my way out of a wet bunch of willows, and you" (11 Oct. 1949; PUL). All other cited letters to Lanham are at Princeton unless otherwise noted.

2. When Hemingway's middle son, Patrick, became ill at the Finca in April 1947, and Pauline came from Key West to assist in his care, she and Mary Hemingway became good friends. In the four remaining years of Pauline's life, they spent a good deal of time together, with Mary visiting her in Key West and California, and Pauline returning to the Finca occasionally. During her restoration of the Key West house Pauline had acquired some expertise in construction, and although Mary does not acknowledge the fact in *How It Was*, it was she *and* Pauline who drew the plans for the tower at the Finca in the summer of 1947; and Pauline came from Key West to check on its progress while Ernest and Mary were in Idaho during the winter of 1947–48. Pauline's letter of 21 January 1948 to Ernest and Mary (which Mary misdated as 1945) opens "Dear Men," a greeting she had used for Ernest and Hadley twenty-three years earlier. For about eighteen months after meeting Mary, Pauline continued to visit the Finca more often than anyone knew until the opening of her letters at the Kennedy Library in 1992.

   With a lesbian sister, Jinny, to whom she was very close, Pauline seems also to have been comfortable with bisexuality. Her letters to Mary suggest that a special relationship existed between them, and those to Ernest are replete with praise for Mary's physical beauty, good nature, and competence. I have been denied permission to quote Pauline's correspondence with Mary; however in a letter to Mary which is at the Kennedy Library (and is labeled "May/June 1949" in Mary's hand) Pauline tells Mary of her forthcoming trip to Europe. It is a document that seems to have an erotic subtext. Mary's letters to Pauline have not surfaced.

Further suggestion of an erotic relationship between Pauline and Mary can be seen in a Hemingway letter of 24 May 1947 to Buck Lanham describing the renewed intensity of his sex life with Mary and how well Mary and Pauline get along. The letter testifies to a supercharged erotic atmosphere at the Finca during the beginning of Pauline and Mary's friendship which may indicate a reprise of events in 1926 when Pauline and Hadley seem to have been in a similar configuration around Ernest.

Peter Griffin indicated that Hadley told her first biographer (Alice Sokoloff) on tape that Pauline liked to crawl in bed with her and Ernest at Schruns and Juan-les-Pins in 1926 (Mark Spilka, 358, n. 14). Hadley's most recent biographer, Gioia Dilberto, speaking to the Friends of the Hemingway Collection in 1992, dismissed this as the trio's sharing breakfast in bed. Several things seems relevant in judging the credibility of such an interpretation: the first that Ernest and Hadley were both large people and beds of the time, unless custom made, were simply double beds – ca. fifty-nine inches wide. Further, if the cozy mornings at Schruns continued at Juan-les-Pins the following summer, as Hadley's statement to Sokoloff indicates, they occurred *after* Hadley had learned in late April or early May that Pauline and Ernest were involved. (The Hemingways announced their separation in August.) Hadley's letters to Ernest, published by James Nagel in 1988, shed additional and puzzling light on this period, showing what seems a culpable willingness on Hadley's part to tolerate, or even welcome, Pauline's attentions to her husband (see James Nagel, "Kitten to Waxin").

That Hemingway may have orchestrated a *ménage à trois,* and then used it as the creative basis of incidents in *Eden* seems even more likely in view of the fact that the letter to Lanham which describes the amity between Pauline and Mary closes with "(KEEP ALL THIS UNDER YOUR HAT TOO)." Further, Hemingway's letters of 13 August and 6 September 1948 to Charles Scribner display considerable and unexplained hostility toward Pauline during the time when she and Mary were closest, suggesting that he may have later resented the friendship he had earlier encouraged (PUL).

Additional evidence of the threat Hemingway seems to have felt when a conjunction that he could not control occurred between his ex-wives is the fact that in 1949 he was furious on finding that Pauline and Martha had met in Venice, a city that he considered his own (EH-Charles Scribner, 26 Aug. and 10 Oct. 1949; PUL).

The first evidence that Hemingway wants to involve Mary in the tonsorial activity that will become part of *Eden* is a letter she has misdated "1946." From internal evidence it was probably written while she was with her parents in Chicago in May 1947, the trip she returned from to find Pauline at the Finca:

My dearest Kittner
    Please never do anything against how you want to do about your beauty lovely hair . . . I'd thought we might fool with something lovely and possibly make mistakes but have *fun* in our one and only lives and correct if we made mistakes . . . . (JFK)

Although Mary told Carlos Baker (*A Life,* 647) that there were six letters concerned with hair styles written at this time, only the one quoted is extant, and she may have been confused, for Hemingway wrote her five other letters about hair-styling that are at the Kennedy Library: three when she was with her parents in Chicago in 1949 (26 and 30 Sept., and 1 Oct.); one when she was with Marlene Dietrich in 1952 (2 Oct.); and one when she was with her parents in Gulfport, Mississippi, in 1954 (15 July).

    In 1948 Hemingway became quite specific in a letter Mary misdated "1945" that was definitely written on 26 August 1948. Mary was at the Finca, and the letter contains directions she is to convey to a stylist, Gustavo Dorio, at Dubic's in Havana:

Tell him you have decided . . . to wear your hair sleek and long instead of short and curly. But you are keeping the same style of hair-cut. You don't want to lose any of the length and you want the very front, that was so short, to grow into the sweep back. You would like the bottom of the hair neatened; trimmed in the same style it is . . . .
    [I]n a week it will look wonderful and chic-er than any dame in Vogue and as it grows (*and does it grow*) it will keep a fine shape.
    Ask Gustavo if there is anything he can recommend . . . to be absolutely harmless to the hair . . . you can use on it to keep it straight and sleek. . . . [T]he girl in my book will have her hair the way you are fixing yours . . . and some 500–000 up people will have d'erections about it. (JFK)

This is the hair style of Barbara Sheldon in the deleted plot of *Eden.*
    In fact, evidence suggests that among Hemingway's four wives, it was only Martha Gellhorn who would not engage in the gender-bending antics that he found erotic, for the phrase that he used to identify the subject of *Eden* to Buck Lanham in a letter of 12 June 1948, "the happiness of the Garden that a man must lose" (Baker, *A Life,* 460), is used in describing Martha in the letter of the same date to Charles Scribner: "She could never depict happiness truly; the happiness of the Garden that you must lose." In the light of this description, Martha's own heretofore cryptic wit in a letter of 26 January (1950) to Charles Scribner, takes on fuller meaning: "Isn't he [EH] odd, the way he believes he invented everything,

even the Guaranty Trust? Ah well, I daresay he will go mad someday and imagine himself Diana, Goddess of the Hunt, and be netted . . ." (PUL).

3. Hemingway was revising the Paris sketches that became *A Moveable Feast* concurrently with *Eden* during the fall and winter of 1958–59. He wrote Charles Scribner on 12 April 1959 from Cuba: "Have had my mss. photostated here (lst two books of this book) and am having the next 42 chapters I shipped from Ketchum to NY either photostated or microfilmed there." Box 24 of Scribner's Archive VI contains that microfilm along with a Certificate of Authenticity issued in New York saying that "Rewrite 16/11/58 p.15 and ending with 'Map . . .' are accurate and complete, etc. and property of Ernest Hemingway." This is dated 13 April 1959 and signed by Alex Moskoni (PUL).

   The microfilmed ms. seems identical to the main *Garden of Eden* manuscript at the Kennedy Library (the File 422.1 series which contains forty-six chapters), although I have not been able to do a page by page comparison because of copying restrictions on the *Eden* manuscript. The microfilm also contains complete texts of Cyril Connolly's *The Unquiet Grave*, several books about elephants and elephant hunting, and a 1953 Michelin Road Guide to Spain and Portugal, suggesting that Hemingway intended to further revise *Eden*, probably in a development of the African stories. A letter of 10 October 1959 to Mary says that on the trip down from Paris he

   made good notes on country for the novel which is in Hendaye and in Spain. Have driven and made notes over every place these unfortunate kids drove except the Riviera part which is so changed it would only kill what you remember. But have gotten the driving impressions and the fast car stuff down and solidly replanted in my head. (JFK)

   The details of Hemingway's accelerating involvement in writing *The Dangerous Summer* and his deteriorating mental and physical condition (discussed in Chapter 6) make it unlikely that he ever worked on *Eden* again.

4. The provisional ending (file 422.2–1) contains a conditional suicide pact and was being written at the same time as the long story with Martha in it "off stage" which became "Cuba" in *Islands*. Hemingway's letter to Lillian Ross (discussed in Chapter 3, n. 39), with its improbable account of an abortive, suicidal dive into the Gulf Stream was, therefore, written near the time he used drowning as a metaphor for Thomas Hudson's emotional vacuum in *Islands* and David Bourne's making of the suicide pact in the provisional ending.

5. In an undated letter of transmission from Tom Jenks to Charles Scribner Jr. which accompanied the copyedited manuscript of *Eden*, Jenks says that he will read the galleys when they come in and continues:

   The preparation of the ms. to show Patrick and then the clubs and so on has been rapid, and while I am confident of the quality of the writing and of the editing, I am also particular about making sure of all the small stitches. So anyone looking at the ms. now for right or whatever should know that there may be some very very small (though perhaps significant) changes made. (PUL)

6. Hemingway's letters often provide indirect evidence for what he was writing during the postwar years. The elephant story has a source in Robert Scott's *Between the Elephant's Eyes,* which Hemingway read (probably while he was on safari) in 1954. On 27 October 1953, Hemingway wrote Wallace Meyer (his editor at Scribner's) from Patrick's farm in Tanganyika, ordering Ernest Jones's *The Life of Freud as a Young Man,* as well as African books from Roland Ward, an English firm. After the plane crash he wrote Meyer to send the books from Nairobi to Cuba in "the usual way," and he says, "About the stories: have some lovely African ones. Some funny. Some very sad" (1 April 1954). By 29 July 1954, he is impatient with the failure of these books to arrive and tells Meyer that he needs them "for work as well as for reading." From August through November 1954 he mentions the African stories to both Charles Scribner and Wallace Meyer, but never gives details except to say that he finished one (7 Aug.) and to complain that after the announcement of his Nobel Prize, people flock to the Finca to see "the old elephant in the zoo" (25 Nov.). At this point he is clearly writing of the old elephant in the unpublished African book (all letters cited, PUL).

   In a letter to Adriana Ivancich, Hemingway says, "I am writing about African and Ngui and Charo [Wakumba men in the African book]. . . . I wrote one good one [of seven stories mentioned], but it is too sad" (30 Jan. 1955, misdated 1954; PUL). This is the elephant story.

7. Even E. L. Doctorow – whose review, "Braver Than We Thought," recognized that *The Garden of Eden* is a novel about creativity, that Catherine Bourne is "a brilliant woman trapped into vicarious participation in someone else's creativity," and that in *Eden* Hemingway may have been writing to transcend the strategies of his own style, but was edited in conformity to the strategies of the style for which he was known – saw the elephant story as only "a threadbare working of a boy's initiation rites" imitative of Faulkner's "The Bear."

   Another serious, sympathetic reviewer who missed the metafictional point is John Updike. Although the elephant tale has received more critical attention than any other single element of *The Garden of Eden,* no one has perceived that Catherine's desire to share in the creative process is linked to the death of the elephant. Critical treatment of the relationship of the framing honeymoon narrative to the African stories displays the same limitations.

   (a) James Nagel sees most clearly just how integral to the novel the elephant tale is, and he considers the story one of Hemingway's best – a judgment with which I agree. See "The Hunting Story in *The Garden of Eden.*"

   (b) Frank Scafella is the only critic to perceive the fusion of the elephant and Catherine in David's mind as he writes. See "Clippings from *The Garden of Eden.*"

(c) John Raeburn, although he considers *Eden* as Hemingway's vision of the incompatibility of sexual tenderness and artistic strength, writes without knowledge of the manuscript and never links Catherine and the slain elephant. See "Sex and Art in *The Garden* . . . "

(d) Gerald Kennedy recognizes that the conflict between Catherine and David is related to the writing and that Catherine's discontent is related to her gender role; but he does not perceive her desire to share the creative act and seems unaware of the significance of the elephant story except that the writing of it is an activity with which David resists androgynous absorption. See "Hemingway's Gender Trouble."

(e) James Hillman, a Jungian analyst, treats the elephant story in a way that reveals splendidly David Bourne's identification with the animal, but the Jungian approach militates against manuscript evidence, for Hillman insists upon an achieved wholeness for David Bourne at the closure of the novel that the manuscripts will not support. See "The Elephant in *The Garden of Eden.*"

(f) Three critics consider the elephant story an interpolation rather than integral to the problem of David Bourne's inability to reconcile writing and intimate relationships in the rest of the novel: Kathy Cackett, "*The Garden of Eden*"; Kenneth Lynn, *Hemingway,* 541; and Mark Spilka, *Hemingway's Quarrel,* 280. Two other essays are hostile to the novel in ways that obviate a balanced consideration of it: to Robert Jones, "Mimesis and Metafiction," Catherine is "malevolent, willful and castrating"; and to K. J. Peters, "Thematic Integrity," she is "deviant."

In 1987, Scribner's severed the elephant tale from the novel and published it as "An African Story" in *The Complete Short Stories.* Inexplicably, the text omits the reference to *bibis,* the women with whom David finds his father and Juma at the *shamba.*

8. While there may have been no photographs or reproductions of the statue in the 1920s, there were when *Eden* was in progress. See Mark Spilka, *Hemingway's Quarrel,* chapter 11. Rodin's sculptures were inspired by Ovid's *Metamorphoses* and Baudelaire's *Les fleurs du mal,* and his illustrations of "The Gates of Hell" group appear in a French volume of Baudelaire that Hemingway owned (Brasch and Sigman, *Hemingway's Library,* no. 425). A plate of the embracing women also appeared in *Rodin Skulpturen* in 1953 (plate 52).

9. The haircut which Barbara Sheldon gives Nick, and its effect on their erotic life and his creative accomplishment, is described almost identically to the tonsorial/erotic adventures of Thomas Hudson discussed in Chapter 3 (Files 112, 113; JFK).

10. Files 650–52; Kennedy Library. Detailed discussion of the endings of *A Farewell to Arms,* which have much the quality of personal metaphor that Catherine's destruction of the African stories has in *Eden,* appears in Michael Reynolds, *Hemingway's First War,* chapter 1.

11. See Robert Fleming, "The Endings of Hemingway's *Garden of Eden*," and Mark Spilka, *Hemingway's Quarrel*, 308–10. Because I began using the *Eden* manuscripts in October 1990, my citations differ from those of Fleming and Spilka, who used the manuscripts at an earlier time when they were differently classified.

12. I refer here to the concept that true androgyny is the possession of, and a balance between, maleness and femaleness; it is manifest in uninhibited access to the emotional and behavioral range that is expected of both males and females in the culture and the period under consideration.

     In Hemingway's life and in his work – early as well as late – it is clear that he was attracted by the potential exchange and/or combination of culturally male and female traits – dominance roles, activities, physical appearance, and sexual positions. The "tough women/tender men" elements of Brett and Jake in *The Sun Also Rises* and of Pilar and Robert Jordan in *For Whom the Bell Tolls*, along with the sympathetic morning sickness Frederic Henry experiences and the offer of Catherine Barkley to cut her hair short if Frederic will let his grow, are but a few examples of this androgynous awareness.

     David Bourne is extremely uncomfortable with his attraction to the visible manifestations of androgyny; and the remorse he experiences after each of his and Catherine's exploits (hair cutting and bleaching, reversed sexual positions) suggests that his attraction to true androgyny is both ambivalent and defensive.

     And I believe that it was Hemingway's own ambivalence which kept him from bringing this narrative together into a completed novel.

13. In correspondence with Carlos Baker, Buck Lanham indicated that Hemingway was still telling the story of Hadley's loss of his early manuscripts during his sixtieth birthday party in 1959 (PUL).

14. Spilka's is a longitudinal study of the Hemingway family, of Hemingway's childhood, of his dependent relationships with women, and of the representation of his serial marriages within his fiction. Another outstanding discussion of the ways in which art and life occupied the same space in Ernest Hemingway's existence is Millicent Bell's essay "*A Farewell to Arms:* Pseudoautobiography and Personal Metaphor."

15. Fredrick Crews in *The New York Review of Books*, Barbara Probst Solomon in *The New Republic*, and John Updike in *The New Yorker* all assume unity of author, narrator, and character. Solomon's review seriously misrepresents the manuscript and asserts inaccurately that in it David Bourne returns as Hemingway at sixty. Crews accepted her assertion as fact in framing his review of Kenneth Lynn's Hemingway biography the year following the publication of the novel.

16. In *A Moveable Feast*, which the unpublished preface makes clear is the predecessor of *Eden*, Hemingway wrote of the end of his first marriage:

     [It is] the oldest trick there is. It is that an unmarried young woman becomes the temporary best friend of another young woman who is married, goes to live with the husband and wife and then unknowingly, innocently and unrelentingly sets out to marry the husband. When the husband is a writer and doing difficult work so that he is occupied much of the time and is not a good companion or partner to his wife for a big part of the day, the arrangement has advantages until you know how it works out. The husband has two attractive girls around when he has finished work. One is new and strange and if he has bad luck he gets to love them both. (MF, 209–10)

17. See Bernice Kert, *The Hemingway Women*.
18. The deleted "Miami" section of *Islands*, written in 1945–46, testifies to the wound this loss had become to the artist after nearly a quarter of a century. Roger Davis, the writer friend of Thomas Hudson, tells his young woman companion (who wants a writing partnership with him) of returning to Paris from Chamby in disbelief that the carbons too had been lost. He links that loss with the exaggeratedly proportioned genitals in the pornographic picture of a woman, and relates his reaction to the loss in images of castration:

> I felt almost as though I could not breathe when I saw that there really were no folders . . . and then I locked the door of the cupboard and went into the next room, which was the bedroom and lay down on the bed and put a pillow between my legs and my arms around another pillow and lay there very quietly. I had never put a pillow between my legs before and I had never lain with my arms around a pillow but now I needed them very badly. (*Complete Short Stories*, 647–48)

19. See Jeffrey Meyers, *Hemingway*, 252. Dr. Lawrence Kubie offered his psychoanalytic attempt to *Saturday Review of Literature* and to Scribner's without success. It was ultimately published in *American Imago* in 1984.
20. Hemingway's fascination with hair began early and continued throughout his life. As early as May 1933 he had used peroxide on his own hair and asked Pauline how to get it from the red it had become to blond (Pauline-EH; JFK). His focus becomes especially visible as work on *Eden* gets under way (see note 2). In her memoir, *How It Was*, Mary Hemingway recounts that on the last night of his life her husband joined her from another room as she sang "Tutti Mi Chiamondo Bionda" (They all call me blond) (502).
21. I will use the categories introduced by Elaine Showalter in *A Literature of Their Own* (13–36), which are now standard in feminist criticism. Showalter divides the history of literature by women into three phases: feminine, feminist, female – a division that is also useful in examining female characterizations in fiction which transcends historical periods. In the *feminine* mode the character achieves her ends by using traits and behavior that the culture assigns to females. In the *feminist* mode the character protests the powerlessness to which the culture relegates women; and she frequently forms a sisterhood relationship with other women in an at-

tempt to mitigate her lack of power. In the *female* mode the character no longer needs to achieve her ends through the power of the male; nor is her energy consumed in protesting her powerlessness: she is able to act for herself.

22. Two important works dealing with the female's struggle to tell her own story perceived as a form of madness by the male who would suppress it are Charlotte Perkins Gilman's "The Yellow Wallpaper" and Jean Rhys's *The Wide Sargasso Sea* (a book for which Martha Gellhorn's *Liana* was one source). J. M. Coetzee gives the conflict yet another twist in *Foe*, where a woman who was on the island with Robinson Crusoe is considered threatening as she follows the author around London demanding that Defoe tell her story too.

23. Bernice Kert, *The Hemingway Women*, 199, 458. Pauline also expressed her sense of relief after the divorce from Hemingway in a letter of December 1941 to Grace (HRC).

24. The terms used here describe the same relationship of character to culturally constructed gender roles as in note 22. The *masculine* mode accepts the culture's definition of male behavior; the *masculinist* mode rejects and protests against it.

25. Boyle is a mysterious figure, a harbinger of the worst possibilities for David. In the manuscript, David questions his advice about the get being no good, saying that such theories are discredited. Boyle replies, "I'm not theorizing, *J'ai constante* [I am certain]" (422.1–8, p. 35). At a slightly later point the manuscript bears Hemingway's notation to bring Boyle in again "at la Napoule[,] at the bad time" (422.1–9, p. 35). But Boyle never returns, and in the typescript opened at the Kennedy Library in January 1988 (422.8), the entire Madrid scene with him is missing.

Although I am aware of the consensus that Boyle has been created from Charles Sweeny (see, e.g., Reynolds, *The Paris Years*, 325 and n. 12), I believe that Boyle is more closely related to the older Hemingway. Deletions from the manuscript at the two points just cited give to Boyle the quasi-military experiences in intelligence gathering and the raising of mercenaries that both Sweeny and Hemingway had participated in, and that Hemingway attributed to Thomas Hudson in *Islands*.

Further, Boyle seems to be named for John Boyes, one of the bloodiest of the elephant hunters, whose book, *The Company of Adventurers*, Hemingway owned. In the manuscript, the job that Boyle offers David is the leading of black mercenaries. Ernest Moore writes in *Ivory: Scourge of Africa* (which Hemingway also owned) that John Boyes was an ivory poacher, a German-educated Englishman who had his own "well-organized, well-armed khaki-clad and disciplined native force; a little army that made him too much for the British government" (185). Boyes discusses bee tubs as the bride price among East African tribes, and Colonel Boyle of *Eden* says that he never liked the term "honeymoon" because it sounds sticky.

Boyle's absence from the 1988 typescript, where David has a number of tiresomely repetitive war stories of the kind Hemingway told – and

about which Catherine taunts him, adds strength to the view of Boyle as
an archetype of the older Hemingway. So too does the fact that in the
1988 typescript David is given to angry, misogynistic outbursts that both
echo Boyle's prophecy ("the get's no good") and suggest that Boyle has
foreseen the problems David will have with women and with writing
(422.8–13).

26. This is an echo of the warning Hemingway gave Fitzgerald about the
writer's vocation as sexually suspect in the "use the hurt" letter – "We are
all bitched from the start . . ." (*Letters* 408). See Mark Spilka, *Hemingway's
Quarrel*, 282–84, for discussion of the reflections of the Hemingway-
Fitzgerald relationship in *Eden*.

27. In "Miami," the deleted part of *Islands* from which thematic elements were
incorporated into *Eden*, Roger Davis thinks of his Hollywood writing period as masturbating into a test tube.

John Irwin explains David's isolated and isolating creative endeavor:

> The relationship of the masculine self with the masculine-feminine work
> is also an autoerotic act . . . in which through the use of the phallic pen
> on the 'pure space' of the virgin page . . . the self is continually spent and
> wasted." (*Doubling and Incest*, 163)

28. Rowland Ward's *Records of Big Game*, which Hemingway owned and which
Catherine says in the manuscript she balanced on her head for posture
training, has several photos that reveal the aptness of Hemingway's metaphor of the dead elephant lying in a wrinkled pile (325–28). It also
establishes that the elephant in the tale is indeed a treasure if its tusks
weigh 200 pounds each, for only two other animals in *Records* have tusks
larger.

29. The phrase "lust for ivory" was a cliché among writers who deplored the
slaughter of elephants and the evils of the slave trade that were connected
with it. In *Ivory: Scourge of Africa*, Ernest Moore contends that elephant
hunters sometimes colluded in obtaining human flesh for the cannibals
who carried their ivory. Juma has filed teeth that reveal his cannibal
origins.

30. Robert Scott, *Between the Elephant's Eyes*. Hemingway owned books on many
areas of African life, art, geography, history, tribal organizations, and
literature – some of them published in the nineteenth century; thus,
David's statement that he writes about "a country that has no literature[,]
where no one has written to guide . . ." can only be metaphorical.

31. In the *Garden of Eden* manuscript opened in 1988 (422.8–14) Marita's
assurance that they can have sexual "variety without perversion" seems to
be yet another ending although it has not been considered as such by
either Mark Spilka or Robert Fleming (who may not have had access to
that typescript). Just how much Marita will become an accessory in David's
self-comforting fantasy is clearer if we remember that the variety she offers
him puts her in the subservient, impersonal, position of an Arab boy, and
if we know that in the Madrid scene of the manuscript where Catherine

voices her own yearning to paint or write, she asks Andy, "[D]o you believe it about women for breeding, boys for pleasure and melons for delight?" (422.1–6, p. 14).

A further sense of how much David's union with Marita will continue his dichotomized life is inscribed in the background of her plea to David, "Can't I read it [the elephant tale] so I can feel like you do and not just happy because you're happy like I was your dog?" (GE, 203). She is echoing a letter Pauline wrote to Hemingway on 20 April 1937 (while he was at the Florida Hotel in Madrid with Martha Gellhorn): "Oh dear Papa please come home as soon as you can. Wish I could follow you around like a little dog myself" (JFK).

32. Gregory Hemingway's *Papa: A Personal Memoir* relates the real-life basis of some of the boys' drinking practices in *Islands* and discusses their hunting rituals.

33. This lamentation seems to chart a kind of learning curve in which, for Hemingway's male characters, the knowledge always comes *after* it is needed

In *Farewell*, the last long paragraph of chapter 3 is Frederic Henry's meditation on the difference between his own joyless debauchery and the serene celibacy of the priest who invites him to visit his family in Abruzzi: "He [the priest] had always known what I did not know and what, when I learned it, I was always able to forget. But I did not know that then . . . ."

In *Islands*, chapter 15 opens with Thomas Hudson on the *Ile de France* bound for the funeral of his sons:

He had gone aboard the ship early, thinking of it, he now knew, as a refuge. . . . He thought that on the ship he would come to terms with his sorrow, not knowing, yet, that there are no terms to be made with sorrow. (IS, 197)

THE AFRICAN BOOK

1. The African book is closed to researchers at the Kennedy Library. My references are to a typescript at Princeton, and will be identified as AM. About half of the African Book appeared in magazines, but there are large elisions and some rearranging of incidents in the periodical publications:

   (a) Excerpts appeared in *Look*, 25 January 1954 as "*Safari*," and 20 and 27 April 1954 as "*The Christmas Gift.*" These contain some fine photographs.

   (b) Much larger segments of the manuscript appeared (unpaginated) in *Sports Illustrated* as *The African Journal*, 20 and 27 December 1971 and 2 January 1972. They will be cited as (AJ:1, 2, or 3). Ray Cave, who wrote the introduction, also made the editing decisions which are clearly set out (Earl Rovit, *Ernest Hemingway*, 154–55 and n. 5, 192).

2. The correspondence between Charles Scribner and Hemingway gives a running account of his anger toward both Martha and Pauline. On more

than one occasion Scribner counseled Hemingway to drop his feud with Martha, and at least once he returned a letter Hemingway had asked him to pass on to her. See Hemingway's letter of 25–26 August 1949 for his reaction to Martha and Pauline's discussing him in Venice (*Letters*, 669). An unpublished letter to Scribner a few weeks later is filled with invective toward both women. In 1950 Martha learned that Hemingway had recently told mutual friends that he was paying her $500 a month alimony, which was not true. It is an interesting figure, for that is what he paid Pauline for child support *and* alimony, with the sum reduced by $100 per month as each of their two sons reached his twenty-first birthday.

3. Gianfranco Ivancich, Adriana's brother, came to Cuba in early 1949 to take a position with Sidarma, a shipping company with offices in Havana, and lived in the guest house at the Finca for nearly three years. He was very close to Mary, and she seems to have turned to him for affection during the most difficult period of Hemingway's emotional involvement with Adriana. A note from Mary to Gianfranco, whom she called "Bunney" because of his diminutive size, is in the Carlos Baker files at Princeton:

> Bunney-Bunney-
> It is curious how it doesn't get any better - the hurting and longing in the bones and blood and skin and eyes and ears and nose. Sometimes, hurting strong, I ask myself "Was it worth this - that joy, this misery?" And the answer is always "*Yes.*" *Dearest Huomino* [little man].

A note in Baker's hand is attached to the sheet of blue paper saying, "To be —— [unclear] by Jean Preston and not to be read by scholars until after Mary Hemingway's death" (PUL). Strong loyalty remained between Mary and Gianfranco after his marriage, and he went to her side immediately upon hearing of Ernest's death. In the summer of 1992, a scholar who had seen Gianfranco recently, and who harbored considerable antipathy toward Mary, told me (during the International Hemingway Conference in Pamplona) that Gianfranco had expressed respect and affection for Mary, and had alluded to the difficulty of her life during the years he lived at the Finca.
   Hemingway arranged financing for a farm Gianfranco bought in Cuba (which was repaid) and in 1953 gave him a manuscript of *The Old Man and the Sea*. He procured design work for Adriana, whom he considered making his literary agent in Italy (Hemingway-Ivancich Correspondence, HRC).

4. Bill Walton saw the Nick Adams movie with Hemingway in New York and recalled the "best work" remark in an interview. It is about this time (early 1952) that Hemingway began the last of his Nick Adams stories, the unfinished "The Last Good Country."

5. Hemingway's belief that by barring the release of *Across the River* in Italy it would remain unread there, seems either naive or disingenuous, particularly since his English publisher, Jonathan Cape, issued the book without its dedication to Mary and without the usual "All characters are fictitious"

disclaimer. On 20 October, while Adriana and her mother were on the ship to Cuba, Hemingway was informed that *Across the River* had been released in Italy. A few days later he learned that the book, in the Cape edition, had been given a full-page, very favorable review by Paolo Monelli in the most prominent paper in northern Italy (EH-Charles Scribner; PUL).

6. Santiago's flawed humanity is discussed in an interesting light in Gerry Brenner's *"The Old Man and the Sea": A Reader's Companion to the Novel.*

7. The translation of Marcello Camilucci's review, from *L'Osservatore Romano,* is included in a letter of Carlos Baker to Robert Morgan Brown which is at the Humanities Research Center. No date for the original publication appears.

8. See note 1 for locating information.

9. A letter to Hemingway from Wallace Meyer indicates that Meyer had several contacts with Earl Theisen in early 1954 and that Theisen had written that Gardner Cowles at *Look* agreed to the project if *Look* got credit for the pictures (2 March 1954). In September 1954 Charles Scribner writes that Bill Lowe (who had left *Look* shortly after the safari) is making a preliminary selection of photographs for the book (PUL). A greeting card from Hemingway to Mary bears the note "Finish the pix in '56," establishing that some work was done on the project (JFK). A good many of these photos are now in the archives at the Kennedy Library, but since they did not arrive there in a manuscript format, it is impossible to tell if all of those that the Hemingways intended to use are accounted for.

10. The Baker biography gives a fine detailed account of the safari (508–25). My debts here are both to Baker and to Bill Walton, whose memories of Denis Zaphiro's 1957 visit to him in Washington are recorded in the 1992 interview that is at the Kennedy Library.

    John Raeburn's *Fame Became Him* is a carefully researched account of Hemingway's life in the public eye and conveys something of the power of the Hemingway image.

11. In 1940 Hemingway (ironically suffering from a hangover) had written Max Perkins a rationalization of why he had left Key West for Cuba a month earlier:

> You couldn't shoot anymore. The government took over all the Keys and put bird wardens on them. If you did a good days work (a miracle with people bothering all the time, with people always comeing to swim in the pool and your hearing every word they said like from a sounding board) there was nothing to do except go down to Mr. Josie's place and drink, Christ I was getting to be a rummy there. (28 Jan.; PUL)

As early as 1952 Hemingway was complaining of the lawlessness in Cuba and thinking of giving up writing and going to Kenya to live near his son Patrick, who remained in East Africa until 1975 (EH-Wallace Meyer, 20 Oct. 1952; PUL). By the time he left Cuba for the safari, there had been two burglaries at the Finca Vigia, one in which Hemingway wounded a man who had escaped through his bedroom window.

12. Just how proud Hemingway was of this title is indicated by his signature on a letter to Luiz Mendez Mercado nearly two years later: "Ernest Hemingway/Honorary Game Warden, Kenya" (18 Oct. 1956; JFK).

13. The crashes and their aftermath are recounted in a comic tone that ignores the seriousness of Hemingway's injuries in the second of the excerpts featured in *Look* (20 April 1954). Ray Bradbury wrote a wonderful story, "The Kilimanjaro Machine," re-visioning Hemingway's death in the crash of 24 January 1954.

14. There is no explanation of Hemingway's giving Philip Percival a fictional name, but retaining Denis Zaphiro's. In the *The Sun Also Rises*, the kind, older Englishman of the Burguete episode is "Wilson-Harris," and the resonance of his decency and generosity helps to characterize the white hunter in the African book.

15. In 1952 books about Hemingway were published by John Atkins, Carlos Baker, and Philip Young. Hemingway had cooperated with Baker, but had tried to prevent Young's psychoanalytically oriented work from reaching print. The difficulties that Robert Morgan Brown was having in getting his dissertation topic approved at New York University were in part a legacy of the problems the Philip Young book had created there, where Young had failed to win tenure because of Hemingway's initial withholding of permissions for his book.

    Excerpts from Charles Fenton's forthcoming work had been serialized in *Atlantic* in March, April, and May of 1954 – where Hemingway undoubtedly read them. He had taken a personal dislike to Fenton and had been furious about having his early years scrutinized; but Fenton's book was fine work and remains valuable today.

16. To the reader who is unfamiliar with the concept of gender differences in language usage, I recommend Pamela Smiley's essay, "Gender-linked Miscommunication in 'Hills Like White Elephants.' " The process by which Smiley examines the dialogue of a single story is very useful in understanding what is happening beneath the surface in much of Hemingway's writing.

17. Pop's last name is also that of the squadron captain in an unfinished story about flying with the R.A.F. which is in the Scribner's vertical file at Princeton. This fragment is the only evidence of Hemingway's beginning the air section of his "Land, Sea, and Air Book."

18. Directed by Jamie Uys, 1984.

19. Denis Zaphiro to Bill Walton, 1957.

20. Hemingway owned and was referring to *Kamba Customary Law* by D. J. Penwill while he worked on the African manuscript. He has incorporated Penwill's account of tribal rules for at least four situations: giving beer to one's prospective father-in-law; the assignment of a protector to a widow; the rule on beer drinking for young males; and the fines that allow one to sleep with an unmarried woman without serious consequences.

21. In letters to Adriana written during this period Hemingway uses the phrase to comment on his loneliness, sometimes making a pun on her street address, Calle Remedico (HRC). Hemingway last saw Adriana when she came to see him and Mary off at Genoa on 5 June 1954 (Adriana-Mary Hemingway, 10 June 1954; and EH-Adriana, 15 June 1954, JFK).

22. *Mzee* is also spelled with a single "e." *Ndofu* (or *ndovu*) means tusk, and used together they signify an aged elephant. See L. Krapf, *A Dictionary of the Swahili Language.*

     Note that Hemingway does not draw analogies between the old writer and the old elephant, just as he did not draw analogies between the powerless child and the powerless old elephant in *Eden.* Rather, in both instances he makes the kind of simple statement about the burden of the elephant's ivory that compels the reader to *feel* the weight of their significance – a form of what in 1922 he called "writ[ing] one true sentence" that is the very essence of Hemingway's style (MF, 12). The essential nature of the genius in this ability is discussed by Paul Smith in "Impressions of Ernest Hemingway."

23. Bill Walton recalls that when Mary Welsh met Ernest Hemingway in 1944, she maintained she had never read any of his books. Walton decided that might be more truth than pose, for she hadn't read anything else either (author's interview).

24. There has long been skepticism about Hemingway's finding manuscripts because the mentions of recovering them had come from others (Leonard Lyons, and later, Mary Hemingway). However, I recently found a letter of 19 January 1957, in Hemingway's hand, and on Ritz Hotel paper, verifying the find. This will be discussed in the chapter on *Feast.*

25. The correspondence makes clear that Hemingway had longed for such an escape for more than a decade. We know that he had wanted to make Martha Gellhorn his protégée, and that she resisted being the writer in the family so that he could retire at forty-four. Further, the newly opened Scribner's correspondence reveals that for several years before the death of Charles Scribner Sr. (in February 1952), Hemingway was searching for a role in which he could work with creative writing, but not be bound to producing his own. As Scribner confided his health problems to him, Hemingway offered to come to New York and take over his job so that Scribner could have an extended rest. He also tried to create a mentor relationship with a number of younger aspiring writers, including Gianfranco Ivancich. Scribner read several manuscripts that Hemingway sent him, including one by Gianfranco, but found them unpromising. Carlos Baker tried without success to help Gianfranco market a short story on life at the Finca, which is in the Baker-Hemingway file at Princeton.

A MOVEABLE FEAST

1. The letters were to be quoted in "The Making of *The Making of Americans*" which Donald Gallup published the next year in *New Colophon.*

2. In May 1957, *Atlantic* asked Hemingway for a contribution to its centenary issue. He contemplated using a Fitzgerald sketch which he had at hand (probably the first chapter on Fitzgerald in *Feast*), then changed his mind – out of loyalty to Fitzgerald's memory, he said – and submitted two other stories ("A Man of the World" and "Get a Seeing-Eyed Dog.") See also Jacqueline Tavernier-Courbin, *The Making of a Myth*, p. 84 and p. 233, n. 57.

3. Rumors that Hemingway had recently recovered early manuscripts in Paris appeared first in Leonard Lyons's column in *The New York Post* in 1957, and again in 1964, when Lyons suggested the Paris origins of Hemingway's forthcoming posthumous book. Mary Hemingway's first statement about the matter was made in the *New York Times Book Review* on 10 May 1964:

> They [the Ritz Hotel trunks] were two small, fabric-covered, rectangular boxes both opening at the seams [containing] blue- and yellow-covered penciled notebooks and sheaves of typed papers, ancient newspaper cuttings, . . . Ernest had not seen the stuff since 1927, when he packed it and left it at the hotel before going to Key West. (26–27)

4. By 1989 A. E. Hotchner claimed to have been with Hemingway when Charles Ritz discovered that Ernest had left a trunk in the hotel's basement where it had gone unnoticed for twenty years. Note that this is not the thirty years that Hemingway reported to Lee Samuels in a letter to be discussed shortly. Hotchner says, "We opened the trunk, and it was a treasure trove of manuscripts, in fact some of the material that later was to constitute a major part of . . . *A Moveable Feast*" (*Hemingway and His World*, 163).

   However, since Hotchner is the anonymous friend invoked in the epigraph Mary added to the manuscript, and since he has more than once claimed that the title originated in a discussion he had with Hemingway, I think it unlikely that he would have remained silent while the very existence of the Ritz Hotel papers was being debated over the quarter of a century between the publication of *Feast* and his own book if, as he claims, he was present at their discovery.

5. I owe the language of this perfect trope to a discussion of the Hemingway-Fitzgerald symbiosis with Max Westbrook. Matthew Bruccoli has documented the symbiosis quite fully in *Scott and Ernest*.

6. The letter, which I found in the summer of 1993, was included in a larger gift Samuels made to the Humanities Research Center in 1963 with the stipulation that the correspondence be closed to researchers for twenty-five years.

7. The Samuels family were partners in the Havana firm of Rothschild, Samuels, and Duigan. Samuels's letters and papers at the Kennedy Library show that on several occasions he loaned Hemingway money for as long as five years on notes that are marked "Noninterest bearing." Part of

Hemingway's Nobel Prize money was used to pay old debts to Samuels. His Hemingway bibliography was published by Scribner's in 1951.

8. Tavernier-Courbin is resistant to the possibility that Hemingway *had* recovered papers in 1956 or 1957 and gives Mary Hemingway's statements on the matter a rather narrow interpretation. While she worked without access to the Scribner's Archives at Princeton which cover this period and contain Hemingway's correspondence with Scribner's about the Paris book, she would have found no mention there of the 1957 recovery.

9. The credibility of Hemingway's list is increased by the fact that when Gus Pfeiffer asked him for the manuscripts of "The Undefeated" and "Fifty Grand," he replied in a letter of 16 March 1928 – the day before he and Pauline sailed for Key West – that he could not find either, was sure they were in storage, and would look for them "when we return in the fall" (JFK). He is writing from the apartment on the rue Ferou that Pfeiffer had helped them to lease, and it is to this apartment that they will return: the phrasing makes it clear that what he has stored is elsewhere.

When he and Pauline married in May 1927, Hemingway's papers were scattered among at least three places: the apartment he and Hadley had occupied on the Notre-Dame-de-Champs (on which he retained the lease until July 1927); Gerald Murphy's studio at 69 rue Froidevaux (where he moved when he separated from Hadley on his return to Paris in mid-August 1926); and the apartment that he and Pauline had leased.

10. A facsimile of the mutilated holograph fragment appears in Bruccoli, *Scott and Ernest*, 39.

11. The liability is mentioned in a letter of 8 November 1959 to Bill Davis, with whom Hemingway had stayed during the past summer while gathering material for the bullfighting piece that was to appear in *Life*. If, as I am trying to ascertain, the tax liability resulted from the sale of the holographs recovered in Paris, there is certainly an ironic connection between the bullfight material that became *The Dangerous Summer* and the Paris book, for in a letter to Davis of 9 May 1960, Hemingway blames his tax lawyer (Alfred Rice) for an error that left him short of cash and resulted in his taking the advance of $30,000 from *Life*. He now regrets his commitment to *Life* because it is interfering with his finishing the Paris book (Bruccoli, *Hemingway at Auction*, no.304, p. 124; no. 312, p. 127).

12. On 3 November 1959, Hemingway had delivered twelve of his proposed thirteen chapters of the Paris book to Scribner's. On 18 November, Harry Brague returned them with the comment that they were very exciting. On 3 December, Charles Scribner wrote:

> I keep thinking of the marvelous Paris stories you let me see, and what a fine controlled thermo-nuclear reaction we will have when they are published. I am absolutely certain that the reception is going to be unparalleled.

By 8 February 1960, Hemingway was back in Cuba, and a letter to Brague promises to "start going over the Paris book" when the income tax is organized; however, on 31 March, he wrote Scribner to remove the book from the fall list.

On 20 June 1959, Scribner wrote, revealing his eagerness to get the publication started:

You know how enthusiastic I am about the Paris pieces. In my opinion, this is some of the finest writing you have ever done. Mightn't it be a good idea to publish some of these in magazines this fall. They should be very strong in first-serialization and that would not impair book sales – particularly if a few were held exclusively for the book . . . . (PUL)

13. **(a)** Hemingway's letter of 26 March 1961 to Lee Samuels accompanied a copy of the Paris manuscript which Hemingway was very anxious to get into Samuels's hands. His handwriting and phrasing suggest his deteriorating state:

Air mail was gone when could get this off starting instantly when you left hung up. No air-mail except for Lodge to Pocatello tomorrow possibly – Mary insisted on *calling* Mss. [emphasis in the original] incompleted. I disagreed but she was typeing . . . . (HRC)

Mary placed the retained copy of the Paris book in a safe deposit box in Hailey, Idaho, shortly after Hemingway's return to the Mayo Clinic on 23 April (*How It Was*, 499).
(b) Whatever Mary said in the presence of Bill Davis is suggested in Hemingway's letter of 8 November 1959 to him:

I let Charlie Scribner and Harry Brague read the Paris stuff and they felt about it the way you and Val and Annie did. Also Hotch felt that way . . . I always knew we had a winner but Mary saying what she did about them had touted me off. (Bruccoli, *Hemingway at Auction*, no. 304, p. 122)

14. Blaise Pascal, *Pensées*.
15. In September 1992 Bill Walton recounted Hemingway's comments about Mary's lack of friends and of background knowledge about art and literature: "He [Ernest] would say, 'Where did you ever find this girl? She doesn't know anybody in the world. You've got all your friends; I've got all my friends. She doesn't have any' " (author's interview).
16. The untitled holograph text of Kennedy Library File 648a [Philip Haines Was a Writer . . .] was edited by Donald Junkins and appeared in the *Hemingway Review* (Spring 1990) along with a variant and apparently earlier manuscript, File 648b. The 648b version has as protagonist James Allen, a blocked writer turned painter who is in a domestic limbo similar to that of Haines; and both manuscripts echo the concerns of Roger Davis and Thomas Hudson in the "Bimini" section of *Islands*. Each of the men lives alone in Paris, separated from a wife while waiting out a complicated divorce in order to marry a woman who is in America – and neither can work while alone. Some phrases in the "Philip Haines" story appear in the letter of 14 September 1954 to Robert Brown quoted in Chapter 5,

suggesting that Hemingway was writing the "Haines" and the "James Allen" fragments then. The "James Allen" piece is particularly interesting for the murderous rage that Allen feels toward the woman he is going to marry, but whose absence seems to have made him unable to create.

17. Bill Walton recounts what was told to him by both Mary Welsh and Irwin Shaw – that they were together in the Ritz Hotel Bar in late 1945 when Mary asked Irwin if he intended to marry her. He replied, "Certainly not. What ever made you think that?" to which she responded, "All right, then I'm going to marry Ernest" (author's interview).

18. In fact, once Hemingway had decided to return to Cuba in early 1945, he went to Charles Wertenbaker, foreign editor for *Time* – without Mary's knowledge – and asked that Mary be relieved of her assignment in Europe in order to come to Cuba as soon as possible after he left Europe (EH-Mary, 26 Dec. 1944; Norberto Fuentes, *Hemingway in Cuba*, 374).

19. Bill Walton, who had every reason to count himself as a friend of both Mary and Ernest, said that early in the marriage he witnessed Hemingway's treating Mary in ways that would have caused any self-respecting woman to say, "Fuck you," and walk out (author's interview).

20. The single exception to Mary's refusal to analyze Hemingway's behavior appears in her letter to Charles Scribner (quoted in Chapter 2, note 34), where she relates Hemingway's abuse to her inability to have a child. That letter continues:

> It has always seemed to me that the reason people continued living together in spite of difficulties and private failures toward each other was that a certain amount of respect and affection survived the hurdles. The reason I have to leave Ernest – not easy for me since I have no other home and no money – is that in his program of being a tough guy, he has destroyed what I used to think was an inexhaustable supply of devotion to him. He has been truculent, brutal, abusive and extremely childish. It has been more than a year since he has actually hit me; but when my cousin (age 65 or there about and the only member of my family he has ever permitted to visit here) was visiting, he brought a whore to lunch aboard the Pilar, anchored at the yacht club. . . . At table his favorite and frequent means of protesting any word, glance, gesture or food he doesn't like is to put his full, freshly served plate on the floor. The other day he dumped the entire plate of bread and crackers on top of my plate. . . .
>
> But don't bother answering this in general – Ernest is inclined to open my mail before I see it. (12 Oct. 1950; PUL)

Both before the marriage and after, Buck Lanham had pointed out to Hemingway occasions on which he felt Mary had been neglected or mistreated when he was present: for example, as early as a shooting party at Winston Guest's estate on Gardiners Island in 1946 and as late as the summer of 1959 when Lanham went to Spain for Hemingway's sixtieth birthday party. The Hemingway-Lanham correspondence shows that he always rejected the validity of Lanham's perceptions (JFK and PUL). In the 1960s Lanham told Carlos Baker, as he was preparing his biography of Hemingway, that Mary once told him that if she opposed Ernest in any way, including the matter of his relationships with other women, he would leave her, and that she was determined to be the last Mrs. Hemingway (Baker-Hemingway File; PUL).

21. In August 1993 Bill Walton told me of accompanying Mary on a Baltic cruise in 1976 (the year her memoir was published). Much of the time she remained in her cabin, drinking heavily; and when they reached Odessa, she refused to accompany him into the city. Finding the steps where Eisenstein had filmed the descent of the baby carriage in *The Battleship Potemkin*, Walton walked down to the waterfront where, hanging over the bar in a seamen's pub, he saw the Karsh photograph of Hemingway.

22. The pattern of Hemingway's interference with Mary's writing is well documented in their correspondence at the Kennedy Library. For example, in 1950, when she was getting her parents settled in Gulfport, Mississippi, he forwarded her mail – after opening it – and advised her about how she should price her writing for popular magazines, saying:

This article business sounds about as complicated as the prize fight racket. Those magazines must be very big business. I never split with anybody and managed myself and collected when Scribner's and lawyers couldn't. . . . I thought your piece was very good. Asking too much money is not smart. Take a smaller amount and write another piece. (14 Aug. 1950; JFK)

This is disingenuous commentary from a man who had dealt with, among other popular magazines, *Cosmopolitan* and *Esquire,* and who had always held out for top dollar. A month later he again urges her to accept an offer on which she has told her agent (Carl Brandt) to negotiate further, saying "If I can afford to sell two first class Venetian fables to *Holiday* for $1000[,] you can afford to accept something over $1,000 for a good, easily written piece" (26 Sept. 1950; JFK).

When *Cosmopolitan* angered him by offering $10,000 for *The Old Man and the Sea,* Hemingway again tried to use a comparison to coerce Mary's selling to them a story she was doing on a fishing tournament: "I don't think if they are budgeted so they can only pay $10,000 for the old man piece which is over 20,000, or close to, words they can be expected to pay more than $1000 for the tournament piece" (7 July 1951; JFK).

In July 1952, *Modern Woman* offered Mary $750 for a story about life with Hemingway (published as "Living with a Genius" in September 1953). Hemingway opened the letter from Hotchner to Mary in which the offer was included, then forwarded it with the remark that "that ought to be an easy seven fifty. I'll try to work hard to be a good seven fifty subject. Hotch is awfully nice to think about you." Two months later, basking in the glory that publication of *Old Man* had created, Hemingway sent Mary the final contract from *Modern Woman,* telling her to retain all but first serial rights because "$750 is small enough price for the article what with all recent developments *Life* with OMAS." He was anticipating a sale to *Reader's Digest* which Hotchner was negotiating (9 Jul. and 27 Sept. 1952; JFK).

23. Bill Walton recounted President Kennedy's amused and exasperated response to the foreign policy advice Mary offered him during the dinner (author's interview).

24. See Bernice Kert's perceptions of Mary Hemingway's last years in *The Hemingway Women.*

25. Although Mary had put the guns in a basement closet after the series of suicide attempts that resulted in Hemingway's return to the Mayo Clinic on 23 April 1961, she left the keys on the window sill above the kitchen sink, where they remained on 30 June when the Hemingways returned from his second hospitalization at the Mayo Clinic. Her reasoning after his death – which until 1966 she insisted was an accident – was that she would not have dreamed of depriving Hemingway of access to his own property. However, as will be discussed later in this chapter, Mary's need and determination to distance herself from Hemingway can now be traced to the last months of 1959 when she reacted to his humiliation of her in Spain. For Mary Hemingway, as for the heroine of a Victorian novel, death had done the work of the divorce court; and I have no doubt that – exhausted and without help from Hemingway's family – she saw, but could not bear to admit, that his suicide was the only release for either of them. Further, in the fall of 1959, Hemingway described Mary's determination to separate part of her life from his as a tactic aimed at driving him to suicide (letter; private collection).

    When I said to Bill Walton in August 1993, "Unconsciously, Mary wanted him to do it," Walton replied, "Now that you have said it, I will say what I have never said before, but have known since Mary called me a few hours after Ernest's death: yes, she did."

26. The rebounding power of juxtaposed material was very much on Hemingway's mind when he arranged *In Our Time* in 1925, and again as he was ordering the stories for *Winner Take Nothing* in 1933 when he wrote Max Perkins:

    A book of stories, that is a good one, is just as much a unit as a novel. You get the overtones by the juxtaposition of the stories or by what you put in between them. (8 April; PUL)

27. The word *remise* (a place of storage) forms another significant link between *Eden* and *Feast*, for I can find it used in only two places in all of Hemingway's work: (1) in *Eden* Catherine burns David's African stories in a petro drum near the *remise* where they store their bicycles. (2) In attempting to create a closure for the Paris book Hemingway writes several variant statements that the book "contains certain material from the *remises* of my memory and of my heart" (File 123; JFK). Another sheet in this file bears names and episode notes for *Eden,* and lists a title, apparently for

the Paris book, which has been lined out – "The Garden of the Very Poor and Free."

28. A sentence Hemingway wrote as he tried to frame the statement that the book was fiction (File 122; JFK).

29. The girl in the café is, as Paul Smith suggests, a muse ("Impressions of Ernest Hemingway"). But in another sense she is also a succubus in that she is metonynmically the power of writing that binds the writer to his pencil and makes any other relationship secondary.

30. The story "The Three Day Blow" follows "The End of Something" in *The First Forty-nine*. Like the chapters in *Feast*, the stories comment on one another, for Hemingway arranged them carefully. See Paul Smith, *Reader's Guide to the Short Stories of Ernest Hemingway*.

31. As Bill Walton saw clearly, anything that Grace Hemingway represented or recommended was anathema to Hemingway – but he secretly loved opera and wrote Buck Lanham of the pleasures of listening to it on records; and, of course, he chose to make Thomas Hudson (of *Islands*) a painter.

In his childhood reading, Hemingway had been both the benefactor and the victim of his parents' tastes: Jack London, for example, was banned from their home, while Dinah Craik's sentimental novel of muscular Christianity, *John Halifax, Gentleman,* became a kind of conduct book for his parents' marriage; and the "outward bound" adventure tales of Frederick Marryat are the model that Hemingway tells Max Perkins he used to train his own sons in the sea around Cuba. See Mark Spilka's *Hemingway's Quarrel* for a discussion of the influence of Hemingway's childhood reading on his fiction.

32. The three Fitzgerald chapters are nearly 25% of the published work. A fourth chapter was omitted: Kennedy Library File 182 is about going to a Princeton football game with Scott and Zelda in October 1928, and was probably not used because by that time Hemingway was married to Pauline, and in *Feast* he had decided to leave her presence equivocal. The break in continuity with the Paris years is another plausible reason for eliminating this well-developed chapter; but the quantity of material about Fitzgerald both verifies how present he was in Hemingway's mind and gives rise to the possibility that Hemingway at some time planned a book on him alone. It is clear from Hemingway's mentions of both Fitzgerald and Thomas Wolfe in his letters to Max Perkins and Charles Scribner that he used these fellow members of the Scribner's stable (as he used James Jones) as a screen on which to project his fears about himself.

33. Despite Max Perkins's belief in Zelda, Hemingway refused to see anything positive about her, and continued to use her as an explanation for Scott's failures. On 23 February 1933 he wrote Perkins:

The only thing that would make a writer of him again would be 1. Zelda's death which might put a term to things in his mind. 2. For his stomach to give out completely so he couldn't drink. He's gone into that cheap Irish love of defeat.

And on 7 September 1935: "Imagine a love affair would help Scott if he has anything left to love with and the woman isn't so awful that he has to kid himself too much" (PUL).

34. In chapter 5, "Genius and Glass," Donaldson discusses Fitzgerald's habit of publishing Zelda's stories, or their joint ventures, as his alone. While this has been known since the Nancy Milford biography of Zelda, Donaldson documents the far more chilling account of creative oppression Fitzgerald excerised after Zelda was institutionalized. Furious that she sent *Save Me the Waltz* directly to Max Perkins instead of asking him to submit it, Fitzgerald told Perkins to do all discussion of the manuscript with him, not Zelda. And when, in the spring of 1933, Zelda began to write about the period of her breakdown and hospitalization in Switzerland, Scott invoked an agreement made between him and two psychiatrists who had treated Zelda (Aldolph Meyer and Thomas Rennie of the Phipps Clinic). He emerged from the confrontational session with Dr. Rennie and Zelda with an agreement that she would cease writing of that period until his novel, *Tender Is the Night*, was published. A transcript of this meeting appears in Matthew Bruccoli, *Some Sort of Epic Grandeur*, 349–53.

35. The central incidents of both the Ford chapter and the "Lost Generation" Stein chapter had been deleted from the manuscript of *The Sun Also Rises*. See Frederic Svoboda, *Hemingway and "The Sun Also Rises."*

36. A list of Hemingway's anecdotes about Zelda's destructive influence on Scott would be a very long one indeed. Simply checking the pages on which she is mentioned in Hemingway's *Selected Letters* is a good start. The archetypal power Zelda possessed for Hemingway is visible in one of his regular tirades against Martha Gellhorn: Zelda died in a fire at Highland Sanitarium near Asheville, North Carolina, on the night of 3 March 1948. In October 1948 Hemingway wrote a long, invective-filled letter about Martha to Charles Scribner, concluding:

> [I]f she were ever burned alive like Scott's poor bloody crazy career destroying wife I would just hope she took a good deep breath quick of the flames and think no more of it. (PUL)

37. In discussing "Mr. and Mrs. Elliot," a short story written during this period, Paul Smith recognizes the evidence that the young Hemingway was very much torn between his sexuality and the conventional morality with which he had grown up. Smith sees, too, that this foreshadows the dilemma of David Bourne in *The Garden of Eden*. See "Impressions of Ernest Hemingway," and "From the Wasteland to the Garden."

38. Pauline is named in Files 147–2, 147–3, and 188 and 189 (JFK). That the decision to leave the "we" unidentified was Hemingway's rather than the editor(s)' is established by his repeated statements in the fragments comprising Files 122–24 that he has left Pauline out.

39. Hadley had made it a condition of the divorce that if Ernest and Pauline stayed apart for 100 days and were still in love, she would agree. It is such a separation that Philip Haines is going through.

40. Fitzgerald read a carbon of the final draft of the novel and his comments resulted in the deletion of about a chapter and a half from the typescript that is largely biographical material about Brett and autobiographical material about Jake. Frederic Svoboda reprints Fitzgerald's ten-page critique in *Hemingway and "The Sun Also Rises*, 137–40.

41. The deleted sentence occurs before the final sentence of the first paragraph on page 201 in the published novel. In the *Eden* ms. this is at 422.1-29, pp. 14–15 (JFK).

42. Two Hemingway letters to Bill Davis (Bruccoli, *Hemingway at Auction*, nos. 303–304, pp. 122–23) include Hemingway's disingenuous account of Mary's reserve when he returned to Cuba on 3 November 1959. He describes his domestic situation as "like Kafka" in letters to Davis and his wife, as well as in a letter to Hotchner, who had been the chief negotiator of Mary's separate peace, and in whose name the apartment in New York was leased. The letter to Hotchner establishes Mary's determination to change the conditions under which she had been living:

> Mary very friendly but holds to same program. Very pleased about flat[,] consents to go to Ketchum to help me out with Carmen and Antonio [Antonio Ordonez was one of the matadors Hemingway had been following in Spain, and he had invited the couple to visit him] on these conditions – A. will not be required to cook – B. That I not ever shoot with Mrs. Gray unless she present.
>
> I've kept reasonable and I hope kind and affectionate although have not much way of judging what that is anymore. . . . OK for Valerie to come over and help me, Christ knows I need her with 92 letters piled on the table. . . . Mary plans to go to Ketchum and help out with Carmen and Antonio then to go to N.Y. in Jan. to flat where won't have to simply do chores and can do her writing. . . What want to do most is get back to writing. Thats one of the big issues too; that I expect other people to subordinate themselves to my writing. (8 Nov. 1959; JFK)

See Baker, *Life Story* (541–50), for an account of Hemingway's behavior in Spain during the summer of 1959.

43. Even when they were in the same house, Mary often wrote notes to Hemingway about matters that had been the source of conflict between them: on 15 December 1959, she comments on his coming to her room in the middle of the night to quarrel and on his complaint that having to help her undress is "maid's work," closing with:

> [I]f you want to get rid of me, please *just say so,* calmly and without all the insinuations and assaults and cruelties. Just say so. But please, let us not go on with the NIGHTLY false accusations and hurts. (JFK)

Hemingway's behavior was an approach he had used with Hadley, Pauline, and Martha, and had tried with Mary when he was newly in love with Adriana, that of making the wife that he wanted to be free of uncomfortable enough to leave him – and he was now infatuated with Valerie

Danby-Smith. His correspondence with Bill Davis indicates that Davis had arranged for Valerie to enter Cuba on or before 8 February 1960, and that as the Hemingways and Valerie prepared to leave Cuba the following July, he became very anxious about getting her into the United States (Bruccoli, *Hemingway at Auction*, no. 310, pp. 125–26). Five years after Hemingway's death, Valerie became the second wife of Hemingway's youngest son.

44. The book would be declared finished at 120,000 words in late May: *Life* had contracted for 10,000. Although the contract was renegotiated in June, Hemingway became more uncertain of what he had written and therefore arranged to return to Spain.

45. The similarities between Hemingway's behavior and his father's during the final year of their lives (extreme depression, paranoia, obsessive attention to detail, irrational projections of penury) compel belief that his genetic heritage of hemochromatosis and chronic depression were among the causes of his deterioration. See Susan Beegel, "Hemingway and Hemochromatosis," and Michael Reynolds, "Hemingway's Home."

46. There is a sharp contrast in the clarity with which Hemingway judges the behavior of Rupert (Bellville) and Sinsky in 1960 and the fact that in 1945 he had slapped Mary for protesting when his drunken friends fouled her bathroom at the Ritz Hotel (*How It Was*, 130–31).

47. All 1960 correspondence between Mary and Hemingway is at the Kennedy Library. The bullfighting piece was serialized in *Life*, beginning with the 5 September 1960 issue, which bears the Loomis Dean photo.

48. Hemingway's medical file at the Kennedy Library contains the offprint of an article from *Current Therapy* by Dr. Richard Steinbilber (a member of the Mayo Clinic staff) inscribed "*Dear Ernie, c'est le guerre*, Dick" in which the phenothiazine derivatives are described as suitable "to aid in control of mental disorder." In the file there are also several articles from the same journal on depression and manic depressive reactions. Kenneth Lynn's assertion that the trycyclic drugs were not available is inaccurate (*Hemingway*, 583–84).

49. In 1926, when it was necessary for Hemingway to have his marriage to Hadley declared invalid in order to marry Pauline Pfeiffer in the Catholic Church, he remembered a battlefield baptism by a priest (after he was wounded in Italy in 1918) that provided the basis in canon law for an annulment of his marriage to Hadley. Catholic teaching distinguishes between *imperfect contrition*, which is sorrow for sin because of the punishment it brings, and *perfect contrition*, which is sorrow for sin because it has offended God and caused injury to another.

50. Hemingway claimed to have written the ending of *A Farewell to Arms* more than fifty times before settling on the one published. This is probably not very much of an exaggeration since a number of those drafts survive at the Kennedy Library. See Michael Reynolds, *Hemingway's First War*.

51. Hemingway took great care in selecting titles, and the evidence of his title searches is preserved in Files 76a, 94b, 120, and 202c at the Kennedy

Library. He never created a title from phrases that he used in casual conversation, and he had used the words Mary chose as title for the Paris book in many situations: (1) "Possible is such a bloody moveable feast" (to Bernard Berenson, 31 Dec. 1950; JFK); (2) "Loneliness is a moveable feast" (to Buck Lanham, 27 Sept. 1950; PUL); (3) "Paris is a moveable feast" (to A. E. Hotchner, *Papa,* 57); (4) "Love is a terrible thing that you would not wish on your neighbor and, as in all countries, it is a moveable feast" (African book manuscript, 511; PUL); and (5) "Happiness . . . is a movable [*sic*] feast" (*Across the River,* 68).

References

Anderson, Lauri. *Hunting Hemingway's Trout*. New York: Atheneum, 1990, 49–71.

Baker, Carlos. *Hemingway: A Life Story*. New York: Scribner's, 1969.

———— *Hemingway: The Writer as Artist*. Princeton: Princeton University Press, 1972.

Beegel, Susan. "Hemingway and Hemochromatosis." *Hemingway Review* 10 (Fall 1990): 57–65.

Bell, Millicent. "*A Farewell to Arms:* Pseudobiography and Personal Metaphor." *The Writer in Context*. Ed. James Nagel. Madison: University of Wisconsin Press, 1984, 110–11.

Boyes, John. *The Company of Adventurers*. London: East Africa Press, 1928.

Brasch, James. "Christ, I Wish I Could Paint": The Correspondence between Ernest Hemingway and Bernard Berenson. *Hemingway in Italy and Other Essays*. Ed. Robert W. Lewis. New York: Praeger, 1990, 49–67.

Brasch, James, and Sigman, Joseph. *Hemingway's Library: A Composite Record*. New York: Garland, 1981.

Brenner, Gerry. "Are We Going to Hemingway's Feast?" *American Literature* 54: 4 (1982): 528–44.

———— "*The Old Man and the Sea*": A Reader's Companion to the Novel. New York: Twayne Publishers, 1991.

Bruccoli, Matthew. *Hemingway at Auction 1930–1973*. Detroit: Gale Research, 1973.

———— *Scott and Ernest: The Authority of Failure and the Authority of Success*. New York: Random House, 1978.

———— *Some Sort of Epic Grandeur*. New York: Random House, 1981.

Burwell, Rose Marie. "Hemingway's *Garden of Eden:* Resistance of Things Past and Protecting the Masculine Text." *Texas Studies in Literature and Language* 35: 2 (Summer 1993): 198–225.

———— Interviews with William Walton, September 1992 and August 1993 (JFK).

———— "The Posthumous Hemingway Puzzle," *Princeton University Library Chronicle* LVI: 1 (Autumn 1994): 25-45.

Cackett, Kathy. "*The Garden of Eden:* Challenging Faulkner's Family Romance." *Hemingway Review* 10 (Spring 1990): 155–69.

Camilucci, Marcello. *L'Osservatore romano.*

Comley, Nancy, and Scholes, Robert. "Tribal Things: Hemingway's Erotics of Truth." *Novel* 25 (1992): 283–97.

Crews, Frederick. "Pressure Under Grace." *New York Review of Books.* Aug. 13, 1987: 30–37.

DeFalco, Joseph. "'Bimini' and the Subject of Hemingway's *Islands in the Stream.*" *Ernest Hemingway: Six Decades of Criticism.* Ed. Linda Wagner-Martin. East Lansing: Michigan State U.P., 1987, 313–24.

Delaney, John. "The Archives of Charles Scribner's Sons." *Princeton University Library Chronicle.* 46: 2 (1985): 137–77.

Desnoyers, Megan Floyd. "Ernest Hemingway: A Storyteller's Legacy." *Prologue.* 24: 4 (Winter 1992): 334–49.

——— "The Hemingways' Friend, Bill Walton." *John F. Kennedy Library Newsletter.* Spring 1993, 4.

Dilberto, Gioia. Friends of the Hemingway Collection Lecture. JFK. March 25, 1992.

Doctorow, E. L. "Braver Than We Thought." *New York Times Book Review,* May 18, 1986: 1, 44–45.

Donaldson, Scott. *By Force of Will.* New York: Viking, 1977.

——— *Fool for Love: F. Scott Fitzgerald.* New York: Congdon & Weed, 1983.

Fleming, Robert. "The Endings of Hemingway's *Garden of Eden.*" *American Literature* 6 (1989): 261–70.

——— "Roger Davis of *Islands:* What the Manuscript Adds." *Hemingway: Essays of Reassessment.* Ed. Frank Scafella. New York: Oxford University Press 1991, 53–60.

Fleming, Robert, and Wheelock, Warren. "Hemingway's Last Word on Stein: A Joke in the Manuscript of Islands." *Hemingway Review* 9 (Spring 1990): 174–75.

——— *The Face in the Mirror: Hemingway's Writers.* Tuscaloosa: University Press of Alabama, 1994.

Fuentes, Norberto. *Hemingway in Cuba.* Secaucus, New Jersey: Lyle Stuart, Inc., 1984.

——— *Hemingway Rediscovered.* New York: Scribner's, 1986.

Gajdusek, Robert. "Elephant Hunt in Eden: A Study of New and Old Myths and Other Strange Beasts in Hemingway's Garden." *Hemingway Review* 7 (Fall 1987): 15–19.

Galantiere, Lewis. "*A Moveable Feast.*" *New York Times Book Review,* May 11, 1964, 1.

Gellhorn, Martha. *Liana.* New York: Scribner's, 1944.

——— "On Apocryphism." *Paris Review,* 23:79 (Spring 1981): 280–301.

Gilbert, Sandra, and Gubar, Susan. *The Madwoman in the Attic: The Woman Writer and the Nineteenth-Century Imagination.* New Haven: Yale University Press, 1979.

Hemingway, Ernest. *Across the River and into the Trees.* New York: Macmillan, 1950.

——— *Across the River and into the Trees* manuscript. JFK.

——— African book manuscript. PUL.

——— *African Journal. Sports Illustrated.* December 20 and 27, 1971; January 2, 1972.

——— "The Christmas Gift." *Look.* April 20 and 27, 1954.

——— *The Complete Short Stories of Ernest Hemingway.* Finca Vigía Ed. New York, Scribner's, 1987.

——— *Death in the Afternoon.* New York: Scribner's, 1932.

——— *The Garden of Eden.* New York: Scribner's, 1986.

——— *The Garden of Eden* manuscripts. JFK and PUL.

——— *Islands in the Stream.* New York: Scribner's, 1970.

——— *Islands in the Stream* manuscripts. JFK and PUL.

——— *Men at War.* New York: Crown Publishers, 1942.

——— *The Nick Adams Stories.* Ed. Philip Young. New York: Scribner's, 1972.

——— *The Old Man and the Sea.* New York: Scribner's, 1952.

——— *The Old Man and the Sea* manuscripts. JFK.

——— "Pamplona Letter." *Transatlantic Review* 2 (October 1924): 300–02.

——— [Philip Haines Was a Writer . . .] manuscripts 648a and 648b. JFK.

——— "Safari." *Look.* January 25, 1954.

——— "The Sea Chase." Caedmon Records. TC 1185.

——— *Selected Letters.* Ed. Carlos Baker. New York: Scribner's, 1981.

——— Unpublished letters. HRC, JFK, PUL, and in private collections.

Hemingway, Grace Hall. *A Record of Ernest Miller Hemingway's Baby Days.* Books 1–5. JFK.

Hemingway, Gregory. *Papa: A Personal Memoir.* Boston: Houghton Mifflin, 1976.

Hemingway, Mary. *How It Was.* New York: Knopf, 1976.

——— "The Making of a Book: A Chronicle and a Memoir," *New York Times Book Review* May 10, 1964: 26–27.

Hemingway, Patrick. "*Islands in the Stream:* A Son Remembers." *Ernest Hemingway: The Writer in Context.* Ed. James Nagel. Madison: University of Wisconsin Press, 1984, 13–18.

Hillman, James. "The Elephant in *The Garden of Eden.*" *Spring: A Journal of Archetype and Culture.* 50 (1990): 93–115.

Hotchner, A. E. *Hemingway and His World.* London: Viking, 1989.

——— *Papa Hemingway.* New York: William Morrow, 1983.

Hovey, Richard. "*Islands in the Stream:* Death and the Artist." *Hemingway: A Revaluation.* Ed. Donald Noble. Troy, NY: Whitson Publishing, 1983, 240–62.

Irwin, John. *Doubling and Incest, Repetition and Revenge.* Baltimore: Johns Hopkins University Press, 1975.

Jones, Robert. "Mimesis and Metafiction in Hemingway's *The Garden of Eden.*" *Hemingway Review* 7 (Fall 1987): 3–13.

Junkins, Donald. "Hemingway's Paris Short Story: A Study in Revising." *Hemingway Review* 10 (Spring 1990): 3–49.

Kazin, Alfred. "Ernest Hemingway as His Own Fable." *Atlantic,* June 1964, 54–57.

Kert, Bernice. *The Hemingway Women.* New York: Norton, 1983.

Krapf, Rev. L. *A Dictionary of the Swahili Language.* Reprint of 1882 Ed., New York: Negro University Press, 1969.

Kennedy, Gerald. "Hemingway's Gender Trouble." *American Literature* 63 (June 1991): 187–207.

Larkin, Philip. *Collected Poems.* Ed. Anthony Thwaite. London: Faber and Faber, 1989, 180.

Lynn, Kenneth. *Hemingway.* New York: Simon & Schuster, 1987.

Lyons, Leonard. "Last Day in Europe." *New York Post.* January 21, 1957, 2, 26.

Meyers, Jeffrey. *Hemingway: A Biography.* New York: Harper & Row, 1985.

Miller, Alice. *Prisoners of Childhood: The Drama of the Gifted Child and the Search for the True Self.* Trans. Ruth Ward. New York: Basic Books, 1981.

Moddelmog, Debra. "Reconstructing Hemingway's Identity: Sexual Politics, the Author, and the Multicultural Classroom." *Narrative* 1: 3 (1993): 187–206.

Moore, Ernest. *Ivory: Scourge of Africa.* New York: Harper, 1931.

Mudrick, Marvin. "A Farewell to Spring and Paris." *Hudson Review* 17 (Winter 1964): 572–79.

Nagel, James. "Kitten to Waxin: Hadley's Letters to Ernest Hemingway." *Journal of Modern Literature.* 15 (Summer 1988): 146–58.

——— "The Hunting Story in *The Garden of Eden.*" *Hemingway's Neglected Short Fiction.* Ed. Susan Beegel. Ann Arbor: University of Michigan Research Press, 1989, 329–38.

L'Osservatore Romano, January 23, 1953.

Penwill, D. J. *Kamba Customary Law.* London: Macmillan, 1951.

Peters, K. J. "The Thematic Integrity of *The Garden of Eden.*" *Hemingway Review.* 11 (Spring 1991): 17–29.

Raeburn, John. *Fame Became Him: Hemingway as Public Writer.* Bloomington: Indiana University Press, 1984.

——— "Sex and Art in *The Garden of Eden.*" *Michigan Quarterly Review.* 29 (Winter 1990): 111–22.

Reynolds, Michael. *Hemingway: An Annotated Chronology.* Detroit: Omni Graphics, 1991.

——— *Hemingway: The American Homecoming.* Oxford: Basil Blackwell, 1992.

——— *Hemingway: The Paris Years.* Oxford: Basil Blackwell, 1989.

——— *Hemingway's First War: The Making of "A Farewell to Arms."* Princeton: Princeton University Press, 1975.

——— "Hemingway's Home: Depression and Suicide." *Ernest Hemingway: Six Decades of Criticism.* Ed. Linda Wagner, East Lansing: Mich. State University Press, 1987, 9–17.

———. *The Young Hemingway.* Oxford, U.K.: Basil Blackwell, 1986.

Rhys, Jean. *The Letters of Jean Rhys.* Ed. Francis Wyndham and Diana Melly. New York: Viking, 1984.

Rollyson, Carl. *Nothing Ever Happens to the Brave.* New York: St. Martins, 1990.

Rowland Ward. *Records of Big Game.* London: Rowland Ward, rpt. 1962.

Rovit, Earl, and Brenner, Gerry. *Ernest Hemingway.* Boston: Twayne Publishers, 1986.

Said, Edward. *Beginnings: Intention and Method.* New York: Basic Books, 1975.

Samuels, Lee. *A Hemingway Checklist.* New York: Scribner's, 1951.

Sanford, Marcelline Hemingway. *At the Hemingways.* Boston: Little Brown, 1962.

——— *At the Hemingways* Manuscripts. Hemingway Museum, Oak Park, Illinois.

Scafella, Frank. "Clippings from *The Garden of Eden.*" *Hemingway Review* 7 (Fall 1987): 21–29.

Scott, Robert. *Between the Elephant's Eyes.* New York: Dodd & Mead, 1954.

Scribner, Charles. *Among Writers.* New York: Scribner's, 1990.

Showalter, Elaine. *A Literature of Their Own.* London: Virago, 1984.

Smith, Paul. "Impressions of Ernest Hemingway." *Hemingway Review* 6 (Spring 1987): 2–10.

——— "From the Waste Land to the Garden with the Elliots." *Hemingway's Neglected Short Fiction.* Ed. Susan Beegel. Ann Arbor: University of Michigan Research Press, 1989, 123–29.

——— *A Reader's Guide to the Short Stories of Ernest Hemingway.* Boston: Hall, 1989.

Sojka, Gregory. "Art and Order in *Islands in the Stream.*" *Hemingway: A Revaluation.* Ed. Donald Noble. Troy, NY: Whitson Publishing, 1983, 263–79.

Solomon, Barbara Probst. *New Republic.* March 9, 1987, 30–34.

Spilka, Mark. *Hemingway's Quarrel with Androgyny.* Lincoln: University of Nebraska Press, 1990.

Svoboda, Frederic. *Hemingway and "The Sun Also Rises."* Lawrence, Kansas: University of Kansas Press, 1983.

Tavernier-Courbin, Jacqueline. *Ernest Hemingway's "A Moveable Feast:" The Making of a Myth.* Boston: Northeastern University Press, 1991.

Updike, John. "The Sinister Sex." *New Yorker.* June 30, 1986, 85–88.

Wagner, Geoffrey. "*A Moveable Feast.*" *Commonweal.* May 29, 1964, 302.

Waldhorn, Arthur. *A Reader's Guide to Ernest Hemingway.* New York: Farrar, Straus, & Giroux, 1981.

Walton, William. Interviews with author. September 1992 and August 1993. JFK.

Westbrook, Max. "Grace Under Pressure: Hemingway and the Summer of 1920." *Ernest Hemingway: The Writer in Context.* Ed. James Nagel. Madison: University of Wisconsin Press, 1984, 77–106.

Young, Philip. *Ernest Hemingway.* New York: Rinehart, 1952.

——— *Ernest Hemingway: A Reconsideration.* University Park: Pennsylvania State University Press, 1966.

——— "Hemingway: The Writer in Decline." *Hemingway: A Revaluation.* Ed. Donald Noble. Troy, NY: Whitson Publishing, 1983, 225–39.

Young, Philip, and Mann, Charles. *The Hemingway Manuscripts: An Inventory.* University Park: Pennsylvania State U.P., 1969.

Bibliography

Atkins, John. *The Art of Ernest Hemingway: His Work and Personality*. London: Peter Nevill, 1952.

Baudelaire, Charles. *Les fleurs du mal*. Illustrated by Auguste Rodin. Paris: Limited Editions Club, 1940.

Buckley, Peter. *Ernest*. New York: Dial Press, 1978.

Cappel Montgomery, Constance. *Hemingway in Michigan*. New York: Fleet Publishing, 1966.

Carpenter, Frederick. "Hemingway Achieves the Fifth Dimension." *Ernest Hemingway: Five Decades of Criticism*. Ed. Linda Welshimer Wagner. East Lansing: Michigan State University Press, 1974, 288–306.

Castillo-Puche, Jose Luis. *Hemingway in Spain*. Garden City, NY: Doubleday, 1974.

Comley, Nancy R. and Scholes, Robert. *Hemingway's Genders*. New Haven: Yale University Press, 1994.

Elsen, Albert. *"The Gates of Hell" by Auguste Rodin*. Stanford: Stanford University Press, 1985.

Fenton, Charles. *The Apprenticeship of Ernest Hemingway*. New York: Farrar, Straus, & Young, 1954.

Gellhorn, Martha. *Travels with Myself and Another*. London: Allen Lane, 1978.

Griffin, Peter. *Along with Youth: Hemingway, the Early Years*. New York: Oxford University Press, 1985.

———— *Less Than a Treason*. New York: Oxford University Press, 1990.

Hemingway, Leicester. *My Brother, Ernest Hemingway*. Cleveland: World, 1962.

Herbst, Josephine. *The Starched Blue Skies of Spain*. New York: HarperCollins, 1992.

Kubie, Lawrence. "Ernest Hemingway: Cyrano and the Matador." *American Imago* 41: 1 (Spring 1984): 9–18.

Mellow, James. *Hemingway: A Life Without Consequences*. New York: Houghton Mifflin, 1992.

Miller, Madelaine Hemingway. *Ernie: Hemingway's Sister "Sunny" Remembers*. New York: Crown, 1975.

Messent, Peter. *Hemingway*. London: Macmillan Press, 1992.

Rodin, Auguste. "The Metamorphoses of Ovid." *Rodin Skulpturen*. London:

Phaidon Press, 1934, 1953. New York: Allen & Unwin; Oxford University Press, 1934.

Smiley, Pamela. "Gender-linked Miscommunication in 'Hills Like White Elephants.' " *Hemingway Review* 8 (Spring 1988): 2–12.

Strychacz, Thomas. "Trophy-hunting as a Trope of Manhood in Ernest Hemingway's *The Green Hills of Africa.*" *Hemingway Review.* 13: 1 (Fall 1993): 36–47.

Whitlow, Roger. *Cassandra's Daughters: The Women in Hemingway.* Westport, Conn.: Greenwood Press, 1984.

Index

Gellhorn, Martha, 2–3, 13, 82, 114;
aggressive pursuit of EH,
198n28; on EH's androgyny,
212–3n2; becomes Scribner's author, 37; believed EH insane, 43;
China assignment, 41; compared
to EH's mother, 170; in text of
"Cuba," 69; disgust with "Crook
Factory," 43, 45–6; feels ill-used
in the marriage, 41–3, 45; friendship with Eleanor Roosevelt, 37,
42; friendship with Charles
Scribner Sr., 36, 40, 41, 45–46,
198–9n29; EH's death wish for,
232n36; hopes for a Hemingway
Nobel, 39–40; inability to bear a
child, 47; *Liana,* 43, 46–7,
199n31, 218n22; marital problems with EH, 27–8, 42, 45–6,
52–3, 199n32; meets EH in Key
West, 34; meets Pauline in Venice, 129; with EH in Spanish Civil
War, 32, 33–47, 197n22; *Travels
With Myself and Another,* 42,
199n31; work conflicts in marriage to EH, 41, 53
Gillman, Charlotte Perkins, 218n22
The Gods Must Be Crazy [film] (Uys),
142
Griffin, Peter, 13
Gurewitsch, David, 197n22

Hayward, Leland, 204n19
Hall, Leicester, 16
Hemingway, Anson, 26
Hemingway, Clarence Edmonds: depression and suicide of, 14, 22;
diabetes of, 29; as disciplinarian,
17, 29; EH's divorce, response
to, 16; EH's writing, response to,
167, 196n19; hemochromatosis
of, 14, 29; mental agitation of,
29, 195n15; muscular Christianity in life of, 15–6, 189–90n4;
parentage of, 26; pioneer vision
of, 189n2; platitudinous lan-

guage of, 196n19; rigidity of, 16,
190n5
Hemingway, Ernest (EH)
Biographical
affairs: with Martha Gellhorn, 2–3,
27; with Jane Mason, 27; with
Pauline Pfeiffer, 27
African safari, 134–6; named honorary game warden, 136,
223n12; plane crashes, 136–7,
223n13
androgyny, 33, 133
apartments and houses: Finca Vigia, 10, 39; Ketchum, Idaho,
179; in Paris, 226n9
biographers, dislike of, 11, 139
biographies of: 13, 189n1
birthday letter from Grace Hemingway, 17–20
boyish wives, preference for, 32
Catholicism, 184, 234n49
cats, fondness for, 23–4
character traits: competitiveness,
156, 228n17; dependency on
women, 27–9, 156–7; dislike of
ambitious women, 170; inability
to sustain intimacy, 10, 70, 76,
82, 160; indifference to small
children, 200n38–9; loneliness,
25–30, 70; mistrust of women,
25–30, 31, 50; narcissism, 10, 25,
157, 162; nourished anger, 52,
149, 202n6, 220–1n2
childhood: discipline in home, 17–
8, 22, 191n9; gender roles in
home, 17; platitudinous language of parents, 196n19; reading, 231n31; twinned with sister,
20–1
China trip, 41
desire for a daughter, 47, 48, 199–
200n36, 200n39, 207n32
desire to paint, 130
elephants: interest in, 22–3, 135,
138
F.B.I. file, 199n35